Lecture Notes in Computer Science   10030

Commenced Publication in 1973
Founding and Former Series Editors:
Gerhard Goos, Juris Hartmanis, and Jan van Leeuwen

More information about this series at http://www.springer.com/series/7408

Peng Liu
Sushil Jajodia
Cliff Wang (Eds.)

Theory and Models for Cyber Situation Awareness

Springer

Editors
Peng Liu
Pennsylvania State University
University Park, PA
USA

Cliff Wang
Army Research Office
Research Triangle Park, NC
USA

Sushil Jajodia
George Mason University
Fairfax, VA
USA

ISSN 0302-9743 ISSN 1611-3349 (electronic)
Lecture Notes in Computer Science
ISBN 978-3-319-61151-8 ISBN 978-3-319-61152-5 (eBook)
DOI 10.1007/978-3-319-61152-5

Library of Congress Control Number: 2017945278

LNCS Sublibrary: SL2 – Programming and Software Engineering

Printed on acid-free paper

This Springer imprint is published by Springer Nature
The registered company is Springer International Publishing AG
The registered company address is: Gewerbestrasse 11, 6330 Cham, Switzerland

Preface

Motivation for the Book

This book seeks to present a summary of recent research advances in cyber situation awareness. A multidisciplinary group of leading researchers from the areas of cyber-security, cognitive science, and decision science offer their viewpoints on recent advances in cyber situation awareness.

Today, when a security incident happens, the top three questions a cyber operation center would ask are: What has happened? Why did it happen? What should I do? Answers to the first two questions form the core of cyber situation awareness (SA). Whether the last question can be satisfactorily addressed is largely dependent on the cyber SA capability of an enterprise.

From the perspective of "data to decisions," cyber SA can be viewed as a main output of a particular data triaging system. Since there are a large variety of sensors monitoring an enterprise network, the cyber operation center will gather a large amount of data coming from these different types of data sources. The data typically represent normal operation status. Stealthy attack-related information could be deeply embedded among the large volume of normal operation data. Thus the signal-to-noise ratio of attack data is normally extremely low. Answering the first two questions through data triaging could be as hard as finding a needle in a haystack.

Although numerous tools have been developed to help security analysts gain a better SA, existing tools are not yet adequate to provide cyber operation centers with highly desirable cyber SA capabilities listed as follows:

- Capability 1: The ability to create problem-solving workflows or processes
- Capability 2: The ability to see the big picture of cyber defense landscape
- Capability 3: The ability to manage uncertainty
- Capability 4: The ability to reason albeit incomplete/noisy knowledge
- Capability 5: The ability to quickly locate needles in haystacks
- Capability 6: The ability to do strategic planning
- Capability 7: The ability to predict the possible next steps an adversary might take

The goal of this work is to present a summary of recent research advances in the development of these highly desirable cyber SA capabilities.

About the Book

Chapters in this book can be roughly divided into the following four areas:

Part I: Overview

- Computer-Aided Human Centric Cyber Situation Awareness

Part II: Computer and Information Science Aspects of the Recent Advances in Cyber Situation Awareness

- An Integrated Framework for Cyber Situational Awareness
- Lessons Learned: Visualizing Cyber Situation Awareness in a Network Security Domain
- Enterprise-Level Cyber Situation Awareness

Part III: Learning and Decision-Making Aspects of the Recent Advances in Cyber Situation Awareness

- Dynamics of Decision-Making in Cyber Defense: Using Multi-Agent Cognitive Modeling to Understand CyberWar
- Studying Analysts Data Triage Operations in Cyber Defense Situational Analysis

Part IV: Cognitive Science Aspects of the Recent Advances in Cyber Situation Awareness

- The Cognitive Sciences of Cyber-Security: A Framework for Advancing Socio-Cyber Systems
- Collaboration on Cybersecurity Situational Awareness

Acknowledgments

We are extremely grateful to all those who contributed to this book. It is a pleasure to acknowledge the authors for their contributions. Special thanks go to Alfred Hofmann, Vice-President Publishing (Editor), Anna Kramer, Assistant Editor, Christine Reiss, Editorial Assistant, and Ingrid Beyer, all from Springer, for their support of this project.

May 2017   Peng Liu
                                                                   Sushil Jajodia
                                                                    Cliff Wang

Contents

Overview

Computer-Aided Human Centric Cyber Situation Awareness

Massimiliano Albanese[1], Nancy Cooke[2], González Coty[3],
David Hall[4], Christopher Healey[5], Sushil Jajodia[1], Peng Liu[4(✉)],
Michael D. McNeese[4], Peng Ning[5], Douglas Reeves[5],
V.S. Subrahmanian[6], Cliff Wang[7], and John Yen[4]

[1] George Mason University, Fairfax, VA, USA
[2] Arizona State University, Mesa, AZ, USA
[3] Carnegie Mellon University, Pittsburg, PA, USA
[4] Pennsylvania State University, University Park, PA, USA
pliu@ist.psu.edu
[5] North Carolina State University, Raleigh, NC, USA
[6] University of Maryland, College Park, MD, USA
[7] Army Research Office, Raleigh, NC, USA

Abstract. In this chapter, we provide an overview of Cyber Situational Awareness, an emerging research area in the broad field of cyber security, and discuss, at least at a high level, how to gain Cyber Situation Awareness. Our discussion focuses on answering the following questions: What is Cyber Situation Awareness? Why is research needed? What are the current research objectives and inspiring scientific principles? Why should one take a multidisciplinary approach? How could one take an end-to-end holistic approach? What are the future research directions?

1 What Is Cyber Situation Awareness

Cyber operations – in the context of mission assurance – give rise – especially within large enterprises - to the questions that are at the core of Cyber Situation Awareness (Cyber SA). Without loss of generality, the process of situational awareness can be viewed as a three-phase process: situation perception, situation comprehension, and situation projection. *Perception* gains awareness about the status, attributes, and dynamics of relevant elements within the enterprise networks. *Comprehension* of the situation encompasses how analysts combine, correlate, and interpret information. *Projection* of the situation into the near future encompasses the ability to make predictions based on the knowledge acquired through perception and comprehension.

Figure 1 shows a simplified illustration of cyber operations in a large enterprise. Essentially, cyber operations are centered on answering four key questions whenever an adversary is launching a cyber-attack:

- What has happened to the networked enterprise information systems ("enterprise networks" for short)?
- What is the impact?

© Springer International Publishing AG 2017
P. Liu et al. (Eds.): Cyber Sitation Awareness, LNCS 10030, pp. 3–25, 2017.
DOI: 10.1007/978-3-319-61152-5_1

- Why did it happen?
- What should we do?

In our viewpoint, the first three questions form the "core" of Cyber SA, and Cyber SA serves as a key enabler for answering the last question, "What should we do". In other words, Cyber SA is geared towards gaining awareness about what has happened or what the adversary has done, the impact of the cyber-attacks, and how the current situation was determined. Here, the impact includes at least two aspects: damage assessment and mission impact analysis. Regarding why the current situation is what it is, the security analysts should identify the exploited vulnerabilities. In many cases, the exploited vulnerabilities include both known and unknown vulnerabilities associated with the enterprise networks.

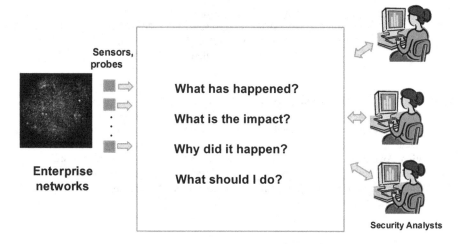

Fig. 1. Cyber operations for mission assurance

From the perspective of "data to decisions," Cyber SA can be viewed as a particular data triaging system. As illustrated in Fig. 2, the output of any sensor shown in Fig. 1 can be viewed as a *data source*. Because there are a large variety of sensors out there, there are actually many kinds of data sources. Here, we roughly classify the data sources as follows:

- **Class A:** in-band data
  - A1: static data. In this class, the data are seldom updated. For example, network topology, naming data, routing tables, vulnerability scan data (e.g., NESSUS reports), attack graphs, and certain host configurations belong to this class.
  - A2: dynamic data. In this class, the data are either data streams or dynamically updated data. Each data item is explicitly or implicitly associated with a timestamp. The timestamps clearly show the stateful nature of cyber SA.

A2.1: raw data (e.g., traffic dumps, OS audit logs, firewall logs)

A2.2: IDS (Intrusion Detection System) alerts (e.g., Snort alerts, tripwire alerts)

A2.3: attack-neutral enterprise system behavior data (e.g., operating system level dependency graphs)

- A3: the communications among security analysts. In this class, the data include the incident reports which are manually generated by analysts.

- **Class B:** out-of-band intelligence
  - In this class, the data include the intelligence feeds from outside. By "outside", we mean that (a) there exists information sharing between the enterprise itself and a set of other partner organizations (e.g., CERT, other sister enterprises); and that (b) the in-band data do not play a role in generating these intelligence feeds.

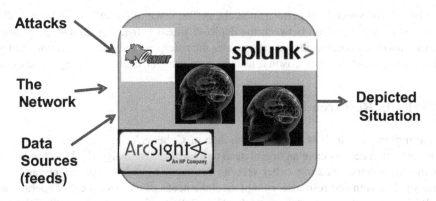

Fig. 2. Cyber SA as a data triaging system

As shown in Fig. 2, we view both Class A and Class B data sources as an *input* to the data triaging system (which is placed at the center of Fig. 2). In addition, we view the depicted situation as the main output of the data triaging system. We note that the data triaging system may also generate other outputs or effects such as new experiences and new SIEM (Secure Information and Event Management) rules.

In our viewpoint, a data triaging system is a hybrid human-cyber system. On one hand, the human part of the system includes the brains (of the security analysts) and how the brains interact with each other. Here, the brains are not only an information process unit, but also a cognitive neural network which holds memories (e.g., domain knowledge, past experiences) and human learning capacity. On the other hand, the cyber part of the system includes unbounded possibilities of software, hardware and HCI (Human Computer Interaction) designs. Nowadays, alert correlation tools and SIEM systems are already being used by security analysts. In the future, intelligent software agents and robotic systems are certainly likely to be developed.

As defined in [ZYL17], a data triaging system is a dynamic human-cyber system. At time t, the state of this dynamic system includes the following elements [ZYL17]:

- The set of attack activities in each attack chain happening on the enterprise network.
- The data sources collected (so far) from multiple sensors.
- A set of incidents detected (so far) by the analysts. The incidents are described by the involved network events and the temporal and causal relationships between these events.
- The analysts' domain knowledge about the network and attacks at time t, as well as their experience knowledge of data analysis.
- Each analyst's mental model at time t. Each mental model holds both a set of hypotheses about possible attacks and the relationships between these hypotheses.
- A set of data triage operations conducted by the analysts at time t. As defined in [ZYL17], the main data triage operations include data filtering, data search, hypothesis generation, and hypothesis confirming or denying.

From the perspective of performance, the performance of Cyber SA can be partially evaluated by a comparison between the depicted situation (see Fig. 2) and the ground truth situation. Of course, since in many cases the enterprise only has partial knowledge of the ground truth, the comparison is usually done using an estimate of the ground truth.

2   Why Is Research Needed

Regarding why research is needed in the area of Cyber SA, on one hand, real-world cyber operation centers have an urgent need to improve their analysts' job performance. On the other hand, existing cyber-security research, especially current research on intrusion detection and response, cannot meet the needs of real-world cyber operations.

With respect to the first aspect, the United States has more than 20 CNDSPs (Computer Network Defense Service Providers) whose operations are relying on human analysts. Currently, these CNDSPs face critical challenges:

- The job performance of analysts is inconsistent.
- It is hard for analysts to get the big picture: there are "walls" between functional domains.
- Better analytics and tools are needed to improve the job performance of analysts.

With respect to the second aspect, we found that big gaps exist between available intrusion detection and response tools and the desired Cyber SA capabilities.

Although a lot of tools have been developed, including vulnerability scanners, event logging tools, traffic classification tools, intrusion detection systems, alert correlation tools, signature generation tools, static and dynamic taint analysis tools, intrusion root back-tracking tools, integrity checkers, static analysis tools, bug finders, attack graph tools, symbolic execution tools, sandboxing tools, and VM monitors, the existing tools are not yet adequate to provide cyber operation centers (e.g., CNDSPs) with the following highly desirable Cyber SA capabilities:

- **Capability 1:** The ability to create problem-solving workflows or processes.
- **Capability 2:** The ability to see the big picture of cyber defense landscape.
- **Capability 3:** The ability to manage uncertainty.
- **Capability 4:** The ability to reason albeit incomplete/noisy knowledge.
- **Capability 5:** The ability to quickly locate needles in haystacks.
- **Capability 6:** The ability to do strategic planning.
- **Capability 7:** The ability to predict possible next steps an adversary might take.

For instance, consider Capability 1. For different attack chains or attack campaigns, different problem-solving workflows are often needed in a cyber operation center. An executable *problem-solving workflow* must clearly tell the analysts when to use which tools against which data sources in which ways. Mathematically, a problem-solving workflow is a partial order among analysts' data triage operations.

Although many intrusion detection and diagnosis tools are available today, no general-purpose toolkit has been developed to automatically generate differentiated problem-solving workflows for different attack campaigns. Putting a set of tools into a "basket" does not automatically enable the set of tools to "learn" from each other and address the problem-solving workflow "puzzle". In fact, real-world cyber operation centers heavily rely on human analysts and their expertise/experiences to generate the suitable problem-solving workflows on-the-fly in the midst of a not-seen-before attack campaign.

3 Research Objectives and Scientific Principles

Motivated by the gaps between existing intrusion detection and response tools and the desired Cyber SA capabilities, the main research objectives in the area of Cyber SA should include the following.

Objective A: Develop a deep understanding about:

- Why the job performance gap between expert and rookie analysts is so different? How can we bridge this performance gap?
- Why many tools cannot effectively improve job performance?
- What models, tools and analytics are needed to effectively boost job performance?

Objective B: Develop a new paradigm of Cyber SA system design, implementation, and evaluation.

Scientific barriers. In achieving these research objectives, the following scientific barriers should be paid particular attention.

- The tension between massive amounts of sensed information and that these information is currently being poorly used by many analysts.
- The mismatch between silicon-speed info sensing and neuron-speed human cognition.
- The tension between the need for "big picture awareness" and that stove piped sensing is largely the state of the practice in cyber operation centers. Besides stove piped sensing, human stovepipes also exist in real world. Organizations tend not to share information with other organizations, and individual analysts within an organization tend not to share with each other.

- The concept of "knowledge of us" [TS09] has not yet been paid sufficient attention by researchers and cyber operation centers.
- The tension between lack of ground-truth and the need for scientifically sound models.
- The tension between unknown adversary intent and publicly-known vulnerability categories.

On one hand, the above scientific barriers bring daunting challenges to the research community. On the other hand, these barriers also create many exciting research opportunities. By crossing these scientific barriers, the potential scientific advances include the following:

- Understanding the nature of human analysts' Cyber SA cognition and decision making.
- Inspiring the design of innovative Cyber SA systems that capture the nature of the human cognitive processes.
- Breaking both vertical (between compartments) and horizontal (between abstraction layers) stovepipes.
- Enabling the advancement of mission assurance analytics (e.g., asset map, damage, impact, mitigation, recovery).
- Discovering blind spot situation knowledge.
- Making adversary intent an integral part of Cyber SA analytics.

Principles. In making these potential scientific advances, we believe the following scientific principles should be followed:

Principle 1. Cyber security research shows a new trend: moving from qualitative to quantitative science; from data-insufficient science to data-abundant science.

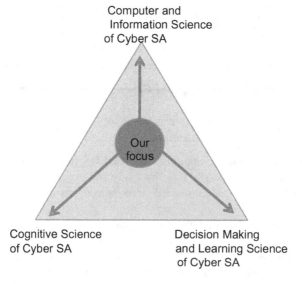

Fig. 3. Taking a multidisciplinary approach to research Cyber SA

The availability of sensed cyber security information opens up fascinating opportunities to understand both mission and adversary activity through modeling and analytics. This would require creative mission-aware analysis of heterogeneous data with cross-compartment and cross-abstraction-layer dependencies in the presence of significant uncertainty and untrustworthiness.

Principle 2. Cyber *SA tools should incorporate human cognition and decision making characteristics at the design stage.*

4   The Need for a Multidisciplinary Approach

We argue that an effective research strategy to tackle the scientific barriers pointed out in the previous section is to take a multidisciplinary approach. In particular, we found that several fundamental Cyber SA research questions cannot be systematically answered by a single-disciplinary approach. For example, the three questions listed below are important research questions, but cannot be adequately answered by restricting the research effort inside a single discipline.

- Q1: What are the differences between an expert analyst and a rookie analyst?
- Q2: What analytics and tools are needed to effectively boost job performance?
- Q3: How can we develop better tools?

For instance, consider question Q1. As illustrated in Fig. 3, the differences between expert and rookie security analyst scan be analyzed and grouped with respect to three different points of view.

- From the perspective of Computer and Information Science, the differences may include the following: (a) expert analysts might use tools a rookie analyst does not use; (b) expert analysts have a much deeper understanding of the inner workings of a tool; (c) expert analysts can create a new tool chain to diagnose a never-seen-before attack campaign, but a rookie analyst cannot.
- From the perspective of Cognitive Science [Gardner87], the differences between expert and rookie analysts may include the following: (a) expert and rookie analysts have different cognitive processes and mental states, even when they are diagnosing the same attack campaign; (b) the reasoning processes of expert analysts are more sophisticated and less error-prone; (c) expert and rookie analysts have different team cognition behaviors.
- From the perspective of Decision Making and Learning Science, the differences between expert and rookie analysts may include the following: (a) expert and rookie analysts generate different "networks" of hypotheses, even when they are diagnosing the same attack campaign; (b) expert and rookie analysts have different instance-based learning behaviors in performing intrusion detection analysis.

Hence, in the MURI project titled "Computer-aided Human Centric Cyber Situation Awareness," which the authors of this chapter have carried out from 2009 to 2015, the primary focus was on the integration of these three perspectives, rather than on a deeper investigation of a single perspective.

5   An End-to-End Holistic Approach

As pointed out in [TS09], Cyber SA is a process involving inter-dependent operations. When a Cyber SA system is viewed as a data triage system, as shown in Fig. 2, the data triage system uses hybrid data triage processes to generate the designated outputs.

Accordingly, in the MURI project mentioned earlier, we took an end-to-end holistic approach to addressing the Cyber SA problem.

As shown in Fig. 4, the proposed end-to-end solution is a "coin" with two sides:

- The *life-cycle side* of the "coin" shows the Cyber SA tasks in each stage of Cyber SA, including the sensing stage (at the computer network), the data conditioning & association stage, the information aggregation & fusion stage, the automated reasoning stage, the human-computer interaction stage (i.e., the interaction between analysts and automated reasoning).
- The *computer-aided cognition side* of the "coin" includes the development of the Cyber SA specific cognition models and cognition-friendly Cyber SA tools.
- To approach research on the two-sided "coin", using testbeds (replications of the analyst task environment) (a) allowed us to learn about the cognitive science underlying cyber analysis; (b) allowed us to learn about the cognitive science underlying collaboration; (c) provided ground truth; and (d) allowed us to test technology solutions with humans in the loop.

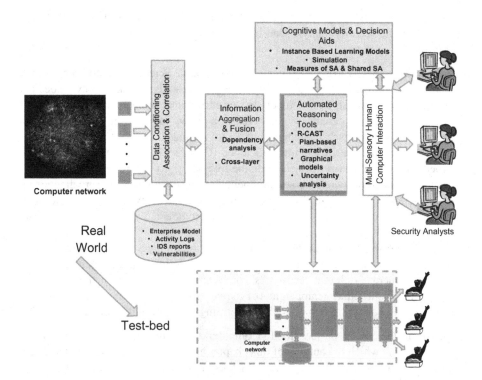

Fig. 4. An end-to-end approach to Cyber SA

The goal of the computer-aided cognition "side" of the proposed solution is to draw new insights from cognitive task analysis, simulations, modeling of analysts' cognition and decision making, and the associated research findings.

The goal of the life-cycle "side" of the proposed solution is to use the insights gained through the computer-aided cognition "side" to develop a new paradigm of computer-aided Cyber SA. This new paradigm includes new analytics and better tools, letting tools and analysts work in concert, and bridging the gap between analysts' cognition and Cyber SA sensors and tools.

6 The MURI Project's Cyber SA Vision

The end-to-end holistic approach we took is inspired by a Cyber SA vision we had when starting to work on the MURI project.

Part 1 of the vision states that today's Cyber SA practice has two fundamental limitations:

- Existence of a huge gap between human cognition and Cyber SA tools and algorithms: the amount of information contained in "raw" situation data collected by Cyber SA tools is several orders of magnitude greater than the "cognition throughput" of human analysts, and critical "links" from data to decision are missing.
- Existence of major "blind spots": existing cyber SA tools and systems – including auditing, vulnerability scanners, attack graph tools, intrusion detection systems, damage assessment tools, and forensics tools – still have significant "blind spots" in their "views" of the cyber situation landscape.

Part 2 of the vision indicates how the two limitations would be addressed in the MURI project. In particular,

- The project would address the first limitation by building the missing links through innovations in Cyber SA specific information and knowledge fusion, cognition automation, artificial intelligence, and visual analytics. One envisioned research direction is to integrate human intelligence with artificial intelligence.
- The project would address the second limitation through breaking both the horizontal and vertical stovepipes. The envisioned techniques include cross-layer dependency analysis and knowledge fusion, cross-compartment dependency analysis and knowledge fusion, probabilistic graphical models to perform uncertainty analysis and management, and integrating "knowledge of us" with "our knowledge of the attack campaign".

7 The MURI Project's Main Research Thrusts

Guided by the MURI project's Cyber SA vision, the project had conducted research along the following thrusts.

- **Thrust 1:** Cognition Automation
  - Developing interactive Cyber SA systems that exhibit intelligent behavior.
  - StudyingCyber SA specific cognitive behaviors.
  - Tracing security analysts' data triage operations and reasoning processes.
  - Developing techniques to do experience-based automatic situation recognition and projection.
  - Developing intelligent agents assisting human analysts in gaining Cyber SA: the intelligent agents should be capable of learning from human data triage operations and reasoning processes.
  - Performing Cyber SA specific cognition throughput evaluation.
  - Discovering bottlenecks in team-based Cyber SA.
- **Thrust 2:** "Blind Spots" Monitoring
  - Performing cross-layer dependency analysis and impact assessment (e.g., [NNL12] and [PNJ12]).
  - Performing cross-compartment dependency analysis and impact assessment.
  - Performing cross-data-source security event correlation.
  - Conducting game-theoretic analysis.
  - Applying big data analytics and machine learning techniques.
- **Thrust 3:** Situation Knowledge Fusion
  - Developing cyber situation knowledge reference models for situation knowledge representation and management [DSL12].
  - Building probabilistic graphical models to perform uncertainty analysis and management.
- **Thrust 4:** Visual Analytics
  - Developing Cyber SA specific visual analytics.

8 Key Research Outcomes of the MURI Project

8.1 Thrust 1 Research Outcomes

8.1.1 A Methodology for Research on the Cognitive Science of Cyber Defense

Our MURI team adhered to the living lab approach. This approach involves a cyclic methodology that begins and ends in the real world. The team would attempt to understand the task of the cyber analyst through interviews with subject matter experts, looking at documentation and the literature, and observing cyber exercises. This information was used to build laboratory versions of the cyber analyst task [RSC11]. Scenarios were developed which included attacks to a network. Because we developed the scenarios, we knew the ground truth. Human participants were recruited and trained on the test bed task. Some scenarios required participants with a background in information assurance. The test bed was equipped with measures of individual and team performance and cognition and provided ways to manipulate the scenario. Findings from these test bed experiments can feed back to the field in the form of user-centered tools, algorithms, or models.

8.1.2   Building a Hybrid Human-Cyber Data Triage System for Cyber SA

Many prominent companies, government organizations and military departments have invested significant financial resources to construct their cyber defense system. Typically, they set up a Security Operations Center (SOC) to perform 24/7 monitoring, intrusion detection, and diagnosis (on what is actually happening). SOCs usually employ multiple automated security tools, such as traffic monitors, firewalls, vulnerability scanners, Intrusion Detection/Prevention System (IDS/IPS). Besides, SOCs rely heavily on cyber security analysts to investigate the data generated from security tools to identify the true "signals" from them and "connect the dots" to answer some higher-level questions about the cyber situation, for example, whether the network is under an attack; what did the attackers do; and what might be their next steps. SOCs cannot be fully automated because the security tools are in many cases unable to "comprehend" sophisticated cyber-attack strategies even through advanced correlated diagnosis. Specifically, analysts need to conduct a series of analysis, including data triage, escalation analysis, correlation analysis, threat analysis, incident response and forensic analysis.

Our MURI team built an innovative hybrid human-cyber data triage system (e.g., [CLY12, ZK13, ZSY14]) for gaining Cyber SA. Data triage encompasses examining the details of a variety of data sources (e.g., IDS alerts, firewall logs, OS audit trails, vulnerability reports, and packet dumps), weeding out the false positives, grouping the related indicators so that different attack campaigns (i.e., attack plots) can be separated from each other. Data triage provides a basis for closer inspection in the following analysis to finally generate confidence-bounded attack incident reports. These incident reports will serve as the primary basis for further decision-making regarding how to change current security configuration and act against the attacks. Data triage is the most fundamental but the most time consuming stage in gaining Cyber SA. Although Security Information Event Management (SIEM) systems take a big leap forward in generating more powerful data triage automatons, SIEM systems are extremely expensive and every organization needs to use a tailored SIEM system. SIEM systems involve a tremendous amount of manual effort.

We aimed to leverage Artificial Intelligence techniques to dramatically reduce the cost of generating data triage automatons. We aimed to automatically learn data triage automatons from analysts' working experience and data triage operation traces. To this end, we leveraged a computer-aided cognitive process tracing method to capture expert analysts' operations while they are performing data triage. We developed a 3-step approach to automatically learn data triage automatons from the traces.

- **Step 1.** We represented the analysts' data triage operations captured in traces and their temporal and logical relationships in a newly defined Characteristic Constraint Graph (CC-Graph).
- **Step 2.** We mined useful SIEM rule ingredients. We analyzed the CC-Graphs to find the key data characteristic constraints. The key constraints were further correlated with the data sources to identify the "can-happen-before" relationships among them. The key constraints and their "can-happen-before" relationships represented various attack patterns, named "Attack Path Pattern". Each attack path pattern, which was formally represented, had a semantic meaning that defines a

class of network connections indicating multi-step attacks. Analysts can review, modify and extend them.

- **Step 3.** We directly used the formally represented attack path patterns to build a finite state machine for conducting automated data triage, just as adding rules to a SIEM system.

We evaluated our approach in a human-in-the-loop case study. 30 professional security analysts were recruited in the study and asked to complete a cyber-attack analysis task with their task operations being traced. Selecting several sets of traces, rule sets were discovered from each set of traces and used to construct a set of data triage state machines. False positive and false negative rates were calculated to evaluate the performance of the state machines by comparing their data triage results with the ground truth. The results show that all the state machines were able to finish processing a much larger data set within several minutes.

8.1.3   Observations of Team Communication and Coordination in Cyber Defense Analysis

Over the course of the MURI project, our team observed several cyber defense exercises and administered surveys to those conducting cyber security for the DoD and industry (e.g., the study in [JCR12]). Insights from these field studies not only led to the development of a test bed and raised various research questions pertaining to teamwork in cyber defense, but also highlighted some general observations. For instance, stove-piping was observed in exercises - both in DoD organizations and in the industry – but was particularly apparent in the DoD. We also observed that analysts in all sectors were not eager to initiate collaboration or share information with each other. Survey data from analysts allowed us to model organizational structure for cyber defense within the industry and the military. These models revealed both large and subtle differences in organizational structure between military and industry cyber security operations.

Field observations and surveys from analysts informed development of the human-in-loop test bed called *CyberCog*. This test bed was used to conduct lab-based experiments on teamwork on two related detection tasks: triage analysis and correlation analysis. Teamwork and information sharing was found to significantly reduce analysts' workload during triage analysis. We found that analysts could achieve higher triage analysis performance by handing-off and collaborating on uncertain alerts/events with other appropriate analysts to leverage each other's unique expertise, instead of trying to reason and analyze all of the alerts individually. Although, collaborating to analyze all alerts may also be detrimental to performance. Our experiments also found evidence of a cognitive bias among teams conducting correlational analyses [JCR16]. Pooling novel information from team members through collaboration is pivotal to correlation analyses. However, teams were found to repeatedly discuss and pool information which is also commonly known to the majority of team members causing sub-optimal decision making.

We found that cyber defense teams have to be facilitated with operator centric collaboration tools to mitigate or reduce such cognitive biases (e.g., information pooling bias and confirmation bias) [RC16]. Carefully designed team training methods are necessary to help analysts determine: when to initiate collaboration with team members, who to collaborate with and when to pursue analyses individually.

8.1.4   Capturing Human Cognition in Cyber-Security Simulations with CYNETS

We built CYNETS (e.g., [GM13]), a simulator to capture human cognition in performing Cyber SA tasks. We conducted a large number of CYNETS simulations, using students as human subjects. During the simulations, the Cyber SA tasks for human subjects were as follows. The subjects were given remote access to two servers to defend from live "red-team" attackers. They were also provided dynamic injects of tasks they were asked to perform – typical systems administration tasks, account creation, database updates, etc. Typical tasks included enumerating and securing accounts with administrative access (changing from default passwords), identifying and updating software with patches, modifying configuration of software to turn off unneeded services, etc. During the exercise, the human subjects needed to identify what was wrong (configuration, patches accounts, services), figure out if attackers were utilizing those vulnerabilities to compromise systems, and turn off attacker access if they were able to locate that the attacker had gained access.

Data Creation. The experimental simulation data was created in a lab environment. The simulated data was fabricated from a network of computers in the laboratory that simulates an active network of computers from a fictitious organization called "ABC". During a 24-hour period, accounts were logged on and off of computer systems to create actual log entries in the Windows Security Log of the server. The data set that was presented to human subjects had some level of normal noise, but generally was limited to successful logon, successful logoff and unsuccessful logon events. Embedded in the presented authentication data was a series of failed logon attempts, followed by an eventually successful event.

Additionally, the same 24-hour period was used and a number of viruses were copied on to the computers. The antivirus program was allowed to detect these files and take appropriate action – either delete or quarantine the files with the malicious code. Together with the updates of new antivirus definitions, these two types of records were presented in the antivirus data.

The final set of data is patch management. In this case, we created a set of records of normally applied updates.

Methods. Three triad teams were recruited. Each individual was randomly assigned to one role for the simulation, either (i) Windows Authentication Analyst (WAA), (ii) Anti-Virus Analyst (AVA), or (iii) Windows Update Analyst (WUA). When the first training scenario was finished, the participants were given a survey to quantify their individual situation awareness using NASA-TLX [HS88] and SART [Taylor90].

After the survey was completed, participants were given a second training scenario followed by another individual SA survey. Following both training scenarios, the participants were given a quick debrief about the scenario and the proper response. Next, the first performance scenario was started and once complete was followed by the same individual SA measures but with the added Shared SA Inventory (SSAI) [SST09]. Subsequently, participants were asked to complete the second performance scenario and the same individual SA and SSAI surveys.

Results. The simulation was tested initially with 3 teams to assess feasibility and capture the performance measures mentioned above. Everything worked well in the simulation, and students were able to perform in the role of individual and team cyber analyst duties in determining routine and threat activities as part of their task.

Implications. The CYNETS scaled world simulation represents the development of a challenging cyber operations environment that emulates real world threat assessment that involves distributed cognition across individual and teamwork functions.

8.1.5   Cognitively Modeling Detection of Cyber Attacks with Instance-Based Learning Theory

The Instance-Based Learning Theory (IBLT) presents decision making as a dynamic process in which analysts interacts with an environment under limited information and uncertainty, and must rely on his/her experience to make decisions. This line of work applied IBLT to gaining Cyber SA.

Cyber-attacks cause major work disruption. It is important to understand how a defender's behavior (experience and tolerance to threats), as well as adversarial behavior (attack strategy), might impact the detection of threats. In this work [DAG13], we used cognitive modeling to make predictions regarding these factors. Different model types representing a defender, based on Instance-Based Learning Theory (IBLT), faced different adversarial behaviors. A defender's model was defined by the analyst's experience of threats: threat-prone (90% threats and 10% non-threats) and non threat-prone (10% threats and 90% non-threats); and different tolerance levels to threats: risk-averse (model declares a cyber-attack after perceiving one threat out of eight total) and risk-seeking (model declares a cyber-attack after perceiving seven threats out of eight total). Adversarial behavior is simulated by considering different attack strategies: patient (threats occur late) and impatient (threats occur early).

For an impatient strategy, risk-averse models with threat-prone experiences show improved detection compared with risk-seeking models with non threat-prone experiences. However, the same is not true for a patient strategy. Based upon model predictions, a defender's prior threat experiences and her/his tolerance to threats are likely to predict detection accuracy, but considering the nature of adversarial behavior is also important.

8.2   Thrust 2 Research Outcomes

8.2.1   A Mission-Centric Framework for Cyber Situational Awareness

Our MURI team proposed a mission-centric framework for Cyber SA, which was mainly motivated by the limitations of attack graphs. First, attack graphs do not provide mechanisms for evaluating the likelihood of each attack pattern or its impact on the enterprise or mission. Second, scalability of alert correlation has not been fully addressed.

The proposed solution (e.g., [AJN12]) is a novel framework to analyze massive amounts of raw security data in real time. It envisions the capability of automatically answering a number of questions the analyst may ask about current situation, impact and evolution of an attack, behavior of the attackers, forensics, quality of available information and models, and prediction of future attacks. In practice, the proposed framework provides security analysts with a high-level view of the cyber situation.

The key components of this framework are as follows. First, we introduced the notion of *generalized dependency graph*, which captures how network components depend on one other. Second, we extended the classical definition of attack graph with the notion of *time span distribution*, which encodes probabilistic knowledge of the attacker's behavior. Third, we introduced the notion of *attack scenario graph*, which combines dependency and attack graphs, bridging the gap between known vulnerabilities and the missions or services that could be ultimately affected. Fourth, we proposed efficient algorithms for both detection and prediction, and showed that they scale well for large graphs and large volumes of alerts. Fifth, we developed an efficient approach for assessing the risk of zero-day vulnerabilities, based on methods for generating partial attack graphs on-demand. Sixth, to answer the questions the analyst may ask, it is critical to define security metrics to capture and quantify several aspects of the system being defended, such us robustness to zero-day attacks. Accordingly, we developed a suite of metrics for measuring network-wide cyber security risk based on attack graphs: we investigated network diversity as a security metric, and evaluated its impact on the robustness of networks against zero-day attacks.

8.2.2 Automatically Explaining Security Alerts

In real-world enterprises, security managers are usually swamped with the large number of alerts they receive, and any effort that helps explain what is happening is very helpful. We developed the novel new notion of a *hypergraph alert mechanism* (HAM) and showed how a HAM can be learned automatically from a set of SNORT rules. We then showed that using sophisticated graph reachability properties, suitably modified to handle time constraints and hypergraph structure, we could generate appropriate explanations of a given set of alerts that an analyst sees in front of him.

In the HAM framework (e.g., [AMP11, AMP14, MMP14]), we assumed that SNORT rules are responsible for generating alerts. A hypergraph alert mechanism consists of certain types of nodes and certain specialized types of hyper-edges.

- A node is a pair (m, a), and represent the fact that SNORT generated an alert a on a machine m *in the enterprise network*.
- A hyper-edge is a triple $e = (H, n, \delta)$ where H is a set of nodes; n is a specific node; and $\delta_{\{e\}}$ is a mapping that associates, with each $n' \in H$, a non-negative real number.

Intuitively, a hyper-edge e indicates that all events in H tend to occur more or less together, with a temporal delay between the time the events in H occur and the time n occurs. For a given event $n' \in H$, $\delta_{\{e\}}(n')$ denotes the amount of time between the occurrence of n' and the occurrence of n.

We developed a formal theoretical model of HAM that is able to provide explanations of an alert, given a history of alerts generated in the past, not just for the current machine, but other machines as well. We also developed an algorithm to take existing SNORT rules together with the enterprise network topology as input and automatically generate a set of HAMs from them.

In addition, we worked on the following problem. Given a set of alerts $A = \{a_1, \ldots, a_k\}$ that have actually happened, what is the best explanation of this set of alerts? An explanation E is a set of hyper-edges with various properties. To solve this problem, we developed a formal definition of an explanation for a given set of alerts; we defined several metrics to evaluate each explanation; we also linked these metrics to NIST's National Vulnerability Database and MITRE's Common Weakness Scoring System. Using these metrics, we developed an initial algorithm able to find the set of best explanations according to all different measures, by using prefixed order relation among the metrics or via Pareto optimality.

8.2.3   Game-Theoretic Analysis of Patch Deployment Using the National Vulnerability Database

Most enterprise security managers today have tons of software within their enterprise. Because of time and cost constraints, they only typically apply patches to the software that is deemed most vulnerable (e.g., by the NIST National Vulnerability Database).

The goal of the proposed game-theoretic analysis [SJP15] is to anticipate how the adversary can behave, and use that information to provide an advantage to the defender. We proposed a framework based on Stackelberg games by which the defender (enterprise security manager) can choose the set of patches to apply within his cost/time constraints that minimize the expected damage caused by the attacker's maximally damaging strategy.

Through game-theoretic analysis, we were able to prove theoretically that the attacker's best strategy (in terms of which known vulnerabilities to exploit) can easily penetrate such defenses. We developed a formal concept of the best strategy for an attacker, showed that for him to find an optimal strategy is intractable, and developed algorithms that an attacker can use.

In addition, we asked the following question: given a set of publicly known information such as the cost of patching vulnerabilities (which can be readily inferred by anyone), what is the strategy that an intelligent attacker would use in order to maximize the expected damage he can cause? With this in hand, the defender can come up with defensive strategies that minimize the expected damage the attacker can inflict. We allowed the defender to do two things: (i) deactivate certain products (e.g., if they have serious vulnerabilities)which could reduce the impact of attacks; and (ii) apply patches to certain vulnerabilities. The first method has a potential impact on productivity of the enterprise while the second has a time/cost implication. We defined the optimal strategy of the defender as a Pareto optimization problem and showed how to find the set of all optimal strategies for the defender. We derived a number of complexity results associated with the attacker's goal of finding an attack that maximizes his expected impact, and also the defender's goal of taking steps to minimize the maximal impact the attacker can have.

We implemented our algorithms and tested them on four real-world vulnerability dependency graphs (a more general version of attack graphs). Our results showed that our algorithms work in reasonable amounts of time on real-world networks and provide options to enterprise security managers that represent different combinations of maximizing productivity and minimizing expected attack impact. Our prototype implementation showed that run-times of our computations are all within acceptable time bounds even for large vulnerability dependency graphs containing 30 K edges and that the balance between productivity and impact of attacks is also acceptable.

8.2.4 Automatic Policy Analysis and Refinement for Security Enhanced Android via Large-Scale Semi-supervised Learning

In this line of work, we focused on automated analysis of audit logs generated by access control systems. For a large population of users, over a period of time measured in months or years, such logs can run into many millions of entries, or greater. The intended output of such automated analysis is a security policy that can be parsed and enforced by some form of mandatory access control.

Mandatory access control (MAC), which is enforced by SELinux, has a number of advantages over discretionary access control (DAC). However, because of the difficulty of creating, understanding, optimizing, and maintaining security policies, MAC is typically turned off, or a weak, generic policy is used which is not very effective at preventing misuse. In theory, if it was possible to identify in advance every potential non-malicious access operation executed by every piece of installable software, an appropriate security policy could be derived that would permit these operations, and no more. This unfortunately is not a realistic goal.

It is, however, realistic to capture from a large population of users, over a sufficient interval of time, most of the access operations that are needed in practice, and to process this information to derive a security policy. There are several research questions that must be answered in doing so:

1. Is it possible to distinguish the operations executed by normal users and software from operations executed by malicious software?
2. Is it possible to generate automatically a security policy that allows normal accesses and prevents malicious accesses, in a way that makes the policy both human readable and efficient to enforce?
3. Will such a method scale to information captured from millions of users over extended periods of time?
4. Will the quality of the generated security policy, as judged by security analysts, be equal to or better than the quality of manually derived policies?

We investigated this issue using as a demonstration system an Android smartphone. Through a partnership with Samsung, we obtained access to a rich dataset of user access operations, collected from millions of users (with their permission). We proposed and evaluated a method for automatically creating security policies which can be enforced by the MAC layer (SEAndroid) of Android devices. This approach answers the above research questions in the affirmative, with some limitations.

Semi-supervised learning is a type of machine learning that trains on both labeled data (used by supervised learning) and unlabeled data (used by unsupervised learning). It is typically used when labeled data is insufficient and expensive to collect, and a large set of unlabeled data is available. By correlating the features in unlabeled data with labeled data, a semi-supervised learner infers the labels of the unlabeled instances with strong correlation. This labeling increases the size of labeled data set, which can be used to further re-train and improve the learning accuracy. Semi-supervised learning is popular for information extraction and knowledge base construction. We hypothesized that the process of developing and refining security policies is analogous to semi-supervised learning. Human analysts encode their knowledge about various access patterns into a policy, and refine that knowledge based on examination of audit logs. Because of the difficulty of doing this accurately and in a timely fashion, security policies are generally overly permissive. Semi-supervised learning can automate this process to achieve scalability in policy refinement.

The input to learning is an existing security policy (if there is one), and a set of access events logged from user devices. Each access event entry identifies the subject (i.e., the process or application), the object (i.e., the file or system resource), and the type of execution requested by the subject on that object. Note that audit logs may contain attempted accesses by malicious as well as non-malicious software and users. A main intuition is that non-malicious accesses are much more common than malicious access attempts, and malicious accesses have distinctive features that can be learned by an automated method.

The proposed method used three machine learning algorithms that consider different perspectives of the knowledge base and audit logs. The output of these algorithms is fed into a combiner that combines and appends the new knowledge into the knowledge base. This learning process is iterated multiple times until no additional new knowledge can be learned from the current audit log input. Finally, the policy generator suggests refinements to the security policy. This proposed method was tested on the SEAndroid platform, with an input dataset consisting of over 14 M denied access events, and an initial security policy containing over 5,000 security rules. The results showed that the method classified as malicious more than 200 types of accesses that are currently allowed by SEAndroid. A number of these accesses have been confirmed as previously unrecognized (and therefore unprevented) attacks on Android devices.

8.3   Thrust 3 Research Outcomes

8.3.1   Using Bayesian Networks to Gain Cyber SA

We explored two ways of using Bayesian Networks to gain Cyber SA (e.g., [XLO10]): (1) building cross-layer Bayesian networks to infer the stealthy bridges between enterprise network islands in clouds; (2) using Bayesian networks to perform automated *heterogeneous* evidence fusion towards detection of zero-day attack paths.

(1) Inferring the stealthy bridges in clouds
Gaining Cyber SA in cloud environments is a very important and emerging research area in Cyber SA. Enterprises have begun to move parts of their IT systems (such as web server, mail server, etc.) from traditional infrastructure into cloud computing environments. A public cloud can provide virtual infrastructures to many enterprises. Except for some public services, enterprise networks are expected to be like isolated islands in the cloud: connections from the outside network to the protected internal network should be prohibited. Consequently, an attack path that shows a multi-step exploitation sequence in an enterprise network should also be confined inside this island. However, as enterprise networks migrate into the cloud and replace traditional physical hosts with virtual machines, some "stealthy bridges" could be created between the isolated enterprise network islands. With the stealthy bridges, the attack path confined inside an enterprise network is able to traverse to another enterprise network in the cloud. In other words, stealthy bridges are stealthy information tunnels existing between disparate networks in a cloud that are unknown to security sensors and should

have been forbidden. Stealthy bridges are developed mainly by exploiting vulnerabilities that are unknown to vulnerability scanners. Isolated enterprise network islands are connected via these stealthy tunnels, through which information (data, commands, etc.) can be acquired, transmitted or exchanged illegally.

In this line of work, we built cross-Layer Bayesian Networks to infer the stealthy bridges between enterprise network islands in clouds. In particular, our main contributions are as follows. First, we found that the creation of "stealthy bridges" is enabled by two unique features of the public cloud: (i) cloud users are allowed to create and share virtual machine images (VMIs) with other users; and (ii) virtual machines owned by different tenants may co-reside on the same physical host machine. Second, we built a cloud-level attack graph by crafting new interaction rules in MulVAL, an attack graph generation tool. The cloud-level attack graph can capture the potential attacks enabled by stealthy bridges and reveal possible hidden attack paths that are previously missed by individual enterprise network attack graphs. Third, based on the cloud-level attack graph built by us, a cross-layer Bayesian Network (BN) was constructed by identifying four types of uncertainties. The cross-layer BN is able to infer the existence of stealthy bridges given supporting evidence from other intrusion steps. The BN has two inputs: the network deployment model (network connection, host configuration, and vulnerability information, etc.) and the evidence. The output of the BN is the probability of specific events, such as the probability of stealthy bridges being established, or the probability of a web server being compromised.

In our evaluation experiments, we considered three major enterprise networks, say A, B, and C. A and B are all implemented within the cloud, while C is implemented partially in the cloud and partially as a traditional infrastructure(e.g., the servers are located in the cloud and the workstations are in a traditional network). The attack includes seven steps conducted by attacker. In this scenario, two stealthy bridges were established: one is from the Internet to enterprise network A through exploitation of an unknown vulnerability, the other one is between enterprise networks B and C by leveraging virtual machine co-residency. The attack path crosses over three enterprise networks that reside in the same cloud, and extends to C's traditional network. A concrete cross-layer BN is constructed and it takes into account the existence of stealthy bridges; the cloud-level attack graph has the capability of revealing potential hidden attack paths. We conducted four sets of simulation experiments, each with a specific purpose. The results showed that (a) the probability of stealthy bridge existence is initially very low, and increases from 34% to 88% as more evidence is collected; (b) the BN can provide relatively correct answer by combining the overall evidence set; and (c) the BN can still produce reliable results in the presence of changing evidence order.

(2) Detecting zero-day attack paths

Since Cyber SA in large enterprise networks is gained through synthesized analysis of multiple data sources, evidence fusion is a fundamentally important Cyber SA capability. In the literature, a variety of homogeneous evidence fusion techniques (e.g., alert correlation) have been developed. However, automated *heterogeneous* evidence fusion is an under-investigated research area. In practice, heterogeneous evidence fusion is primarily relying on SIEM rules manually developed by security analysts. Unfortunately, it is extremely expensive to generate high quality SIEM rules.

In this line of work, we took the first steps towards using Bayesian Networks to perform evidence fusion towards detection of zero-day attack paths in enterprise networks. Detecting zero-day attacks is one of the most fundamentally challenging Cyber SA problems yet to be solved. Zero-day attacks are usually enabled by unknown vulnerabilities. The information asymmetry between what the attacker knows and what the defender knows makes zero-day exploits extremely hard to detect. Signature-based detection assumes that a signature is already available for each exploit, therefore it fails to detect unknown exploits. Anomaly detection may detect zero-day exploits, but this solution has to cope with high false positive rates.

Considering the extreme difficulty of detecting individual zero-day exploits, a substantially more viable strategy is to identify zero-day attack paths. In real world, attack campaigns are relying on a chain of attack actions, which forms an attack path. Each attack chain is a partial order of exploits and each exploit is exploiting a particular vulnerability. A zero day attack path is a multi-step attack path that includes one or more zero-day exploits. A key insight in dealing with zero-day attack paths is to analyze the chaining effect. Typically, it is not very likely for a zero-day attack chain to be 100% zero-day, namely having every exploit in the chain be a zero-day exploit. Hence, defenders can assume that (i) the non-zero-day exploits in the chain are detectable; and (ii) these detectable exploits have certain chaining relationships with the zero-day exploits in the chain. As a result, connecting the detected non-zero-day segments through a path is an effective way of revealing the zero-day segments on the same chain.

Both alert correlation and attack graphs are possible solutions for generating potential attack paths, but they are still very limited in revealing the zero-day ones. A main reason for this is that they both perform homogeneous evidence fusion and they both have very limited capability to perform *heterogeneous* evidence fusion. A key observation is that zero-day attack path detection requires heterogeneous evidence fusion, whereas homogeneous evidence fusion is simply not adequate.

We observed that Bayesian networks can incorporate literally all kinds of knowledge the defender has about the zero-day attack paths; we also observed that a Bayesian network based approach is elastic. Whenever new knowledge is gained about zero-day attacks, such new knowledge can be incorporated into the Bayesian network. Whenever erroneous knowledge is identified, one can easily remove it. Based on these observations, we developed an innovative technique which uses Bayesian Networks to perform heterogeneous evidence fusion towards detection of zero-day attack paths in enterprise networks. We proposed constructing Bayesian networks at the system object level by introducing the object instance graph. We designed, implemented and evaluated a system prototype named ZePro, which can effectively and automatically identify zero-day attack paths.

8.4   Thrust 4 Research Outcomes

8.4.1   Web-Based Visualization of Snort Alert Data Using Ensemble Approaches

We firstly developed a netflow visualization tool [HH16]. This tool visualizes correlated netflows and Snort alerts as charts (e.g., bar charts, scatter plots), a simple design rational that was chosen because it is well recognized and well understood by the analysts, and because it has been shown to be effective for the types of tasks the analysts perform. Based on our model of construction tools designed to fit our analysts' workflow and mental models, each analyst has full control to define the data attributes on the graph's axes, as well as which data to aggregate at different graph positions.

We further extended our investigation of how ensemble visualization techniques can be applied within our visualization tool. Ensemble visualization studies the problem of visualizing very large datasets made up of "members" that represent events or episodic repetition within the data. In the physical science community, ensembles often encode simulation data, where each member is a simulation run with specific input parameters. In a cyber security environment, an ensemble might be a collection of network data, where each member represents a particular type of suspected attack or collection of network traffic associated with a specific category of class of activity.

We then developed a prototype web-based application, based on our original chart-based netflow visualization tool, to represent netflows and Snort alerts as ensemble members, and to then apply ensemble visualization approaches to present this data. This involved two important challenges: (i) designing a method to represent network security data in a way that fits the "ensemble of members" input requirements for ensemble visualization techniques; and (ii) building off existing ensemble visualization methods to visually present netflow and Snort alert data in ways that can efficiently and effectively support network analysts.

To address these challenges, we developed methods to identify patterns in time-varying ensemble members in two different ways. This makes the ensemble approach much more applicable to cyber situation data, since all analysis on network data requires consideration of a time dimension. These techniques were extended and integrated into our ensemble-based network analysis framework.

9   Conclusions

In this chapter, we provided an overview of Cyber Situational Awareness, an emerging research area in the broad field of cyber security, and discuss, at least at a high level, how to gain Cyber Situation Awareness. Our discussion focused on answering the following questions: What is cyber situation awareness? Why is research needed? What are the research objectives and scientific principles? Why should one take a multidisciplinary approach? How could one take an end-to-end holistic approach? What are the future research directions?

Acknowledgements. We would like to thank the Army Research Office (ARO) for sponsoring this MURI project. This work was supported by ARO award W911NF-09-1-0525.

References

[ACJ14]   Albanese, M., Cam, H., Jajodia, S.: Automated cyber situation awareness tools for improving analyst performance. In: Pino, R.E., Kott, A., Shevenell, M. (eds.) Cybersecurity Systems for Human Cognition Augmentation. Advances in Information Security, vol. 61, pp. 47–60. Springer, Cham (2014)

[AJN12]   Albanese, M., Jajodia, S., Noel, S.: Time-efficient and cost-effective network hardening using attack graphs. In: Proceedings of the 42nd Annual IEEE/IFIP International Conference on Dependable Systems and Networks (DSN 2012), 25–28 June, Boston, Massachusetts, USA (2012)

[AMP11]   Albanese, M., Molinaro, C., Persia, F., Picariello, A., Subrahmanian, V.S.: Finding unexplained activities in video. In: Proceedings of 2011 International Joint Conference on Artificial Intelligence, accepted for both a talk and poster presentation, Barcelona, July 2011

[AMP14]   Albanese, M., Molinaro, C., Persia, F., Picariello, A., Subrahmanian, V.S.: Discovering the top-k unexplained sequences in time-stamped observation data. IEEE Trans. Knowl. Data Eng. **26**(3), 577–594 (2014)

[CLY12]   Chen, P.-C., Liu, P., Yen, J., Mullen, T.: Experience-based cyber situation recognition using relaxable logic patterns. In: The 2nd IEEE International Conference on Cognitive Methods in Situation Awareness and Decision Support (CogSIMA 2012), New Orleans, LA, 6–8 March 2012 (2012)

[DAG13]   Dutt, V., Ahn, Y., Gonzalez, C.: Cyber situation awareness: modeling detection of cyber attacks with instance-based learning theory. Hum. Factors **55**(3), 605–618 (2013)

[DSL12]   Dai, J., Sun, X., Liu, P., Giacobe, N.: Gaining big picture awareness through an interconnected cross-layer situation knowledge reference model. In: ASE International Conference on Cyber Security, Washington DC, 14–16 December (2012)

[Gardner87] Gardner, H.: The Mind's New Science: A History of the Cognitive Revolution. Basic Books, New York (1987)

[GM13]   Giacobe, N.A., McNeese, M.D., Mancuso, V.F., Minotra, D.: Capturing human cognition in cyber-security simulations with NETS. In: 2013 IEEE International Conference on Intelligence and Security Informatics (ISI), 4–7 June 2013, pp. 284–288 (2013)

[HH16]   Healey, C.G., Hao, L., Hutchinson, S.E.: Visualizations and analysts. In: Erbacher, R., Kott, A., Wang, C. (eds.) Cyber Defense and Situational Awareness. Advances in Information Security, vol. 62, pp. 145–165. Springer, Cham (2016)

[HS88]   Hart, S.G., Staveland, L.E.: Development of NASA-TLX (Task Load Index): results of empirical and theoretical research. Adv. Psychol. **52**, 139–183 (1988)

[JCR12]   Jariwala, S., Champion, M., Rajivan, P., Cooke, N.J.: Influence of team communication and coordination on the performance of teams at the iCTF competition. In: Proceedings of the 56th Annual Conference of the Human Factors and Ergonomics Society, Human Factors and Ergonomics Society, Santa Monica (2012)

[JCR16]   Jariwala, S., Champion, M., Rajivan, P., Cooke, N.J.: Influence of team communication and coordination on the performance of teams at the iCTF competition. In: Proceedings of the 56th Annual Conference of the Human Factors and Ergonomics Society, Human Factors and Ergonomics Society, Santa Monica (2016)

[MGL15]   Zhao, M., Grossklags, J., Liu, P.: An empirical study of web vulnerability discovery ecosystems. In: ACM CCS (2015)

[MMP14] Molinaro, C., Moscato, V., Picariello, A., Pugliese, A., Rullo, A., Subrahmanian, V.S.: PADUA: a parallel architecture to detect unexplained activities. ACM Trans. Internet Technol. **14**, 3 (2014)

[NNL12] Natrajan, A., Ning, P., Liu, Y., Jajodia, S., Hutchinson, S.E.: NSDMine: automated discovery of network service dependencies. In: Proceedings of the 31st Annual International Conference on Computer Communications (INFOCOM 2012), 25–30 March 2012, Orlando, Florida (2012)

[PNJ12] Peddycord III, B., Ning, P., Jajodia, S.: On the accurate identification of network service dependencies in distributed systems. In: Proceedings of the USENIX 26th Large Installation System Administration Conference (LISA 2012), San Diego, CA, 9–14 December (2012)

[RB14] Rimland, J., Ballora, M.: Using complex event processing (CEP) and vocal synthesis techniques to improve comprehension of sonified human-centric data. In: Proceedings of the SPIE Conference on Sensing Technology and Applications, vol. 9122, June 2014

[RC16] Rajivan, P., Cooke, N.J.: A methodology for research on the cognitive science of cyber defense. J. Cognit. Eng. Decis. Making Special Issue on Cybersecurity Decision Making (2016)

[RSC11] Rajivan, P., Shankaranarayanan, V., Cooke, N.J.: CyberCog: a synthetic task environment for studies of cyber situation awareness. In: Presentation and Proceedings of 10th International Conference on Naturalistic Decision Making (NDM), May 31-June 3, Orlando, FL (2011)

[SJP15] Serra, E., Jajodia, S., Pugliese, A., Rullo, A., Subrahmanian, V.S.: Pareto-optimal adversarial defense of enterprise systems. ACM Trans. Inf. Syst. Secur. 17(3) (2015)

[SST09] Scielzo, S., Strater, L.D., Tinsley, M.L., Ungvarsky, D.M., Endsley, M.R.: Developing a subjective shared situation awareness inventory for teams. In: Proceedings of the Human Factors and Ergonomics Society Annual Meeting, vol. 53, no. 4, pp. 289–293. SAGE Publications, Los Angeles (2009)

[Taylor90] Taylor, R.M.: Situational awareness rating technique (SART): the development of a tool for aircrew systems design. In: Situational Awareness in Aerospace Operations (AGARD-CP-478), pp. 3/1–3/17, Neuilly Sur Seine, NATO – AGARD, France (1990)

[TS09] Tadda, G.P., Salerno, J.S.: Overview of cyber situation awareness. In: Jajodia, S., Liu, P., Swarup, V., Wang, C. (eds.) Cyber Situational Awareness. Advances in Information Security, vol. 46, pp. 15–35. Springer, Heidelberg (2009)

[WNX13] Wang, R., Ning, P., Xie, T., Chen, Q.: MetaSymploit: day-one defense against script-bases attacks with security-enhanced symbolic analysis. In: Proceedings of 22nd USENIX Security Symposium (Security 2013), August 2013

[XLO10] Xie, P., Li, J.H., Ou, X., Liu, P., Levy, R.: Using bayesian networks for cyber security analysis. In: Proceedings of IEEE DSN-DCCS (2010)

[ZK13] Zhong, C., Kirubakaran, D.S., Yen, J., Liu, P., Hutchinson, S., Cam, H.: How to use experience in cyber analysis: an analytical reasoning support system. In: Proceedings of IEEE Conference on Intelligence and Security Informatics (ISI) (2013)

[ZSY14] Zhong, C., Samuel, D., Yen, J., Liu, P., Erbacher, R., Hutchinson, S., Etoty, R., Cam, H., Glodek, W.: RankAOH: context-driven similarity-based retrieval of experiences in cyber analysis. In: Proceedings of IEEE CogSIMA Conference (2014)

[ZYL17] Zhong, C., et al.: Studying analysts data triage operations in cyber defense situational analysis. In: Liu, P., Jajodia, S., Wang, C. (eds) Theory and Models for Cyber Situation Awareness. LNCS, vol. 10030, pp. 128–169. Springer, Cham (2017)

Computer and Information Science

An Integrated Framework for Cyber Situation Awareness

Sushil Jajodia and Massimiliano Albanese(⊠)

Center for Secure Information Systems, George Mason University,
Fairfax, VA 22030, USA
{jajodia,malbanes}@gmu.edu

Abstract. In this chapter, we present a framework that integrates an array of techniques and automated tools designed with the objective of drastically enhancing the Cyber Situation Awareness process. This framework incorporates the theory and the tools we developed to answer – *automatically* and *efficiently* – some of the fundamental questions security analysts may need to ask in the context of Cyber Situation Awareness. Most of the work presented in this chapter is the result of the research effort conducted by the authors as part of a the Multidisciplinary University Research Initiative project sponsored by the Army Research Office that was mentioned in the introductory chapter. We present the key challenges the research community has been called to address in this space, and describe our major accomplishments in tackling those challenges.

1 Introduction

Without loss of generality, the process of situation awareness can be viewed as a three-phase process: situation perception, situation comprehension, and situation projection [1]. *Perception* provides information about the status, attributes, and dynamics of relevant elements within the environment. *Comprehension* of the situation encompasses how people combine, interpret, store, and retain information. *Projection* of the elements of the environment (situation) into the near future encompasses the ability to make predictions based on the knowledge acquired through perception and comprehension.

In order to make informed decisions, security analysts need to be aware of the current situation, the impact and evolution of an attack, the behavior of the attackers, the quality of available information and models, and the plausible futures of the current situation. Some of the questions they may ask are: Is there any ongoing attack? If so, where is the attacker? Are available attack models sufficient to understand what is observed? Can they predict an attacker's goal? If so, how can they prevent that goal from being reached?

This work was supported in part by the Army Research Office MURI awards number W911NF-09-1-0525 and W911NF-13-1-0421 and by the Office of Naval Research grant number N00014-15-1-2007.

P. Liu et al. (Eds.): Cyber Sitation Awareness, LNCS 10030, pp. 29–46, 2017.
DOI: 10.1007/978-3-319-61152-5_2

In this chapter, we describe several techniques, mechanisms, and tools that can help form and leverage specific types of cyber situation awareness. This framework aims at enhancing the traditional cyber defense process by automating many of the capabilities that have traditionally required a significant involvement of human analysts and other individuals. Ideally, we envision the evolution of the current human-in-the-loop approach to cyber defense into a human-on-the-loop approach, where human analysts would only be responsible for examining and validating or sanitizing the results generated by automated tools, rather than being forced to comb through daunting amounts of log entries and security alerts.

The remainder of this chapter is organized as follows. Section 2 discusses the overall process of Cyber Situation Awareness, and Sect. 3 presents a motivating example we use throughout the chapter. Section 4 introduces the proposed framework, whereas Sect. 5 discusses our scientific progress and major research accomplishments in more detail. Finally, Sect. 6 gives some concluding remarks.

2   The Process of Cyber Situation Awareness

The security analyst – or cyber defense analyst – plays a major role in all the operational aspects of maintaining the security of an enterprise. Security analysts are also responsible for studying the threat landscape with an eye towards emerging threats to the organization. Unfortunately, given the current state of the art in the area of automation, the operational aspects of IT security may still be too time-consuming to allow this type of outward looking focus in most realistic scenarios. Therefore, the scenario we envision – where automated tools would gather and preprocess large amounts of data on behalf of the analyst – is a highly desirable one. Ideally, such tools should be able to automatically answer most, if not all, the questions an analyst may ask about the current situation, the impact and evolution of an attack, the behavior of the attackers, the quality of available information and models, and the plausible futures of the current situation. In the following, we define the fundamental questions that an effective Cyber Situation Awareness framework must be able to help answer. For each question, we identify the inputs as well the outputs of the Cyber Situation Awareness process, and we also briefly comment on the life cycle of the situation awareness gained in response to each question.

1. **Current situation.** *Is there any ongoing attack? If yes, what is the stage of the intrusion and where is the attacker?*
   Answering this set of questions implies the capability of effectively detecting ongoing intrusions, and identifying the assets that might have been already compromised. With respect to these questions, the input to the CSA process is represented by IDS logs, firewall logs, and data from other security monitoring tools. On the other hand, the product of the CSA process is a detailed mapping of current intrusive activities. This type of CSA may quickly become obsolete – if not acted upon timely or updated frequently – as the intruder progresses within the system.

2. **Impact.** *How is the attack impacting the organization or mission? Can we assess the damage?*
   Answering this set of questions implies the capability of accurately assessing the impact, so far, of ongoing attacks. In this case, the CSA process requires knowledge of the organization's assets along with some measure of each asset's value. Based on this information, the output of the CSA process is an estimate of the damage caused so far by ongoing intrusive activities. As for the previous case, this type of CSA must be frequently updated to remain useful, because damage will increase as the attack progresses.

3. **Evolution.** *How is the situation evolving? Can we track all the steps of an attack?*
   Answering this set of questions implies the capability of monitoring ongoing attacks, once such attacks have been detected. In this case, the input to the CSA process is the situation awareness generated in response to the first set of questions above, whereas the output is a detailed understanding of how the attack is progressing. Developing this capability can help address the *useful life* limitations highlighted above and *refresh* the situation awareness generated in response to the first two sets of questions.

4. **Behavior.** *How are the attackers expected to behave? What are their strategies?*
   Answering this set of questions implies the capability of modeling the attacker's behavior in order to understand its goals and strategies. Ideally, the output of the CSA process with respect to this set of questions is a set of formal models (e.g., game theoretic models, stochastic models) of the attacker's behavior. The attacker's behavior may change over time, therefore models need to adapt to a changing adversarial landscape.

5. **Forensics.** *How did the attacker reach the current situation? What was he trying to achieve?*
   Answering this set of questions implies the capability of analyzing the logs *after the fact* and correlating observations in order to understand how an attack originated and evolved. Although this is not strictly necessary, the CSA process may benefit, in addressing these questions, from the situation awareness gained in response to the fourth set of questions. In this case, the output of the CSA process includes a detailed understanding of the weaknesses and vulnerabilities that made the attack possible. This information can help security engineers and administrators harden system configurations in order to prevent similar incidents from occurring again in the future.

6. **Prediction.** *Can we predict plausible futures of the current situation?*
   Answering this set of questions implies the capability of predicting possible moves an attacker may take in the future. With respect to this set of questions, the input to the CSA process is represented by the situation awareness gained in response to the first (or third) and fourth sets of questions, namely, knowledge about the current situation (and its evolution) and knowledge about the attacker's behavior. The output is a set of possible alternative scenarios that may materialize in the future.

7. **Information.** *What information sources can we rely upon? Can we assess their quality?*
Answering this set of questions implies the capability of assessing the quality of the information sources all other tasks depend upon. With respect to this set of questions, the goal of the CSA process is to generate a detailed under-standing of how to weight all different sources when processing information in order to answer all other sets of question the overall CSA process is aiming to address. Being able to assess the reliability of each information source would enable automated tools to attach a confidence level to each finding.

It is clear from our discussion that some of these questions are strictly cor-related, and the ability to answer some of them may depend on the ability to answer other questions. For instance, as we have discussed above, the capability of predicting possible moves an attacker may take depends on the capability of modeling the attacker's behavior. A cross-cutting issue that affects all other aspects of the CSA process is *scalability*. Given the volumes of data involved in answering all these questions, we need to define approaches that are not only effective, but also computationally efficient. In most circumstances, determining a good course of action in a reasonable amount of time may be preferable to determining the best course of action, if this cannot be done in a timely manner.

In conclusion, the situation awareness process in the context of cyber defense entails the generation and maintenance of a body of knowledge that informs and is augmented by all the main functions of the cyber defense process [1]. Situation awareness is generated or used by different mechanisms and tools aimed at addressing the seven classes of questions that security analysts may routinely ask while performing their work tasks.

3   Motivating Example

Throughout this chapter, we will often refer to the network depicted in Fig. 1 as a motivating example. This network offers two public-facing services, namely *Online Shopping* and *Mobile Order Tracking*, and consists of three subnetworks separated by firewalls. The first two subnetworks implement the two services, and each of them includes a host accessible from the Internet. The third subnetwork implements the core business logic, and includes a central database server. An attacker who wants to steal sensitive data from the main database server will need to breach multiple firewalls and gain privileges on several hosts before reaching the target.

As attackers can leverage the complex interdependencies of network con-figurations and vulnerabilities to penetrate seemingly well-guarded networks, in-depth analysis of network vulnerabilities must consider attacker exploits not merely in isolation, but in combination. For this reason, in order to study the vul-nerability landscape of any enterprise network, we extensively use attack graphs, which reveal potential threats by enumerating paths that attackers can take to penetrate a network [8].

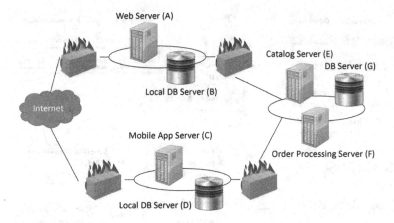

Fig. 1. Motivating example: enterprise network offering two public-facing services

The attack graph for the network of Fig. 1 is shown in Fig. 2. This attack graph shows that, once a vulnerability V_C on the Mobile Application Server (host h_C) has been exploited, we can expect the attacker to exploit either vulnerability V_D on host h_D or vulnerability V_F on host h_F. However, the attack graph alone does not answer the following important questions: Which vulnerability has the highest probability of being exploited? Which attack pattern will have the largest impact on the two services that the network provides? How can we mitigate the risk? Our framework is designed to answer these questions efficiently.

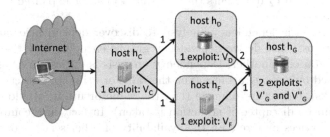

Fig. 2. The attack graph for the motivating example network

4   The Cyber Situation Awareness Framework

The proposed Cyber Situation Awareness framework is illustrated in Fig. 3. We start from analyzing the topology of the network, known vulnerabilities, possible zero-day vulnerabilities – these must be hypothesized – and their interdependencies. Vulnerabilities are often interdependent, making traditional point-wise vulnerability analysis ineffective. Our topological approach to vulnerability analysis

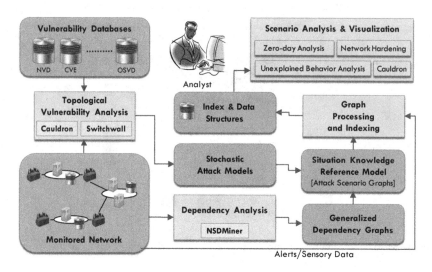

Fig. 3. The proposed Cyber Situation Awareness framework

allows to generate accurate attack graphs showing all the possible attack paths within the network.

A node in an attack graph represents – depending on the level of abstraction – an exploitable vulnerability (or family of exploitable vulnerabilities) in either a subnetwork, an individual host, or an individual software application. Edges represent causal relationships between vulnerabilities. For instance, an edge from a node V_1 to a node V_2 represents the fact that V_2 can be exploited after V_1 has been exploited.

We also perform dependency analysis to discover dependencies among services and/or hosts and derive dependency graphs encoding how these components depend on one another. Dependency analysis is critical to assess current damage caused by ongoing attacks (i.e., the value or utility of services disrupted by the attacks) and future damage (i.e., the value or utility of additional services that will be disrupted if no action is taken). In fact, in a complex enterprise, many services may rely on the availability of other services or resources. Therefore, they may be indirectly affected by the compromise of the services or resources they rely upon.

The dependency graph for the network of Fig. 1 is shown in Fig. 4. This graph shows that the two services *Online Shopping* and *Mobile Order Tracking* rely upon hosts h_A and h_C respectively. In turn, host h_A relies upon local database server h_B and host h_E, whereas host h_C relies upon local database server h_D and host h_F. Similarly, h_B, h_D, h_E, and h_F rely upon database server h_G, which then appears to be the most critical resource.

By combining the information contained in the dependency and attack graphs in what we call the *attack scenario graph*, we can then compute an estimate of the future damage that ongoing attacks might cause for each possible outcome

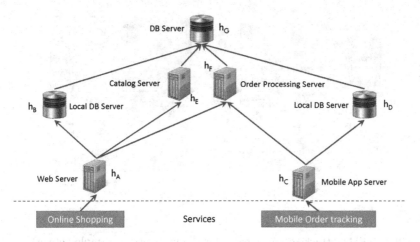

Fig. 4. The dependency graph for the motivating example network

of the current situation. In practice, the proposed attack scenario graph bridges the semantic gap between known vulnerabilities – the lowest abstraction level – and the missions or services that could be ultimately affected by the exploitation of such vulnerabilities – the highest abstraction level. The attack scenario graph for the network of Fig. 1 is shown in Fig. 5. In this figure, the graph on the left is an attack graph modeling all the vulnerabilities in the system and their relationships, whereas the graph on the right is a dependency graph capturing all the explicit and implicit dependencies between services and hosts. The edges from nodes in the attack graph to nodes in the dependency graph indicate which services or hosts are directly impacted by a successful vulnerability exploit, and are labeled with the corresponding exposure factor, that is the percentage loss the affected asset would experience upon successful execution of the exploit.

In order to enable concurrent monitoring of multiple attack types, we developed novel graph-based data structures and an index structure to index large amounts of alerts and event data in real-time. We also developed efficient algorithms to analyze such data structures and help automatically answers questions about the current cyber landscape and its evolution.

Moreover, the novel capabilities described so far have been leveraged to develop a suite of additional capabilities and tools, including but not limited to: topological vulnerability analysis [6], network hardening [3], and zero-day analysis [5]. Some of these capabilities and tools are discussed in the following section.

In summary, the proposed framework can provide security analysts with a high-level view of the cyber situation. From the simple example of Fig. 5 – which models a system including only a few hosts and services – it is clear that manual analysis could be extremely time-consuming even for relatively small systems. Instead, the graph of Fig. 5 provides analysts with a visual and very clear understanding of the situation, thus enabling them to focus on higher-level tasks that

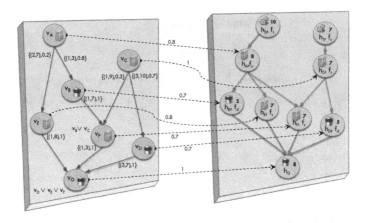

Fig. 5. The attack scenario graph for the motivating example network

require experience and intuition, and thus are more difficult to automate. Additionally, other classes of automated analytical processes may be developed within this framework to support the analyst during these higher-level tasks as well. For instance, based on the model of Fig. 5, we could automatically generate a ranked list of recommendations on the best course of action analysts should take to minimize the impact of ongoing and future attacks (e.g., sets of network hardening actions).

5   Scientific Progress and Major Accomplishments

In this section, we highlight major accomplishments achieved during the execution of the research project that led to the development of the framework discussed in the previous section.

5.1   Topological Vulnerability Analysis

Situation awareness, as defined in the previous sections, implies knowledge and understanding of both the defender (*knowledge of us*) and the attacker (*knowledge of them*). In turn, this implies knowledge and understanding of all the weaknesses existing in the computing infrastructure we aim to defend. By their very nature, security concerns on networks are highly interdependent. Each host's susceptibility to attack depends on the vulnerabilities of other hosts in the network. Attackers can combine vulnerabilities in unexpected ways, allowing them to incrementally penetrate a network and compromise critical systems. To protect our critical infrastructure networks, we must understand not only individual system vulnerabilities, but also their interdependencies. While we cannot predict the origin and timing of attacks, we can reduce their impact by knowing the possible attack paths through our networks. We need to transform raw security data into roadmaps that let us proactively prepare for attacks, manage vulnerability risks, and have real-time situation awareness. We cannot rely on manual processes and mental models. Instead, we need automated tools to analyze and visualize vulnerability dependencies and attack paths, so we can understand our overall security posture, providing context over the full security life cycle.

A viable approach to such full-context security is called topological vulnerability analysis (TVA) [6]. TVA monitors the state of network assets, maintains models of network vulnerabilities and residual risk, and combines these to produce models that convey the impact of individual and combined vulnerabilities on the overall security posture. The core element of this tool is an attack graph showing all possible ways an attacker can penetrate the network. Topological vulnerability analysis looks at vulnerabilities and their protective measures within the context of overall network security by modeling their interdependencies via attack graphs. This approach provides a unique new capability, transforming raw security data into a roadmap that lets one proactively prepare for attacks, manage vulnerability risks, and have real-time situation awareness. It supports both offensive (e.g., penetration testing) and defensive (e.g., network hardening) applications. The mapping of attack paths through a network via TVA provides a concrete understanding of how individual and combined vulnerabilities impact overall network security. For example, we can (i) determine whether risk-mitigating efforts have a significant impact on overall security; (ii) determine how much a new vulnerability will impact overall security; and (iii) analyze how changes to individual hosts may increase overall risk to the enterprise.

This approach has been implemented as a security tool – CAULDRON [7] – which transforms raw security data into a model of all possible network attack paths. In developing this tool, several technical challenges have been addressed, including the design of appropriate models, efficient model population, effective visualization and decision support tools, and the development of scalable mathematical representations and algorithms. The result is a working software tool that offers truly unique capabilities.

Figure 6 shows a simplified attack graph for a network of three hosts (referred to as host 0, 1, and 2 respectively). Rectangles represent vulnerabilities that an attacker may exploit, whereas ovals represent security conditions that are either required to exploit a vulnerability (*pre-conditions*) or created as the result of an exploit (*post-conditions*). Purple ovals represent initial conditions – which depend on the initial configuration of the system – whereas blue ovals represent intermediate conditions created as the result of an exploit. In this example, the attacker's objective is to gain administrative privileges on host 2, a condition that is denoted as root(2). In practice, to prevent the attacker from reaching a given security condition, the defender has to prevent exploitation of all vulnerabilities that have that condition as a post-condition. For instance, in the example of Fig. 6, one could prevent the attacker from gaining user privileges on host 1, denoted as user(1), by preventing exploitation of rsh(0,1), rsh(2,1), sshd_bof(0,1), and sshd_bof(2,1). Conversely, to prevent exploitation of a vulnerability, at least one pre-condition must be disabled. For instance, in the example of Fig. 6, one

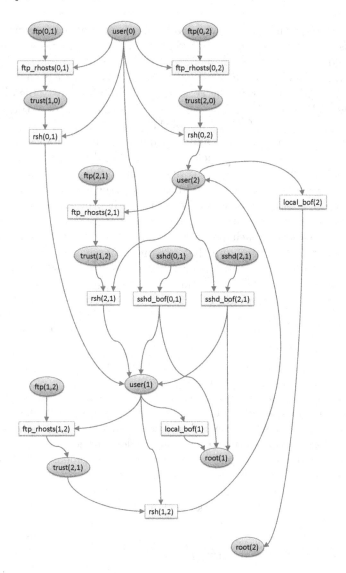

Fig. 6. An example of attack graph (Color figure online)

could prevent the attacker from exploiting rsh(1,2) by disabling either trust(2,1) or user(1).

The analysis of attack graphs provides alternative sets of protective measures that guarantee safety of critical systems. For instance, in the example of Fig. 6, one could prevent the attacker from reaching the target security condition root(2) by disabling one of the following two sets of initial conditions: {ftp(0,2), ftp(1,2)}, or {ftp(0,2), ftp(0,1), sshd(0,1)}.

Through this unique new capability, administrators are able to determine the best sets of protective measures that should be applied in their environment. In fact, each set of protective measures may have a different cost or impact, and administrators can choose the best option with respect to any of these variables.

Still, we must understand that not all attacks can be prevented, and there must usually remain some residual vulnerability even after reasonable protective measures have been applied. We then rely on intrusion detection techniques to identify actual attack instances. But the detection process needs to be tied to residual vulnerabilities, especially ones that lie on paths to critical network resources as discovered by TVA. Tools such as Snort can analyze network traffic and identify attempts to exploit unpatched vulnerabilities in real time, thus enabling timely response and mitigation efforts. Once attacks are detected, comprehensive capabilities are needed to react to them. TVA can reduce the impact of attacks by providing knowledge of the possible vulnerability paths through the network. TVA attack graphs can be used to correlate and aggregate network attack events, across platforms as well as across the network. These attack graphs also provide the necessary context for optimal response to ongoing attacks.

In conclusion, topological analysis of vulnerabilities plays an important role in gaining situation awareness, and more specifically what we earlier defined *knowledge of us*. Without automated tools such as CAULDRON, human analysts would be required to manually perform vulnerability analysis, and this would be an extremely tedious and error-prone task. From the example of Fig. 6, it is clear that even a relatively small network may result in a large and complex attack graph. With the introduction of automated tools such as CAULDRON, the role of the analyst shifts towards higher-level tasks: instead of trying to analyze and correlate individual vulnerabilities, analysts have in front of them a clear picture of existing vulnerability paths; instead of trying to manually map alerts to possible vulnerability exploits, analysts are required to validate the findings of the tool and drill down as needed [4]. The revised role of human analysts – while not changing their ultimate mandate and responsibilities – will require that they are properly trained to use and benefit from the new automated tools. Most likely, as their productivity is expected to increase as a result of automating the most repetitive and time-consuming tasks, fewer analysts will be required to monitor a given infrastructure.

5.2   Zero-Day Analysis

As stated earlier, attackers can leverage complex interdependencies among network configurations and vulnerabilities to penetrate seemingly well-guarded networks. Besides well-known weaknesses, attackers may leverage unknown (zero-day) vulnerabilities, which even developers are not aware of. In-depth analysis of network vulnerabilities must consider attacker exploits not merely in isolation, but in combination. Attack graphs reveal such threats by enumerating potential paths that attackers can take to penetrate networks. This helps determine whether a given set of network hardening measures provides safety of given critical assets. However, attack graphs can only provide qualitative results (i.e., secure or insecure), and this may render resulting hardening recommendations ineffective or far from optimal.

To address these limitations, traditional efforts on network security metrics typically assign numeric scores to vulnerabilities as their relative exploitability or likelihood, based on known facts about each vulnerability. However, this approach is clearly not applicable to zero-day vulnerabilities due to the lack of prior knowledge or experience. In fact, a major criticism of existing efforts on security metrics is that zero-day vulnerabilities are unmeasurable due to the less predictable nature of both the process of introducing software flaws and that of discovering and exploiting vulnerabilities [10]. Recent work addresses the above limitations by proposing a security metric for zero-day vulnerabilities, namely, k-zero day safety [14]. Intuitively, this metric is based on the number of distinct zero-day vulnerabilities that are needed to compromise a given network asset. A larger such number indicates relatively more security, because it is less likely to have a larger number of different unknown vulnerabilities all available at the same time, applicable to the same network, and exploitable by the same attacker. However, as shown in [14], the problem of computing the exact value of k is intractable. Moreover, Wang et al. [14] assume the existence of a complete attack graph, but, unfortunately, generating zero-day attack graphs for large networks is usually infeasible in practice [13]. These facts comprise a major limitation in applying this metric or any other similar metric based on attack graphs.

In order to address the limitations of existing approaches, we proposed a set of efficient solutions [5] to enable zero-day analysis of practical applicability to networks of realistic sizes. This approach – which combines on-demand attack graph generation with the evaluation of k-zero-day safety – starts from the problem of deciding whether a given network asset is at least k-zero-day safe for a given value of k, meaning that it satisfies some baseline security requirements: in other words, in order to penetrate a system, an attacker must be able to exploit at least a relatively high number of zero-day vulnerabilities. Second, it identifies an upper bound on the value of k, intuitively corresponding to the maximum security level that can be achieved with respect to this metric. Finally, if k is large enough, we can assume that the system is sufficiently secure with respect to zero-day attacks. Otherwise, we can compute the exact value of k by efficiently reusing the partial attack graph computed in previous steps.

In conclusion, similarly to what we discussed at the end of the previous section, the capability presented in this section is critical to gain situation awareness, and can be achieved either manually or automatically. However, given the uncertain nature of zero-day vulnerabilities, the results of manual analysis could be more prone to subjective interpretation than any other capability we discuss in this chapter. At the same time, since automated analysis relies on assumptions about the existence of zero-day vulnerabilities, complete reliance on automated tools may not be the best option for this capability, and a human-in-the-loop solution may provide the most benefits. In fact, the solution presented in [5] can be seen as a decision support system where human analysts can play a role in the overall workflow.

5.3   Network Hardening

As discussed earlier, attack graphs reveal threats by enumerating potential paths that attackers can take to penetrate networks. Attack graph analysis can be extended to automatically generate recommendations for hardening networks, which consists in changing network configurations in such a way to make networks resilient to certain attacks and prevent attackers from reaching certain goals. One must consider combinations of network conditions to harden, which has corresponding impact on removing paths in the attack graph. For instance, in Sect. 5.1, we discussed how one could prevent the attacker from reaching the target security condition root(2) in the example of Fig. 6, and we identified two possible hardening solutions. Furthermore, one can generate hardening solutions that are optimal with respect to some notion of cost. Such hardening solutions prevent the attack from succeeding, while minimizing the associated costs. However, the general solution to optimal network hardening scales exponentially as the number of hardening options itself scales exponentially with the size of the attack graph.

In applying network hardening to realistic network environments, it is crucial that the algorithms are able to scale. Progress has been made in reducing the complexity of attack graph manipulation so that it scales quadratically – or linearly within defined security zones [13]. However, many approaches for generating hardening recommendations search for exact solutions [15], which is an intractable problem. Another limitation of most work in this area is the assumption that network conditions are hardened independently. This assumption does not hold true in real network environments. Realistically, network administrators can take actions that affect vulnerabilities across the network, such as pushing patches out to many systems at once. Furthermore, the same hardening results may be obtained through more than one action.

Overall, to provide realistic recommendations, the hardening strategy we proposed in [3] takes such factors into account, and removes the assumption of independent hardening actions. We define a network hardening strategy as a set of allowable atomic actions that administrators can take (e.g., shutting down an ftp server, blacklisting certain IP addresses) and that involve hardening multiple network conditions. A formal cost model is introduced to account for the impact of these hardening actions. Each hardening action has a cost both in terms of implementation and in terms of loss of productivity (e.g., when hardening requires shutting down a vulnerable service). This model allows the definition of hardening costs that accurately reflect realistic network environments. Because computing the minimum-cost hardening solution is intractable, we introduce an approximation algorithm to compute suboptimal hardening solutions. This algorithm finds near-optimal solutions while scaling almost linearly – for certain values of the parameters – with the size of the attack graph, as confirmed by experimental evaluations. Finally, theoretical analysis shows that there is a theoretical upper bound for the worst-case approximation ratio, whereas experimental results show that, in practice, the approximation ratio is much lower than such bound, that is, the solutions found using this approach are not far, in terms of cost, from the optimal solution. In conclusion, automated analysis of network hardening options can greatly improve the performance of a security analyst, by providing a timely list of recommended strategies to prevent attackers from compromising the target system while, at the same time, minimizing the cost for the defender. The analyst will then be responsible solely for validating the recommended strategies and selecting the ones that appear to be the most effective in meeting not only quantitative but also qualitative requirements. For instance, automated analysis may conclude that the most cost-effective hardening solution is one that requires – amongst other things – to temporarily shut down the server hosting the company's web site. Although the website may not be running any revenue-generating services, the potential impact on the company's reputation may make this solution less attractive, and a human analyst looking at the results of the automated tools may opt for the second-best solution after taking into account factors that the tools were not able to capture.

5.4   Probabilistic Temporal Attack Graph

The first step in achieving any level of automation in the situation awareness process is to develop the capability of modeling cyber-attacks and their consequences. This capability is critical to support many of the additional capabilities needed to address the key questions presented earlier in this chapter (e.g., modeling the attacker, predicting future scenarios).

Attack graphs have been widely used to model attack patterns, and to correlate alerts. However, existing approaches typically do not provide mechanisms for evaluating the likelihood of each attack pattern or its impact on the organization or mission. To address this limitation, we extend the attack graph model discussed earlier in this chapter with the notion of *timespan distribution*, which encodes probabilistic knowledge of the attacker's behavior as well as temporal constraints on the unfolding of attacks. We assume that each step of an attack sequence is completed within certain temporal windows after the previous exploit has been executed, each associated with a probability. For instance, suppose an attacker has gained some privileges on host h_E in Fig. 1. Using these privileges, he can then create the conditions to exploit a vulnerability on the main database server. However, this will take a variable amount of time depending on his skill level. The attacker will then have time to exploit the vulnerability until the vulnerability itself is patched, or the attack is discovered.

Leversage and Byres [9] describe how to estimate the *mean time to compromise* a system and relate that to the skill level of the attacker. This approach can be generalized to estimate timespan distributions for individual vulnerability exploits. In fact, we can assume that the time taken to exploit a vulnerability varies with the skill level of the attacker. Additionally, some vulnerabilities are easier to exploit than others, thus exhibiting higher probabilities. Intuitively, a timespan distribution specifies a set of disjoint time intervals when a given exploit might be executed, and an incomplete probability distribution over such time intervals.

In our model, edges in the attack graph are labeled with timespan distributions. For instance, in the attack graph of Fig. 5, the edges from V_A to V_E and V_B are labeled with $\{(2,7), 0.2\}$ and $\{(1,3), 0.8\}$ respectively, meaning that, after exploiting V_A, with 20% probability an attacker will exploit V_E between 2 and 7 time units later, and with 80% probability he will exploit V_B between 1 and 3 time units later.

5.5 Dependency Graph

Government or enterprise networks today host a wide variety of network services, which often depend on one another to provide and support network-based services and applications. Understanding such dependencies is essential for maintaining the well-being of a network and its applications, particularly in the presence of network attacks and failures. In a typical government or enterprise network, which is complex and dynamic in configuration, it is non-trivial to identify all these services and their dependencies. Several techniques have been developed to learn such dependencies automatically. However, they are either too complex to fine-tune or cluttered with false positives and/or false negatives.

We developed several novel techniques as well as a tool named NSDMiner (which stands for Network Service Dependencies Miner) to automatically discover the dependencies between network services from passively collected network traffic [11]. NSDMiner is non-intrusive: it does not require any modification of existing software, or injection of network packets. More importantly, NSDMiner achieves higher accuracy than previous network-based approaches. Our experimental evaluation, which uses network traffic collected from our campus network, shows that NSDMiner outperforms the two best existing solutions by a significant margin.

Specifically, we developed three additional techniques to assist in the automatic identification of network service dependencies through passively monitoring and analyzing network traffic, including a logarithm-based ranking scheme aimed at more accurate detection of network service dependencies with lower false positives, an inference technique for identifying the dependencies involving infrequently used network services, and an approach for automated discovery of clusters of network services configured for load balancing or backup purposes. We performed extensive experimental evaluation of these techniques using real-world traffic collected from a college campus network. The experimental results demonstrate that these techniques advance the state of the art in automated detection and inference of network service dependencies.

5.6 Additional Research Accomplishments

The wide array of accomplishments described in the previous sections is not exhaustive of the work performed as part of the project mentioned earlier in this chapter. In the following, we briefly describe additional lines of research we pursued and the accomplishments we achieved in those areas. We refer the reader to our previous publications for more information.

We studied network diversity as a security property of networks [16]. The interest in diversity as a security mechanism has recently been revived in various applications, such as Moving Target Defense (MTD), resisting worms in sensor networks, and improving the robustness of network routing. However, most existing efforts on formally modeling diversity have focused on a single system running diverse software replicas or variants. At a higher abstraction level, as a global property of the entire network, diversity and its impact on security have received limited attention. In our work, we took the first step towards formally modeling network diversity as a security metric for evaluating the robustness of networks against potential zero-day attacks. Specifically, we first devised a biodiversity-inspired metric based on the effective number of existing distinct resources. We then proposed two complementary diversity metrics, based on the least and average attacker's effort, respectively.

We also proposed a probabilistic framework for assessing the completeness and quality of available attack models [2], both at the intrusion detection level (e.g., IDS signatures) and at the alert correlation level (e.g., attack graphs). Intrusion detection and alert correlation are valuable and complementary techniques for identifying security threats in complex networks. However, both methods rely on models encoding a priori knowledge of either normal or malicious behavior. As a result, these methods are incapable of quantifying how well the underlying models explain what is observed on the network. Our approach overcomes this limitation, and enables us to estimate the probability that an arbitrary sequence of events is not explained by a given set of models. We leverage important mathematical properties of this framework to estimate such probabilities efficiently, and design fast algorithms for identifying sequences of events that are unexplained with a probability above a given threshold. This approach holds promise of identifying zero-day attacks, because such attacks (by definition of zero-day) are likely to be incompatible with all known traffic patterns.

Finally, we developed Switchwall [12], an Ethernet-based network fingerprinting technique that detects unauthorized changes to the L2/L3 network topology, the active devices, and the availability of an enterprise network. The network map is generated at an initial known state and is then periodically verified to detect deviations in a fully automated manner. Switchwall leverages a single vantage point and uses only very common protocols (PING and ARP) without any requirement for new software or hardware. Moreover, no previous knowledge of the topology is required, and our approach works on mixed speed, mixed vendors networks. Switchwall is able to identify a wide-range of changes, and this capability has been validated by our experimental results on both real and simulated networks.

6   Conclusions

As we discussed, the process of situation awareness in the context of cyber defense consists of three phases: situation perception, situation comprehension, and situation projection. Situation awareness is generated and used across these three phases, and cyber analysts must answer several key questions during this process. In this chapter, we outlined an integrated approach to cyber situation awareness, and presented a framework – comprising several mechanisms and automated tools – that can help bridge the semantic gap between the available low-level data and the mental models and cognitive processes of security analysts.

In our project, we focused on techniques and tools for automatically answering the questions the analyst may ask about the current situation, the impact and evolution of an attack, the behavior of the attackers, the quality of available information and models, and the plausible futures of the current situation.

Although this framework represents a first important step in the right direction, a lot of work remains to be done for systems to achieve self-awareness capabilities. Key areas that need to be further investigated include adversarial modeling and reasoning under uncertainty, and promising approaches may include game-theoretic and control-theoretic solutions.

References

1. Albanese, M., Jajodia, S.: Formation of awareness. In: Kott, A., Wang, C., Erbacher, R.F. (eds.) Cyber Defense and Situational Awareness. Advances in Information Security, vol. 62, pp. 47–62. Springer, Cham (2014)
2. Albanese, M., Erbacher, R.F., Jajodia, S., Molinaro, C., Persia, F., Picariello, A., Sperlì, G., Subrahmanian, V.: Recognizing unexplained behavior in network traffic. In: Pino, R.E. (ed.) Network Science and Cybersecurity. Advances in Information Security, vol. 55, pp. 39–62. Springer, New York (2014)
3. Albanese, M., Jajodia, S., Noel, S.: Time-efficient and cost-effective network hardening using attack graphs. In: Proceedings of the 42nd Annual IEEE/IFIP International Conference on Dependable Systems and Networks (DSN 2012), Boston, June 2012
4. Albanese, M., Jajodia, S., Pugliese, A., Subrahmanian, V.S.: Scalable analysis of attack scenarios. In: Atluri, V., Diaz, C. (eds.) ESORICS 2011. LNCS, vol. 6879, pp. 416–433. Springer, Heidelberg (2011). doi:10.1007/978-3-642-23822-2_23
5. Albanese, M., Jajodia, S., Singhal, A., Wang, L.: An efficient approach to assessing the risk of zero-day. In: Samarati, P. (ed.) Proceedings of the 10th International Conference on Security and Cryptography (SECRYPT 2013), pp. 207–218. SciTePress, Reykjavík (2013)
6. Jajodia, S., Noel, S.: Topological vulnerability analysis. In: Jajodia, S., Liu, P., Swarup, V., Wang, C. (eds.) Cyber Situational Awareness. Advances in Information Security, vol. 46, pp. 139–154. Springer, New York (2010)
7. Jajodia, S., Noel, S., Kalapa, P., Albanese, M., Williams, J.: Cauldron: mission-centric cyber situational awareness with defense in depth. In: Proceedings of the Military Communications Conference (MILCOM 2011), Baltimore, pp. 1339–1344, November 2011
8. Jajodia, S., Noel, S., O'Berry, B.: Topological analysis of network attack vulnerability. In: Kumar, V., Srivastava, J., Lazarevic, A. (eds.) Managing Cyber Threats: Issues, Approaches, and Challenges, Massive Computing, vol. 5, pp. 247–266. Springer, New York (2005)

9. Leversage, D.J., Byres, E.J.: Estimating a system's mean time-to-compromise. IEEE Secur. Priv. **6**(1), 52–60 (2008)
10. McHugh, J.: Quality of protection: measuring the unmeasurable? In: Proceedings of the 2nd ACM Workshop on Quality of Protection (QoP 2006), pp. 1–2. ACM, Alexandria, October 2006
11. Natrajan, A., Ning, P., Liu, Y., Jajodia, S., Hutchinson, S.E.: NSDMine: automated discovery of network service dependencies. In: Proceedings of the 31st Annual International Conference on Computer Communications (INFOCOM 2012), Orlando, pp. 2507–2515, March 2012
12. Nazzicari, N., Almillategui, J., Stavrou, A., Jajodia, S.: Switchwall: automated topology fingerprinting and behavior deviation identification. In: Jøsang, A., Samarati, P., Petrocchi, M. (eds.) STM 2012. LNCS, vol. 7783, pp. 161–176. Springer, Heidelberg (2013). doi:10.1007/978-3-642-38004-4_11
13. Noel, S., Jajodia, S.: Managing attack graph complexity through visual hierarchical aggregation. In: Proceedings of the ACM CCS Workshop on Visualization and Data Mining for Computer Security (VizSEC/DMSEC 2004), pp. 109–118. ACM, Fairfax, October 2004
14. Wang, L., Jajodia, S., Singhal, A., Noel, S.: k-zero day safety: measuring the security risk of networks against unknown attacks. In: Gritzalis, D., Preneel, B., Theoharidou, M. (eds.) ESORICS 2010. LNCS, vol. 6345, pp. 573–587. Springer, Heidelberg (2010). doi:10.1007/978-3-642-15497-3_35
15. Wang, L., Noel, S., Jajodia, S.: Minimum-cost network hardening using attack graphs. Comput. Commun. **29**(18), 3812–3824 (2006)
16. Wang, L., Zhang, M., Jajodia, S., Singhal, A., Albanese, M.: Modeling network diversity for evaluating the robustness of networks against zero-day attacks. In: Kutyłowski, M., Vaidya, J. (eds.) ESORICS 2014. LNCS, vol. 8713, pp. 494–511. Springer, Cham (2014). doi:10.1007/978-3-319-11212-1_28

Lessons Learned: Visualizing Cyber Situation Awareness in a Network Security Domain

Christopher G. Healey[1]([✉]), Lihua Hao[1], and Steve E. Hutchinson[2]

[1] Department of Computer Science, North Carolina State University,
Raleigh, NC 27695-8206, USA
healey@ncsu.edu
[2] ICF International, U.S. Army Research Laboratory, Adelphi, USA
http://www.csc.ncsu.edu/faculty/healey

Abstract. This chapter discusses lesson learned working with cyber situation awareness and network security domain experts to integrate visualizations into their current workflows. Working closely with network security experts, we discovered a critical set of requirements that a visualization must meet to be considered for use by the these domain experts. We next present two separate examples of visualizations that address these requirements: a flexible web-based application that visualizes network traffic and security data through analyst-driven correlated charts and graphs, and a set of ensemble-based extensions to visualize network traffic and security alerts using existing and future ensemble visualization algorithms.

1 Introduction

The use of computer networks continues to grow, and with it the rise of sophisticated network attacks. Network security analytics has become an important area of computer science, and more recently data visualization. To maintain the security and stability of a network system, analysts continuously collect vast amount of data that capture important characteristics about their networks, then analyze the data to detect attacks, intrusions, and suspicious activity hidden in the traffic. Visualization has been proposed as an important component of this effort, since it allows for interactive exploration and analysis of large amounts of data, and can help analysts detect unexpected patterns more efficiently and effectively than traditional, text-based representations [3,13,19].

During this MURI project, we collaborated with network security experts from ARL to explore the use of visualization to improve cyber situation awareness in a network security environment. Numerous important findings resulted from this collaboration. In particular, we discovered that visualizations designed for network security analytics must meet a number of unique requirements, if they are to be adopted by network security analysts. Based on these requirements, visualizations that are simple and efficient in their representation of network data can provide powerful tools to support exploration and discovery in an effective and time critical manner. We discuss these requirements in detail,

© Springer International Publishing AG 2017
P. Liu et al. (Eds.): Cyber Sitation Awareness, LNCS 10030, pp. 47–65, 2017.
DOI: 10.1007/978-3-319-61152-5_3

then summarize two approaches we developed to visualize network security data: analyst-drive web-based charts and graphs, and ensemble analysis techniques.

2   Visualization for Cyber Situation Awareness

The visualization community has focused recent attention on the areas of cyber security and cyber situation awareness. Early visual analysis of cyber security data often relied on text-based approaches that present data in text tables or lists. Unfortunately, these approaches do not scale well, and they cannot fully represent important patterns and relationships in complex network or security data. Follow-on work applied more sophisticated visualization approaches like node-link graphs, parallel coordinates, and treemaps to highlight different security properties, patterns in network traffic, and hierarchical data relationships. Because the amount of data generated can be overwhelming, many tools adopt a well-known information visualization approach: overview, zoom and filter, and details on demand. This approach starts by presenting an overview of the data. This allows an analyst to filter and zoom to focus on a subset of the data, then request additional details about the subset as needed. Current security visualization systems often consist of multiple visualizations, each designed to investigate different aspects of a system's security state from different perspectives and at different levels of detail.

2.1   Security Visualization Surveys

Visualization for cyber environments has matured to a point where survey papers on the area are available. These papers provide useful overviews, and also propose ways to organize or categorize techniques along different dimensions.

Shiravi et al.'s survey of visualization techniques for network security provides a useful overview of current visualization systems, and proposes a number of broad categories for data sources and visualization techniques [13]. One axis subdivides techniques by data source: network traces, security events, user and asset context (e.g., vulnerability scans or identity management), network activity, network events, and logs. A second axis considers use cases: host/server monitoring, internal/external monitoring, port activity, attack patterns, and routing behavior. Numerous techniques are described as examples of different data sources and use cases. The authors specifically address the issue of situation awareness in their future work, noting that many visualization systems try to prioritize important situations and project critical events as ways to summarize the massive amounts of data generated within a network. They distinguish between situation awareness, which they define as "a state of knowledge", and situation assessment, defined as "the process of attaining situation awareness." Converting raw data into visual forms is one method of situation assessment, meant to present information to an analyst to enhance their situation awareness.

Dang and Dang also surveyed security visualization techniques, focusing on web-based environments [3]. Dang chose to classify systems based on where they run: client-side, server-side, or web application. Client-side systems are normally simple, focusing on defending web users from attacks like phishing. Server-side visualizations are designed for system administrators or cyber security analysts with an assumed level of technical knowledge. These visualizations are usually larger and more complex, focusing on multivariate displays that present multiple properties of a network to the analyst. Most network security visualization tools fall into the server-side category. A final class of system is security for web applications. This is a complicated problem, since it can involve web developers, administrators, security analysts, and end users. Dang also subdivided server-side visualizations by their main goal: network management, monitoring, analysis, and intrusion detection; by visualization algorithm: pixel, chart, graph, and 3D; and by data source: network packet, NetFlows, and application-generated data. Various techniques exist at the intersection of each category.

New security and cyber situation visualization systems are constantly being proposed. These range from simple visualization approaches like charts and maps [4], node-link graphs [10], and timelines [9,11], to more complex representations like parallel coordinates [1,16], treemaps [7,8], and hierarchical visualizations [2].

Although security visualization systems aim to support more flexible user interactivity and correlation of various data sources, many of them still force an analyst to choose from a fairly limited set of static representations. For example, Phan et al. use charts, but with fixed attributes on the x and y-axes [9]. General purpose commercial visualization systems like Tableau, ArcSight, SpotFire, or SAS VA [6,12,14,15] offer a more flexible collection of visualizations, but they do not include visualization and human perception guidelines, so representing data effectively requires visualization expertise on the part of the analyst. Finally, many systems lack a scalable data management architecture, so the entire dataset must be loaded into memory prior to analysis and visualizing, increasing data transfer cost and limiting dataset size.

3   Visualization Design Philosophy

Our design philosophy is based on discussions with cyber security analysts at various research institutions and government agencies. The analysts overwhelming agreed that, intuitively, visualizations should be very useful. In practice, however, they had rarely realized significant improvements by integrating visualizations into their workflow. A common comment was: "Researchers come to us and say, Here's a visualization tool, let's fit your problem to this tool. But what we really need is a tool built to fit our problem." This is not unique to the security domain, but it suggests that security analysts may be more sensitive to deviations from their existing analysis strategies, and therefore less receptive to general-purpose visualization tools and techniques.

This is not to say, however, that visualization researchers should simply provide what the security analysts ask for. The analysts have high-level suggestions about how they want to visualize their data, but they do not have the visualization experience or expertise to design and evaluate specific solutions to meet their needs. To address these, we initiated a collaboration with colleagues at ARL to build visualizations that: (1) meet the needs of the analysts, but also (2) harness the knowledge and best practices that exist in the visualization community.

Again, this approach is not unique, but it offers an opportunity to study its strengths and weaknesses in the context of a cyber security domain. In particular, we were curious to see which general techniques (if any) we could start with, and how extensively these techniques would need to be modified before they would be useful for an analyst. Seen this way, our approach does not focus explicitly on network security data, but rather on network security analysts. By supporting the analysts' situation awareness needs, we are implicitly addressing the goal of effectively visualizing their data.

From our discussions, we defined a set of requirements for a successful visualization tool. Interestingly, these do not inform explicit design decisions. For example, they do not define which data attributes we should visualize and how those attributes should be represented. Instead, they implicitly constrain a visualization's design through a high-level set of suggestions about what a real analyst is (and is not) likely to use. We summarized these comments into six general categories:

1. **Mental Models.** A visualization must "fit" the mental models the analysts use to investigate problems. Analysts are unlikely to change how they attack a problem in order to use a visualization tool.
2. **Working Environment.** The visualization must integrate into the analyst's current working environment. For example, many analysts use a web browser to view data stored in formats defined by their network monitoring tools.
3. **Configurability.** Static, pre-defined presentations of the data are typically not useful. Analysts need to look at the data from different perspectives that are driven by the problems they are currently investigating.
4. **Accessibility.** The visualizations should be familiar to an analyst. Complex representations with a steep learning curve are unlikely to be used, except in very specific situations where a significant cost-benefit advantage can be found.
5. **Scalability.** The visualizations must support query and retrieval from multiple data sources, each of which may contain very large numbers of records.
6. **Integration.** Analysts will not replace their current problem-solving strategies with new visualization tools. Instead, the visualizations must augment these strategies with useful support.

4   Web-Based Alert Visualization

The configurability, accessibility, scalability, and integration requirements of our design demand flexible user interaction that combines and visualizes multiple large data sources. The working environment requirement further dictates that this happen within the analyst's current workflow. To achieve this, we initially designed and implemented a visualization system that combines MySQL, PHP, HTML5, and JavaScript to generate web-based network security visualizations through combinations of analyst-configurable charts focused on analyzing suspicious network activity.

4.1   Web Visualization

Based on our integration requirement, we built our visualizations as a web application using HTML5's canvas element. This works well, since it requires no external plug-ins and runs in any modern web browser.

We visualize network data using 2D charts. Basic charts are one of the most well known and widely used visualization techniques [17,18]. This supports our accessibility requirement, because: (1) charts are common in other security visualization systems the analysts have seen, and (2) charts are an effective visualization method for presenting the values, trends, patterns, and relationships the analysts want to explore.

Numerous JavaScript-based libraries exist to visualize data as 2D charts, for example, HighCharts, Google Charts, Flot Charts, and RGraph. Unfortunately, these libraries are designed for general information visualization, so they do not support analysis at multiple levels of abstraction or correlation between multiple charts. To address this, we extended RGraph [5] to generate security visualizations with flexible user interaction, data retrieval via MySQL, and the ability to correlate between multiple charts.

RGraph cannot automatically choose chart types based on the data to visualize. This capability might be useful, since analysts do not want to manually select the chart type if this decision is obvious. On the other hand, the analysts do not want to be restricted to specific, pre-defined visualizations. To support these conflicting needs, we classify our charts based on the different use cases in Fig. 1: (1) pie and bar charts for proportion and frequency comparison over a single attribute, (2) bar charts for value comparison over a secondary attribute, (3) scatterplots for correlation between two attributes, and (4) Gantt charts for range value comparisons. A visualization is created based on analysis goals, and not on the specific data being visualized. The analyst is free to change this initial selection, and more importantly, to interactively manipulate which data attributes are mapped to the primary and secondary dimensions.

Once a request is finalized, the system: (1) generates SQL queries to extract the target data from one or more data sources, (2) initializes chart properties like background grids and glyph size, color, and type, and (3) visualizes the data.

4.2   Charts

In a general information visualization tool, the viewer is usually asked to define exactly the visualization they want. We automatically choose an initial chart type based on: (1) existing knowledge on the strengths, limitations, and uses of different types of charts, and (2) the data the analyst chooses to visualize. For example, if the analyst asks to see the distribution of a single data attribute,

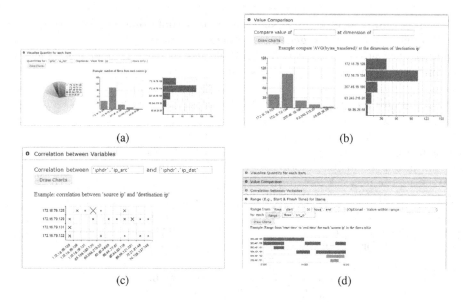

Fig. 1. Charts classified by use case: (a) pie and bar chart, analysis of proportion; (b) bar chart, value comparison along one dimension; (c) scatterplot, correlation analysis; (d) Gantt chart, range in at least one dimension

the system recommends a pie chart or bar chart. If the analyst asks to see the relationship across two data attributes, the system recommends a scatterplot or a Gantt chart.

The axes of the charts are initialized based on properties of the data attributes, for example, a categorical attribute on a bar chart's x-axis and an aggregated count on the y-axis. If the attributes were event timestamp and destination IP, time would be assigned to the x-axis and destination IP to the y-axis of a scatterplot (Fig. 2a). Visualizing start and end times for flows across destination IP produces a Gantt chart with time on the x-axis, destination IP on the y-axis, and rectangular range glyphs representing different flows (Fig. 2b). Or, if two attributes like source and destination IP are selected, the attributes are mapped to a scatterplot's x and y-axes, with data points shown for flows between pairs of values (Fig. 2c, d).

Data elements sharing the same x and y values are grouped together and displayed as a count. For example, in a scatterplot of traffic between source and destination IPs, the size of each tick mark indicates the number of connections between two addresses (Fig. 2c, d). In a Gantt chart, the opacity of each range bar indicates the number of flows that occurred over the time range for a particular destination IP (Fig. 2b).

More importantly, the analyst is free to change any of these initial choices. The system will interpret their modifications similar to the processing we perform for automatically chosen attributes. This allows the analyst to automatically start with the most appropriate chart type (pie, bar, scatterplot, or Gantt) based

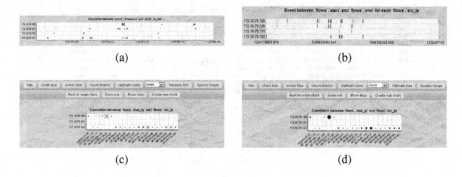

(a) (b)

(c) (d)

Fig. 2. Scatterplot and Gantt chart: (a) a scatterplot of connection counts over time by destination IP; (b) a Gantt chart of time ranges for flows by source IP; (c) a scatterplot with frequency count mapped to the size of an × glyph; (d) a scatterplot with count mapped to circle size

on their analysis task, the properties of the attributes they assign to a chart's axes, and on any secondary information they ask to visualize at each data point.

4.3 Correlation over Multiple Views

Analysts normally conduct a sequence of investigations, pursuing new findings as they are uncovered by correlating multiple data sources and exploring the data at multiple levels of detail. This necessitates visualizations with multiple views and flexible user interaction. We correlate multiple data sources by generating correlated SQL queries and extending the RGraph library to support dependencies between different charts (Fig. 3).

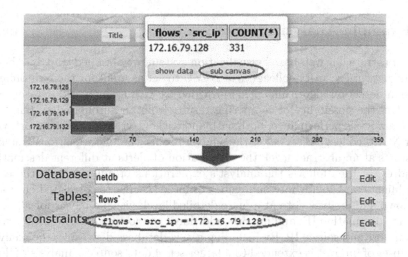

Fig. 3. New constraints to create a correlated chart

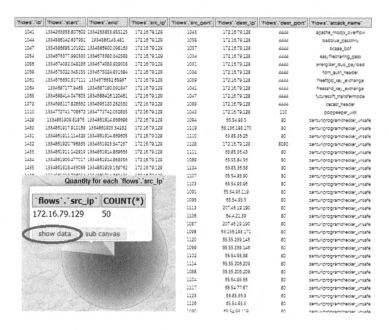

Fig. 4. Pie chart with a raw data spreadsheet

As an analyst examines a chart, they will form new hypothesis about the cause or effect of activity in the network. Correlated charts allow the analyst to immediately generate new visualizations from the current view to explore these hypotheses. In this way, the system allows an analyst to conduct a series of analysis steps, each one building on previous findings, with new visualizations being generated on demand to support the current investigations (Fig. 4).

5   Example Analysis Session

To demonstrate our web-based visualization system, we obtained trap data being used by network security colleagues at NCSU to act as input for their automated intrusion detection algorithms. This provided us with a real-world dataset, and also offers the possibility of comparing results from an automated system to a human analyst's performance, both with and without visualization support. One of our NCSU colleagues served as the analyst in this example scenario. Visualization starts at an abstract level: the distribution of alerts at different destination IP addresses; then follows the analyst's explorations of different hypotheses as he highlights and zooms into subregions of interest, creates correlated charts to drill down and analyze data at a more detailed level: visual analysis for alerts to a specific destination IP; and imports additional supporting data into the visualization: port and source IP. By including a new database flow table, the analysis of a subset of interest is extended to a larger set of data sources: analysis of flows related to interesting alerts. The visualization system supports the analyst by generating different types of charts on demand, based on the analyst's current interest and needs. The analyst can view the data both visually and in raw text form to examine qualitative and quantitative aspects of the current region of interest. The data sources used in this example include:

- **event.** Signature id and timestamp for each alert.
- **flows.** Network flow information, including source and destination IP, port, and start and end time.
- **iphdr.** Source and destination IP and other information related to packet headers.
- **tcphdr.** TCP related information such as source and destination port.

The analyst begins by selecting the database and the tables to use for the first visualization, as well as the constraints needed to correlate the tables and filter the rows to explore. Based on these tables and constraints, the analyst can determine the types of analysis he wants to pursue and the data attributes to visualize. The analyst initially visualizes the number of alerts for each destination IP, selecting *ip_dst* from table *iphdr* as the "aggregate for" attribute. A SQL query is automatically generated to extract data for the chart.

Choosing "Draw Charts" displays the aggregated results as pie and bar charts (Fig. 5). This supports visual analysis of the data from different perspectives. Pie charts highlight the relative number of alerts for different destination IPs, while bar charts facilitate a comparison of the absolute number of alerts by destination IP. The charts are linked: highlighting at a bar in the bar chart will highlight the corresponding section in the pie chart, and vice-versa.

By default, aggregation results are sorted by the number of alerts for different destination IPs in reverse order, allowing the analysts to focus on the first few rows with the largest number of alerts. This is based on the assumption that analysts are more interested in addresses where a significant amount of traffic or number of alerts occurs. The analysts can reverse the sort order to search for low-occurrence events.

The pie and bar charts indicate that the majority of the alerts (910) occur at destination IP 172.16.79.134. Choosing "Show Data" displays all 910 rows as a spreadsheet in a new window (Fig. 6a). To further analyze alerts associated with this destination IP, the analyst chooses "Sub Canvas" to open a new window with the initial query information (the database, tables, and constraints) predefined. The constraint *iphdr.ip_dst* = 172.16.79.134 is added to restrict the query for further analysis over this target destination IP. The analyst can continue to add new constraints or tables to the query as he requests visualizations to continue his analysis.

Next, the analyst chooses to visualize alerts from different source IPs attached to the target destination IP. He uses destination port to analyze the correlation between source and destination through the use of a scatterplot. Figure 6b shows there is only one source IP with alerts related to the target destination IP, and that most alerts are sent to port 21, shown as the large × symbol in the scatterplot.

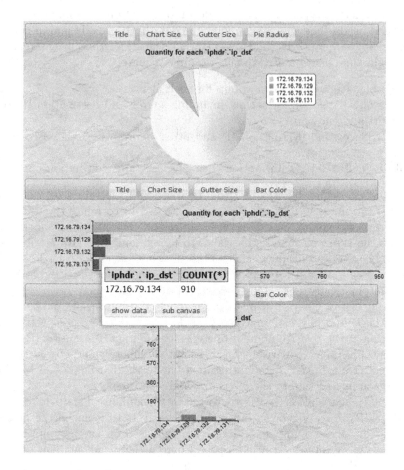

Fig. 5. Aggregated results visualized as a pie chart and horizontal and vertical bar charts

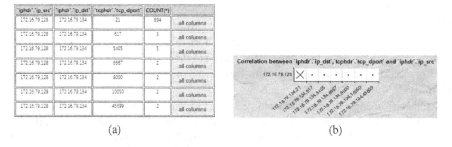

Fig. 6. Detail analysis: (a) raw data spreadsheet; (b) scatterplot of relationships between source IP and destination port correlated to destination IP 172.16.79.134

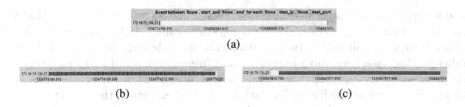

Fig. 7. Gantt chart with alerts for network flows at the destination IP and port of interest; (a) two flows; (b) zoom on the left flow, showing numerous alerts; (c) zoom on the right flow, showing one alert (Color figure online)

The analyst looks more closely at traffic related to the target destination IP on port 21 by visualizing netflows and their associated alerts in a Gantt chart. Collections of overlapping flows are drawn in red with endpoints at the flow set's start and end times. Alerts appear as black vertical bars overlaid on top of the flows at the time the alert was detected. Figure 7a shows most of the flows are distributed over two time ranges. By zooming in on each flow separately (Fig. 7b, c), the analyst realizes that the vast majority of the alerts occur in the left flow (Fig. 7b). The alerts in this flow are considered suspicious, and are flagged for more detailed investigation.

This example demonstrates how our system allows an analyst to follow a sequence of steps based on their own strategies and preferences to investigate alerts. Although it is possible to filter the raw data to "highlight" this result directly, our colleagues suggested it might be difficult to recognize that the majority of the alerts occur for a specific destination IP, source IP, port, and time range from a 910-line alert spreadsheet. The visualizations allow an analyst to follow this pattern step-by-step, uncovering more detailed information as they progress.

6   Ensemble Alert Visualization

A relatively new area of research that has grown rapidly in recent years is ensemble analysis. In numerous disciplines, scientists collect data produced by a series of runs of a simulation or an experiment, each with slightly different initial conditions or parameterizations. This collection of related datasets—an *ensemble*—has been widely used to simulate complex systems, explore unknowns in initial conditions, investigate parameter sensitivity, mitigate uncertainty, and compare structural characteristics of models. Each individual dataset forms a *member* of the ensemble. Ensemble visualization is an active area of research in visualization, specifically designed for exploring and comparing both within and between members of massive ensemble datasets.

Although network security data and ensemble data look quite different at first glance, they are similar in terms of their analytic challenges and goals. Both are large and time-dependent, necessitating analysis in the time dimension and approaches to support scalability. Ensemble visualization focuses on comparison and aggregation of related ensemble members, while security visualization focus on exploration of correlations between network traffic. Although visualization of scientific ensemble and network data at the most detailed level will likely be different, high-level ensemble overviews and frameworks could allow an analyst to quickly identify and drill down on subsets of interesting or suspicious network traffic. If we view network security data as a type of ensemble, there is an important opportunity to apply ongoing and future ensemble visualization research to improve network security analytics.

6.1   Network Ensemble Data

To harness ensemble visualization for network security analytics, we must address the challenge of terminology mapping: defining a network ensemble from security datasets, and dividing the data into a series of related network traffic, analogous to members in an ensemble. We focus on two common types of network security data: alerts and flows. An alerts dataset contains source and destination IP, port, time, protocol, message, and classification. A flows dataset contain source and destination IP, port, flags, start time, end time, protocol, number of packets, and number of bytes. An alert belongs to a flow if it is detected within the flow's time range and has the same source and destination IP. Based on this, we define two types of ensembles: an alert ensemble and a flow ensemble.

To maintain the requirement of configurability, we propose a general framework to construct network data ensembles. This allows analysts to configure details of the ensemble, if they choose to do so. A network ensemble consists of related network traffic (analogous to ensemble members), each representing a temporal sequence of alerts or flows that fall within equal-sized time windows. Analyzing relationships (similarities) between this network traffic is one important goal of cyber situation awareness.

Specifically, we offer two ways to define members in a network ensemble. The first method combines data properties to identify members. For example, we could define source IP and source port to specify members. Now, alerts or flows sent from each source IP+port form a network ensemble member. The second method divides the ensemble time window into a number of smaller time windows, each identifying a member in the ensemble. For example, if the dataset consists of network traffic for a 24-hour period, hourly traffic can represent an ensemble member. Finally, analysts can control the data values stored within each member. For example, we can analyze inter-member relationships in an alert ensemble by comparing changes in the of numbers of alerts over the time dimension.

6.2   Alert Ensembles

To construct an alert ensemble, an analyst defines the SQL tables that contain the alert data of interest, a time dimension column, correlations between the tables if more than one table is selected, and any additional constraints needed to form the ensemble. The system will automatically identify the time window that covers the ensemble's data. The analyst can choose one or more table columns to define ensemble members, or evenly subdivide the ensemble's time window into a number of smaller time periods, each representing a member.

To analyze relationships between members in an alert ensemble, we subdivide the time range of every member into a user-specified number of time-steps and aggregate alerts within each time-step. For example, each destination IP+port combination could form a member in the ensemble. Given a time window divided into 30 time-steps, the number of alerts is calculated at every time-step. Comparing alert members is performed by comparing changes in the number of alerts over time.

6.3   Flow Ensembles

Flow ensembles are defined in a manner similar to alert ensembles. An analyst chooses the SQL tables that contain the data, defines how to correlate alerts and flow traffic, identifies time dimension columns for the alerts and flows, and provides any additional constraints to extract the data to analyze. A flow has start and end times and contains a number of alerts, so comparing pairs of flows is more complicated than comparing numbers of alerts. Instead of aggregating data across time-steps, we view every member in a flow ensemble as a sequence of individual flows. Calculating member similarity aligns flows between pairs of members prior to comparison using dynamic time warping (DTW).

A member m_i in a flow ensemble is a sequence of l_i flows $m_i = (f_{i,1}, f_{i,2}, \ldots, f_{i,l_i})$. Each flow has start time t_s^i and end time t_e^i, and contains zero or more alerts. This makes the comparison of flow traffic more complicated than aggregated alerts. Manhattan distance is not applicable for flow sequence comparison because the sequences may have different lengths and may not be aligned in time. To calculate the DTW distance between flow members, we must first calculate the dissimilarity between pairs of flows. Let $dis(f_u, f_v)$ be the dissimilarity between flows f_u and f_v. We propose a simple flow comparison that calculates $dis(f_u, f_v)$ based on three metrics:

1. **Duration.** Given f_i's duration $dur_i = t_e^i - t_s^i$, the duration dissimilarity between f_u and f_v is

$$dis_{\text{dur}}^{u,v} = \frac{|dur_u - dur_v|}{\max(dur_u, dur_v)} \tag{1}$$

2. **Density.** Given f_i containing n_i alerts, the density of alerts in f_i is $den_i = n_i/dur_i$. The density dissimilarity between f_u and f_v is

$$dis_{\text{den}}^{u,v} = \frac{|den_u - den_v|}{\max(den_u, den_v)} \tag{2}$$

3. **Distribution.** Given start and end times t_s^i and t_e^i for a flow f_i that receives n_i alerts at times $t_1^i, t_2^i, \ldots, t_{n_i}^i$, the intervals between alerts are $I_i = \{t_s^i - t_1^i, t_2^i - t_1^i, \ldots, t_e^i - t_{n_i}^i\}$. We use $\sigma_i = \sum_{i=1}^{n_i}(I_i - I_\mu)^2/n_i$, the variance of the

intervals between alerts, to compute distribution dissimilarity between f_u and f_v as

$$dis_{\text{dist}}^{u,v} = \frac{|\sigma_u - \sigma_u|}{\max(\sigma_u, \sigma_v)} \tag{3}$$

The individual dissimilarities are averaged and normalized to generate an overall dissimilarity between f_u and f_v. We allow an analyst to tune the weights w_{dur}, w_{den}, and w_{dist} during averaging:

$$dis(f_u, f_v) = w_{\text{dur}} dis_{dur}^{u,v} + w_{\text{dens}} dis_{\text{dens}}^{u,v} + w_{\text{dist}} dis_{\text{dist}}^{u,v}$$
$$0 \leq w_{\text{dur}}, w_{\text{dens}}, w_{\text{dist}} \leq 1 \tag{4}$$
$$w_{\text{dur}} + w_{\text{dens}} + w_{\text{dist}} = 1$$

6.4   Ensemble Member Visualization

Ensemble visualization often contains detailed representations of one or more ensemble members. These detailed member visualizations may be very different depending on the types of members contained in a ensemble. To maintain consistency with our existing web-based network security visualization system, we use 2D charts to visualize network traffic. Specifically, we generate line charts to visualize members in an alert ensemble and Gantt charts for members in a flow ensemble.

Alert Member Visualization. An alert ensemble member is a sequence of aggregated alert counts calculated at every time-step. Figure 8a visualizes a 100-member alert ensemble for a single source IP of interest constructed by an analyst. Destination IP+port is used to define individual members. Time unfolds on the x-axis, and the number of alerts at each time step is plotted on the y-axis. Color represents the destination IP of each alert's parent flow.

Figure 8a highlights a number of similar patterns: flows that start with numerous alerts but end with few alerts; flows with two spikes in alerts near their center; and an outlier flow (in orange) with numerous alerts over its center.

The analyst chooses to assign the 100 alerts members to $k = 20$ clusters. Figure 8b visualizes the 20 clusters, averaging the number of alerts within each cluster at every time-step. This visualization provides a general understanding of changes in the numbers of alerts over time. The highlighted purple line at the bottom of the graph represents a large cluster that contains 65 members. A follow-on visualization of this cluster's members (Fig. 8c) confirms that changes in the number of alerts over time among the 65 members are similar.

Flow Member Visualization. We chose to visualize flow traffic and associated alerts using Gantt charts. The x-axis represents time, and the y-axis represents member (e.g., a combined IP+port). Flows are visualized as colored bars with endpoints at the flow's start and end times. Alerts appear as black vertical tick marks at the time the alert was detected.

Analysts choose clusters of flow members to visualize, based on results from flow similarity clustering algorithms. For example, Fig. 9 visualizes two clusters,

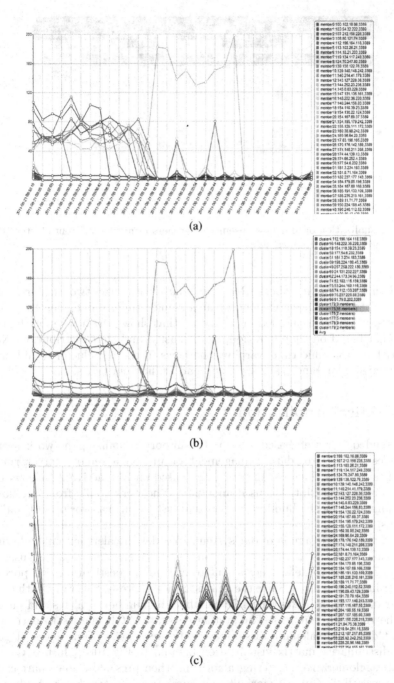

Fig. 8. Alert member visualization: (a) a 100-member ensemble; (b) visualization of members assigned to $k = 20$ clusters; (c) visualizing each alert member in a cluster containing 65 members with similar alert patterns, but from different flows (Color figure online)

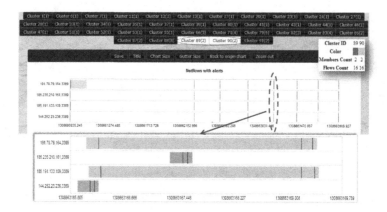

Fig. 9. Visualization of four flow ensemble members from two different clusters shown in blue and red (Color figure online)

each with two flow members. Red and blue identify the two clusters. Zooming into a group of flows that occur at a similar time, but belong to different members, produces a detailed visualization that shows the flows in each cluster are similar based on time duration, alert density, and alert distribution. Notice that without dynamic time warping, the flows in the red cluster would not be considered similar, since they start and end at different times.

7   Practical Application

We extended our web-based system to support visualizing network security ensembles. As before, data management occurs on a remote server running MySQL and PHP. The visualizations are based on interactive 2D charts using HTML5 and Javascript. We used anonymized network traffic from one floor of our Computer Science building to test our system on real-world alert and flow patterns.

As a practical example of our system, consider the alert ensemble discussed above that retrieves alerts data for source IP 64.120.250.242 and uses destination IP+port to define alerts sent to a common destination and port as a member in the ensemble. Since the analyst is not interested in traffic with a small number of alerts, he sorts ensemble members by number of alerts and analyzes only the top 100 members. The system generates SQL queries to extract the relevant data and calculate dissimilarities between pairs of members. It generates a dissimilarity matrix visualization (similar to Fig. 10b), clusters the flows with an agglomerative clustering algorithm, then presents a line chart characterizing overall dissimilarity for different numbers of clusters k. The analyst uses the line chart to study inter-member relationships, combining the 100 members into $k = 20$ clusters, then visualizes the largest cluster, containing 65 members with similar changes in the number of alerts over time (Fig. 8c). Ensemble

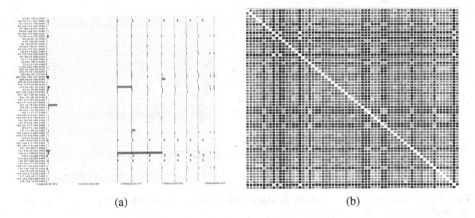

(a)   (b)

Fig. 10. Flow ensemble: (a) visualizing ensemble members in a Gantt chart; (b) dissimilarity matrix for the 65 members

visualization makes it more efficient to detect similar changes in alerts patterns, something that is not as obvious from a general visualization of alert traffic.

To gain a more in-depth understanding of the alert traffic covered by the 65-member cluster, the analyst takes flow traffic into consideration by requesting a flow ensemble visualization. The alert visualization system exports SQL queries to extract the alerts in the 65-alert member. The analyst uses these constraints to retrieve associated flows to construct a flow ensemble. Members in the ensemble are defined by destination IP+port. Equal weights are assigned to the three metrics w_{dur}, w_{dens}, and w_{dist} during flow comparison (Eq. (4)). In this way, every member in the flow ensemble is correlated with the member in the alert ensemble that is sent to the same destination.

Figure 10a visualizes the 65 members in the flow ensemble as 65 individual Gantt charts with time on the x-axis and destination IP+port on the y-axis. At this level of detail, flow traffic for most members looks similar, making it difficult to visually distinguish the flows without zooming in. The dissimilarity matrix (Fig. 10b) indicates that network traffic sent to different destinations are fairly strongly differentiated when we include the flow data (i.e., there are numerous dark cells in the dissimilarity matrix).

Based on the dissimilarity matrix, the analyst decides that members of the ensemble are similar if their dissimilarities are smaller than 0.21. This combines the 65 members into $k = 38$ clusters. As expected, flows in members from the same cluster are similar. For example, in Fig. 11, the flows in a cluster with six members have very similar density and distributions of alerts, and relatively similar durations (as shown in the top-right overview visualization).

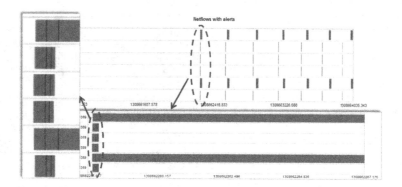

Fig. 11. A cluster of six members in the flows ensemble. Corresponding flows has very similar patterns

8 Conclusions

Data visualization converts raw data into images that allow a viewer to "see" data values and the relationships they form. The images allow viewers to use their visual perception to identify features in the data, to manage ambiguity, and to apply domain knowledge in ways that would be difficult to do algorithmically. Visualization can be formalized as a mapping: data passed through a data–feature mapping generates a visual representation—a visualization—that displays individual data values and the patterns they form.

Numerous situation awareness tools use visualization techniques like charts, maps, and flow diagrams to present information to an analyst. The challenge is to determine how best to integrate visualization techniques into a cyber situation awareness domain. Many tools adopt a well-known information visualization approach: overview, zoom and filter, and details on demand. Techniques utilized recently for the security and situation awareness domains include: charts and maps, node-link graphs, timelines, parallel coordinates, treemaps and hierarchical visualization.

We identified an initial set of requirements for a successful visualization tool. These do not define which data attributes we should visualize or how those attributes should be represented. Instead, they implicitly constrain a visualization's design through a high-level set of suggestions about what a real analyst is, and is not, likely to use. A visualization must "fit" the mental models the analysts use to investigate problems. It must integrate into the analyst's current working environment. Pre-defined presentations of the data are typically not useful. Visualizations should be familiar to an analyst. The system must support query and retrieval from multiple data sources; the visualizations must integrate into existing strategies with useful support. We demonstrate a prototype system for analyzing network alerts based on these guidelines, using both basic charts and graphs, and ensemble approaches to compare and combine alert and flow traffic based on inter-member relationships. In both cases, data retrieval and data-feature mapping are driven by the analyst, to ensure they visualize their current data of interest in ways that highlight exactly the data correlations they want to analyze.

References

1. Bradshaw, J.M., Carvalho, M., Bunch, L., Eskridge, T., Feltovich, P.J., Johnson, M., Kidwell, D.: Sol: an agent-based framework for cyber situation awareness. Künstliche Intellienz **26**(2), 127–140 (2012)
2. Cockburn, A., Karlson, A., Bederson, B.B.: A review of overview+detail zooming and focus+context interfaces. ACM Comput. Surv. **41**(1) (2008). Article 2
3. Dang, T.K., Dang, T.T.: A survey on security visualization techniques for web information systems. Int. J. Web Inf. Syst. **9**(1), 6–31 (2013)
4. Goodall, J., Sowul, M.: VIAssist: visual analytics for cyber defense. In: IEEE Conference on Technologies for Homeland Security (HST 2009), Boston, pp. 143–150 (2009)
5. Heyes, R.: RGraph: HTML5 and JavaScript charts (2017). https://www.rgraph. net
6. HP ArcSight ESM. http://www8.hp.com/us/en/software-solutions/ arcsight-esm-enterprise-security-management/
7. Kan, Z., Hu, C., Wang, Z., Wang, G., Huang, X.: NetVis: a network security management visualization tool based on Treemap. In: 2nd International Conference on Advanced Computer Control (ICACC 2010), Shenyang, pp. 18–21 (2010)
8. Mansmann, F., Fisher, F., Keim, D.A., North, S.C.: Visual support for analyzing network traffic and intrusion detection events using TreeMap and graph representations. In: Symposium on Computer-Human Interaction for Management of Information (CHIMIT 2009), Baltimore, article 3 (2009)
9. McPherson, J., Ma, K., Krystosk, P., Bartoletti, T., Christensen, M.: PortVis: a tool for port-based detection of security events. In: Workshop on Visualization and Data Mining for Computer Security (VizSEC/DMSEC 2004), Washington, DC, pp. 73–81 (2004)
10. Minarik, P., Dymacek, T.: NetFlow data visualization based on graphs. In: Goodall, J.R., Conti, G., Ma, K.-L. (eds.) VizSec 2008. LNCS, vol. 5210, pp. 144–151. Springer, Heidelberg (2008). doi:10.1007/978-3-540-85933-8_14
11. Phan, D., Gerth, J., Lee, M., Paepcke, A., Winograd, T.: Visual analysis of network flow data with timelines and event plots. In: Goodall, J.R., Conti, G., Ma, K.-L. (eds.) VizSEC 2007, pp. 85–99. Springer, Heidelberg (2008)
12. SAS Visual Analytics. http://www.sas.com/en_us/software/business-intelligence/ visual-analytics.html
13. Shiravi, H., Shiravi, A., Ghorbani, A.: A survey of visualization systems for network security. IEEE Trans. Vis. Comput. Graph. **18**(8), 1313–1329 (2012)
14. Tableau Software. http://www.tableau.com
15. Tibco Spotfire. http://spotfire.tibco.com
16. Tricaud, S., Nance, K., Saadé, P.: Visualizing network activity using parallel coordinates. In: 44th Hawaii International Conference on System Sciences (HICSS 2011), Poipu, pp. 1–8 (2011)
17. Tufte, E.R.: The Visual Display of Quantitative Information. Graphics Press, Cheshire (1983)
18. Tufte, E.R.: Envisioning Information. Graphics Press, Cheshire (1990)
19. Zhang, Y., Xiao, Y., Chen, M., Zhang, J., Deng, H.: A survey of security visualization for computer network logs. Secur. Commun. Netw. **5**(4), 404–421 (2012)

Enterprise-Level Cyber Situation Awareness

Xiaoyan Sun[1], Jun Dai[1], Anoop Singhal[2], and Peng Liu[3(✉)]

[1] California State University, Sacramento, CA 95819, USA
[2] National Institute of Science and Technology, Gaithersburg, MD 20899, USA
[3] Penn State University, University Park, PA 16802, USA
pliu@ist.psu.edu

Abstract. This chapter begins with a literature review of situation awareness (SA) concepts, and a study on how to apply SA to the cyber field for enterprise-level network security diagnosis. With the finding that an isolation problem exists between the individual perspectives of different technologies, this chapter introduces a cyber SA model named SKRM, which is proposed to integrate the isolated perspectives into a framework. Based on one of the SKRM layers, called Operating System Layer, this chapter presents a runtime system named Patrol, that reveals zero-day attack paths in the enterprise-level networks. To overcome the limitation of Patrol and achieve better accuracy and efficiency, this chapter further illustrates the usage of Bayesian Networks at the low level of Operating System to reveal zero-day attack paths in a probabilistic way.

1 Cyber Situation Awareness

Complete and accurate cyber situation awareness (cyber SA) is the essential prerequisite for human security analysts to well defend the network: the analysts should clearly know what is going on in the network to aid the decision making process. Much of the work in security analysis is from the individual perspective of the algorithms or tools engaged in vulnerability analysis, intrusion detection, damage and impact assessment, etc. These analytical tools are useful for assessing the network states and facilitating the human analysts' network security management. Taking attack graph for example, by combining the vulnerabilities existing in a network, an attack graph can generate the potential attack paths that show how the attackers may exploit the network. Without attack graph, security analysts have to manually construct the possible attack scenarios by analyzing the vulnerability scan reports provided by vulnerability scanners such as Nessus. This is a daunting task if the analysis target is a large scale enterprise network with hundreds of machines.

While these techniques such as attack graphs provide powerful means to represent complex security systems and ease the analysts' work in some aspects, they tend to focus on the individual perspectives within the techniques. This produces some issues when it comes to the overall cyber situation awareness. First, the individual techniques are usually isolated from each other. Each system is capable of producing a large amount of data, such as the system logs,

P. Liu et al. (Eds.): Cyber Sitation Awareness, LNCS 10030, pp. 66–109, 2017.
DOI: 10.1007/978-3-319-61152-5_4

network traffic information, security alerts, and even business transaction logs. It's a huge challenge for security analysts to find the needed information from this volume of data. Moreover, integrating and interpreting the information generated by the isolated systems is another challenge. Few integration frameworks or models exist for coupling the tools, algorithms, and techniques to enhance the security analysts' situation awareness and improve analysts' effectiveness in addressing complex cyber security problems. Second, the role of the cyber security analyst is rarely considered. This is problematic as human is the core of cyber SA. The output of most tools has to be interpreted within the mind of human security analysts. Questions as follows should be answered with the role of human operators explicitly taken into account: what information should be present to the analysts for better understanding? Are the analysts able to understand the output and correctly correlate the reported events? To what extent can the system ease the human analysts' cognition and enhance the situation awareness? The list goes on. Therefore, to achieve complete and accurate cyber situation awareness, an integration model that couples the existing security techniques and considers the role of human analysts should be established.

1.1   Situation Awareness (SA)

The definition of situation awareness has evolved from the very first ones that are proposed by Dominguez [1] and Fracker [2] in the aircraft piloting domain. Fracker defines situation awareness as "the pilot's knowledge about a zone of interest at a given level of abstraction". Pilots develop the situation awareness by matching the sampled data acquired from the environment to the knowledge structures stored in their long-term memory [2]. Endsley then gives a formal definition of SA in dynamic environments: *"situation awareness is the perception of the elements of the environment within a volume of time and space, the comprehension of their meaning, and the projection of their status in the near future"* [3]. In this definition situation awareness is abstracted into three levels: *perception, comprehension,* and *projection.*

Several mutation definitions of situation awareness are then proposed on basis of Endsley's definition. Salerno et al. [4] introduces a situation awareness model that can be applied to multiple domains. They view the basic process of transforming large amount of data into information and making sense of it as the key component of SA. Since the majority of SA is still being accomplished in the minds of human operators, a gap still exists between the data and the decision support tools. They thus emphasize the importance of situation awareness to the decision process by modifying Endsley's definition into "situation awareness is the perception ... and the projection of their status *in order to enable decision superiority.*" McGuinness and Foy [5] add a fourth level called *resolution* to Endsley's definition. Resolution level is able to specify which path to follow in order to achieve the desired state change. Resolution is not decision making, but provides available options and corresponding consequences that can facilitate decision making. McGuinness and Foy explain the four levels of SA using an analogy: perception means "What are the current facts?"; comprehension asks

"What is actually going on?"; projection represents "What will happen if ...?"; and resolution asks, "What exactly shall I do?".

Alberts et al. [6] informally defines the situational awareness in the context of battlespace. They refer situational awareness as what *"describes the awareness of a situation that exists in part or all of the battle space at a particular point in time"*. For situation in the battlespace, they identify three main components: missions and constraints on missions, capabilities and intentions of relevant forces, and key attributes of the environment. For awareness, they emphasize the role of prior knowledge by pointing out that awareness is *"the result of a complex interaction between prior knowledge and current perceptions of reality"*. Each individual could have a unique awareness given the same situation. Therefore, they mention that professional education and training can be used to ensure that individuals with same data, information, and current knowledge can achieve similar awareness.

In addition, Endsley [7] also discussed the temporal aspects of situation awareness. Three aspects in terms of time are identified: the perception of time (time itself), the temporal dynamics associated with events (e.g. how much time is available until some event occurs), and the dynamic aspect of real-world situations (e.g. the rate at which information is changing). Time is an important part for the comprehension level and projection level of situation awareness. Besides, the dynamic nature of situations also requires the situation awareness to constantly change to keep accurate. Decision makers rely on the previous experience to keep aware of the changing situation, make decisions and take actions. In the OODA (Observe, Orient, Decision, Act) loop [8], decisions and actions provide feedback to the environment and a new cycle begins.

1.2   Apply SA to the Cyber Field

It is a natural yet critical step to apply SA to the cyber field to facilitate security analysis. Cyber security is inherently a battle between attackers and defenders in the cyber space. However, this battle is intrinsically unfair: much of the attack information may be forever hidden from defenders, while lots of defense information is detectable and thus accessible for attackers. That is, information asymmetry exists between the two sides. To win such a challenging battle, defenders have to gain capabilities to effectively dig out useful information out of the data from very limited security sensors. The various analytical tools and algorithms scattered in the security literature are the ones that people can rely on to extract information from data. However, it is found that the "best" tools (in terms of accuracy, efficiency, costs), when used by humans, do not necessarily result in the best SA.

This is due to the fact that most of the current security analytical approaches were not designed with human beings in consideration. Rather, their focus was usually on the technical breakthroughs with attempts to improve the approach's performance at various evaluation metrics, including efficiency, accuracy, overhead or even scalability. But few of them would pay attention to measure how well users could perceive and comprehend their generated data. Furthermore, much of the analytical methods are also found to hold only individual perspectives, and thus isolated from each other. Locked in their own perspectives, isolated tools do not really help human comprehend to gain holistic understanding of the entire scenario.

The above isolations are casting challenges on human beings' limited cognitive capabilities. When human analysts are given rich data, but the data is disconnected from each other due to different sources, the rich data becomes a burden, instead of an advantage, for human cognitions. Overwhelmed in such disconnected data, human analysts will find it hard to comprehend anything. This is so-called human cognition hurdles that people need to take into consideration when they expect human users truly benefit from their outputs.

Compared to traditional security analytics, cyber SA considers potential human cognition hurdles in the loop. That is, based on the rich sensed data, cyber SA makes efforts to ensure human analysts can more effectively perceive and comprehend data so as to make the right decision in a timely fashion. But, how to achieve this? The answer is integration. For the purpose of easing human digestions and facilitating their understanding, it is expected to integrate human beings and the traditional individual perspectives into a macroscopic framework. This integration framework will be a platform that accommodates and offers multi-disciplinary theories, algorithms and toolsets in an integrated fashion. Desired cyber SA capabilities beyond intrusion analysis or post-mortem analysis, such as mission asset damage and impact assessment, can only emerge after the integration framework.

Individual Perspectives. However, such an integration framework is not directly available in the literature in terms of security. To build it, we first need to identify the existing individual perspectives that may be integrated into the framework and enable SA to benefit the overall security analysis.

Security Monitoring. For various purposes, an enterprise network can be under the observation of several monitoring tools. Such tools may include WireShark [13], Ntop [14], TCPdump [15], Bro [16] or Snort [17] for logging the network traffic/flows, Nessus [18], OVAL [19], GFI LanGuard [20], QualysGuard [21] or McAfee FoundStone [22] for scanning out the vulnerabilities, Lumeta IPsonar [23], SteelCentral NetCollector (formerly OPNET NetMapper) [24], Nmap [25] or JANASSURE [26] for discovering the network mapping, Backtracker [27], Shelf [28] or Patrol [29] for intercepting the system calls, Malwarebytes Anti-Exploit [30], AVG AntiVirus [31] or McAfee AntiVirus [32] for capturing runtime security incidences. These monitoring tools, deployed as security sensors in the enterprise networks, can be leveraged to gain perception for cyber SA.

Intrusion Detection. The enterprise network is mainly protected by intrusion detection systems (IDS), which is one of the mechanisms to alert administrators to possible cyber attacks. Host-based IDSs like OSSEC HIDS [33] and Trip-Wire [34] alert administrators for abnormal events on individual hosts, while network-based IDSs like Snort alert them for suspicious packets through the entire network boundary. Signature-based IDSs like Bro and Snort alert administrators to known attacks, while anomaly-based IDSs [35–42] can even alert them to unknown attacks. These techniques gain the capability to detect zero-day exploits by profiling normal behavior and detecting deviations, but they are also found to be hard to cope with false positives.

One of the noticeable intrusion detection methods is the system call-based intrusion detection, which mainly leverages statistical properties of system call sequence [37,38] and system call arguments [40,41]. This method was started from pioneer works by Forrest et al. [35] and Lee et al. [36] for intrusion detection. In addition to the sequences and arguments, Bhatkar et al. further takes into account the temporal properties involving arguments of different system calls [42]. Our system call-based intrusion detection work, Patrol [29] which will be presented in Sect. 3, is to identify zero-day attack paths through network-wide dependencies parsed from system calls. These paths provide network-wide attack contexts, and help detect unknown vulnerability exploitations.

The IDS systems raise alerts when they notice security patterns or anomalies. Hence, IDS is an important tool for us to gain perception for cyber SA. The breakthrough made by Patrol further makes IDS able to facilitate human comprehension for cyber SA.

Alert Correlation. As its name indicates, alert correlation [43,44] is a technique invented to correlate isolated alerts to form potential attack paths. It has high potentials to facilitate human comprehension for cyber SA, but it may induce high false rates at the same time. The false rates are pointed to be twofold [29]: (1) The correlation itself is inaccurate because it attempts to integrate possibly different contexts into a unified "story"; (2) The alerts that the correlation largely depends on genetically inherit false rates from security sensors like IDS. When the two folds of false rates are combined together, the accuracy of the whole solution gets worse.

Event Correlation. The isolation concern is already noticed by part of the security products and research in the community, and they made progress from isolated technologies to holistic picture. Examples are ArcSight [48], QualysGuard [21], NIRVANA [49], etc. Specifically, ArcSight is a leading enterprise security information and event management (SIEM) system, that provides a correlation engine to visualize the security management of user activities, event logs and intrusion alerts. As a web-based vulnerability scanner, QualysGuard combines the business-level view and the network-level view by delivering IT security and compliance as a service. NIRVANA is already designed as a situation awareness tool with graphical model and inference algorithms to help security analysts. Although all these outcomes are only achieving partial big picture awareness, it shows that event correlation is a big facilitate to human comprehension for cyber SA.

Service Dependency Discovery. Service dependency discovery is a subproblem of event correlation, that makes efforts to mine service dependencies from the (network or host) events. Its results may be used to rank the impact weights of mission assets in the enterprise network, and hence it is very important and useful to facilitate human comprehension, projection and even resolution for cyber SA.

Network-based discovery methods usually mine the network service dependencies from network traffic. A technique is developed in [57] to enumerate the interdependencies of application and services, while [58] proposes to use Leslie Graph as the abstraction to describe the complex dependencies between network, host and application components. The co-occurrences of network traffic within a small time window is leveraged in [45] to identify service dependencies, also for the purpose of fault localization. Based on [45], eXpose [46] further filters out traffic that is less likely to lead to dependencies, using a statistical measure. Orion [47] learns dependencies based on the spike detection in delay distribution of flow pairs. Fuzzy-logic algorithms are used in [59] to build an inference engine to classify dependencies from the traffic. The nested network traffic flow observation is leveraged by NSDMiner [60,61] to identify dependencies.

Host-side instrumentation can be performed to monitor the behavior of running processes, which is then used to extract service dependencies. For example, Magpie [50] records fine-grained kernel/middleware/application events, correlates them into execution paths for applications within a computer, and traces them across the network. Pinpoint [51] records component interactions to track the paths that requests follow. X-trace [52] reconstructs trees of events involved in the execution of a task. Constellation [53] installs host-based daemons in a distributed way and then applies networked machine learning. Macroscope [56] combines the information of identified processes that produce traffic with network level packet traces.

Operating System Object Dependency Tracking. Operating system object dependency tracking is first invented by King et al. [27] with the purpose to automatically identify sequences of intrusion steps. The follow-up works [54,55] further propose to integrate system object dependency tracking and alert correlation techniques. Xiong et al. [28] applies it to intrusion recovery. Our work on Patrol takes advantage of this technique to reveal the zero-day attack paths, locating all the known or unknown operating system level mission assets (processes or files) that have been damaged due to the attack. All these works show that the system object dependency tracking technique could be used to facilitate comprehension for cyber SA.

Attack Graph. Another technique that notices the isolation problem (between vulnerabilities) is attack graph, which makes progress to break it by considering vulnerabilities in combination. With the strengths to model and correlate causality dependencies among known vulnerabilities, attack graph is capable to generate all the possible attack paths that show exploit sequences to specific attack goals in the enterprise network. Since Phillips and Swiler [101] in 1998 first proposed a model using attack templates to represent generic steps in known attacks, attack graph has been studied for more than one decade. At the early development stage, state enumeration attack graph becomes the main stream. [62,63,89] by Sheyner et al. [102] by Ramakrishnan et al. [64] by Jha et al. [101]

by Phillips and Swiler, and [65] by Swiler et al. are research works regarding state enumeration attack graph. Because of the serious complexity problem of state enumeration attack graph, researchers began to develop the new dependency attack graph. Examples of research in dependency attack graph are [66] by Noel and Jajodia, TVA [90] and Cauldron [67–69] by Jajodia et al. [103] by Ammann et al., MIT NetSPA [104] by Ingols et al. [70] by Noel et al., MulVAL [91–93] by Ou et al., and NIRVANA [49]. Although attack graph is powerful at vulnerability correlation, it could not capture zero-day attack paths. Notable progress is recent research [71,72], which have pioneered the attack graph based modeling of zero-day vulnerabilities. In short, attack graph shows great potentials to facilitate human comprehension for cyber SA.

Bayesian Networks. Bayesian Networks (BN) have been applied to intrusion detection [105] and cyber security analysis both in traditional networks [106] and the cloud environment [107]. Based on known vulnerabilities and observed alerts, [106] can infer which hosts are likely to be compromised, and [107] leverages BN to infer the stealthy bridges (unknown in nature) between enterprise network islands in the cloud environment. Our work, presented in Sect. 4 employs BN to infer zero-day attack paths in a probabilistic way. These inference capabilities enabled by BN shows that BN is a powerful tool addressing uncertainty to enhance human comprehension and projection for cyber SA.

Integration Framework. Researchers have developed various frameworks or models of situation awareness in different domains. Using the definition of situation awareness provided in [5], Tadda and Salerno [10] establish a situation awareness reference model that provides definitions to concepts such as entity, object, group, event, activity, etc. Salerno et al. [4] propose another situation awareness model based on the Joint Directors of Laboratories (JDL) data fusion model [9] but utilize Endsley's notions of Perception, Comprehension, and Projection (referred as Anticipation in [4]) in the model of SA [3]. The model reflects the basic process of situation awareness, which usually starts with the analyst defining the problem of interest. The analyst then adapts an existing model developed from previous experience. The existing model defines the interested patterns and thus required data to be collected for situation awareness.

However, the above existing SA models do not notice the isolation in-between individual perspectives of the different technologies in a enterprise-level network. The goal of enabling enterprise-level SA is to break such isolation, integrate the individual perspectives, and use the integrated situation awareness to enhance the human security analysts' perception, comprehension and projection of the whole enterprise scenario. Therefore, to gain big picture awareness through interconnecting situation knowledge from isolated techniques, we construct a framework of cyber SA, as shown in Fig. 1 [12], on the basis of the models established by Tadda and Salerno [10] and by Endsley [7]. The key component of this framework is a model we proposed, the *Situation Knowledge Reference Model (SKRM)*, which will be elaborated in Sect. 2. In a word, SKRM is *a model that integrates cyber knowledge from different perspectives by coupling data, information,*

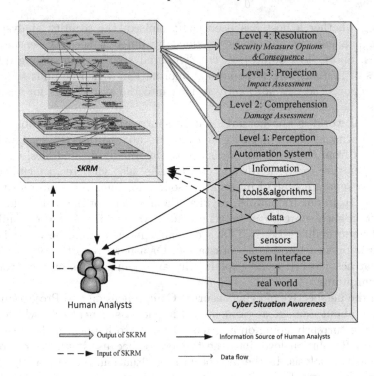

Fig. 1. A model of cyber situation awareness [12].

algorithms and tools, and human knowledge, to enhance cyber analysts' situation awareness [12,73].

In the cyber SA framework in Fig. 1, we utilize McGuinness and Foy's definition of situation awareness [5] which is composed of four levels, perception, comprehension, projection, and resolution. As the core integration model, the SKRM is able to take data, information, tools and algorithms, and even human intelligence as the input, and enhances human security analysts' four levels of situation awareness. Human security analysts can acquire information from a number of sources, including data, information, system interfaces, real world, and the output of SKRM as well, to help the understanding of the situation.

Compared to Tadda and Salerno's model in [10], the perception level in Fig. 1 includes two more elements, system interface and real world, in addition to data and information.

The system interface is one of the main information sources for security analysts to acquire the most relevant information. System design is an important factor affecting the effectiveness of security analysts' situation awareness. A well-designed system (including both good algorithms and interfaces) can greatly ease the information perception and comprehension. Furthermore, the information acquirement is an active process [7], in which the security analysts can choose which information is displayed through the system interface. For example, when evaluating whether a host has been compromised, the security analysts may go through a number of reports provided by different security sensors, such as Nessus, Snort, TCPdump [15], etc. The analysts can shift among different interfaces or systems to get the needed information. When he finds some clues in these reports, he may also actively look into the system logs for suspicious activities.

The real world is another information source that is directly observed by human security analysts. Security analysts are able to directly hear and view information from the environment, such as abnormally deleted files, extremely high temperature in the hardware, etc. Endsley also view team members and others as a separate type of information source for human operator's situation awareness [7]. In our framework, we view them as part of the real world. Information from such sources can be generated in various forms. For example, the financial abnormality discussed in a company meeting may be related to an intrusion happened towards a workstation. Or a news report about a recently popular attack pattern could explain why an organization's own network has similar symptoms.

From the perspective of cyber security, Comprehension and Projection levels are mainly about damage assessment and impact assessment [11], which evaluates what is currently going on and what is likely to happen in the future. We include the Resolution level into the framework because it's a critical part of cyber security analysis. In the face of current situation, security analysts usually have a number of security measures to achieve the desired state change. Such security measures include network hardening, system intrusion recovery, etc. Different countermeasures may require different costs and lead to different consequences. Therefore, Resolution level provides the security analysts with the available options and the corresponding consequences and facilitates the decision making process.

1.3 Organization of This Chapter

The following of this chapter will be structured as follows: Sect. 2 will focus on the introduction to SKRM, which is our proposed cyber SA model to build the integration framework; Sect. 3 will present a runtime system called Patrol, that reveals zero-day attack paths on the Operating System Layer of the SKRM model; Sect. 4 will illustrate the usage of Bayesian Networks at the low level of Operating System to reveal zero-day attack paths in a probabilistic way.

2 SKRM: Gaining Big Picture Awareness Through an Interconnected Cross-Layer Situation Knowledge Reference Model

2.1 Motivation

Cyber security is nowadays facing a "sea" of sensed data, especially in an enterprise environment. Such data may be generated from a variety of technologies (algorithms and tools) that are developed for the purpose of vulnerability analysis, intrusion detection, damage and impact assessment, and system recovery, etc. The rich data opens up fascinating opportunities for us to understand both mission and adversary activities based on modeling and analytics. As pointed out in Sect. 1.2, cyber situation awareness (SA) is one of the outcomes that we demand from the availability of such big data, which is expected to form the prerequisite that cyber decision makers could depend on to infer what intrusions may be going on, what consequences they may have and what actions should be taken.

However, all the information technologies in enterprise security deployment contribute their data in disparate format to the sea, and hence we find that the resultant cyber SA could be "broken" in the form of "isolated" pieces. We mention in [73] that the root cause to account for this is the isolated *individual* perspectives born with technologies, which do not explicitly consider how to enhance human analysts' overall cyber situation awareness. The local views held during the design and implementation of technologies ultimately cause differences, and such differences exist inherently in technology genes which will definitely go to the resultant data as well, such as data granularity, data format, data semantics and data meanings.

Tons of such heterogeneous data is presented from different sources to security experts for analysis. Genetically "locked" in corresponding different and individual perspectives, the data is usually at different levels, ranging from business to network, from network to system, etc. Put together, they are supposed to deliver the most critical knowledge of the current security situation to human analysts. For this purpose, experts with different background and expertise are needed to make efforts together to digest and understand the data. However, it is found that even for the same security topic, experts from different areas are not able to effectively communicate with each other. For example, experienced business managers have the capability to quickly notice unusual financial loss from business-relevant data, but they may not able to tell whether the loss is caused by a buffer overflow attack or a SQL injection attack towards one workstation. In contrast, an operating system expert can immediately notice an abnormal system call from the log data, but cannot tell how this could affect the company's business flow. That is, the cyber knowledge inherits isolation from data during the process of extraction, and thus is also in "locked" mode.

It is pointed out in [73], due to the existence of the above-described lock mode, "an *integration* framework should be established to integrate cyber knowledge from different perspectives by coupling data, information, algorithms and tools, and human knowledge, to enhance cyber analysts' situation awareness". Many cyber SA capabilities need to be based on big-picture awareness that can only be delivered by the macroscopic framework. For example, one of such capabilities is mission damage and impact assessment, which is essential to identify and track the relevant causality relationships during attacks and subsequent damage propagation. Another example is the asset identification (and prioritization), which is expected to identify and classify critical mission assets into categories like "polluted", "clean but in danger", and "clean and safe". These capabilities benefit the security analysts by greatly easing their the decision making process and facilitating the network security management. However, to gain such capabilities, it is needed to conquer the following "stovepipe" problem.

The "Stovepipe" Problem. The above two capabilities both require the SA-level abstraction (perception, comprehension, projection or resolution) from the involved (data and code) elements at different levels of the computer and information system semantics. In specific to cyber security, damage can be possibly identified at the business process level, application/service level, operating system object (file or process) level or instruction level (memory unit, instruction, register and disk sector). However, for the resultant assessment to be more comprehensive, the capabilities both require a multi-level understanding and cross-level awareness. Using the previous example, system experts exactly know which file is added, deleted or modified, but they hardly know how this can impact the business level. On the other hand, business managers can rapidly notice a suspicious financial loss, but they cannot relate it to an dis-allowed system call inside the operating system. That is, the current security solutions are usually restricted and isolated by their corresponding abstraction levels, such as workflow healing [74], intrusion detection [79,80], attack graph analysis [89–92], OS-level dependency tracking [27] and recovery [28], and instruction-level taint analysis [81–83]. When these technologies are applied to cyber SA, we need them to effectively "talk" to each other, and help security analysts achieve overall situation awareness.

Such "isolation" between different knowledge bases is referred to as the "*stovepipe*" problem [73]. The above-mentioned abstraction levels are one kind of stovepipes, as they cause security analytics bound to individual levels of semantics abstraction. Actually, this kind of stovepipes are *horizontal stovepipes*, as non-integrated security tools on the same abstraction level, such as vulnerability scanners, anti-virus/malware sensors, monitors and loggers, IDS, can also be restricted from each other by the compartmentalization (processes, physical machines, network segments). This second type of stovepipes are *vertical stovepipes*. In simple, horizontal stovepipes are due to differences between the abstraction levels, while vertical ones are due to differences on the same abstraction levels.

The stovepipe problem is by nature an important one to be addressed for situation awareness, as today's security analytic approaches and outcomes are inherently stovepiped, either horizontally or vertically. The SAs extracted from the existing individual situation knowledge collectors are just isolated "pieces". Desired SA capabilities cannot be gained without a large picture which requires holistic understanding of the entire scenario. Therefore these pieces of SAs must be stitched together to become an interconnected cross-layer "big picture", which we call as "big picture awareness" in [73].

Challenges and Approachs. There exist several non-trivial challenges in accessing and modeling cross-layer data and applying it in mission-driven analytics: (1) the stovepipes in an enterprise network have to be identified, including both horizontal (e.g., abstraction levels) and vertical (e.g., compartments) ones; (2) analytical technologies have to be recognized to break the corresponding stovepipes, including inter-compartment ones for vertical stovepipes and cross-abstraction-level for horizontal stovepipes; (3) the isolated network situation knowledge needs to be integrated into a "big picture" based on the above two breakthroughs.

To tackle the stovepipe problem, we present an enterprise network situation knowledge reference model (SKRM) with multiple abstraction layers [73]. As a natural and critical "next-step" to achieve big picture awareness, SKRM addresses the above challenges based on the following approaches: (1) We categorize enterprise network situation knowledge and thus identify the abstraction layers of SKRM: the Workflow Layer, App/Service Layer, Operating System Layer and Instruction Layer. Each layer, from top to bottom, is characterized by additional fine-grained granularity. These abstraction layers are regarded as horizontal stovepipes, and the compartments on the corresponding abstraction layer, i.e. business tasks, applications or services, processes or files, memory units or disk sectors, etc., are regarded as vertical stovepipes. (2) To break the vertical stovepipes, inter-compartment data or control dependency tracking technologies are brought and extended into SKRM, including workflow data or control dependency mining [74–76], service dependency discovery [47,84], OS-level dependency tracking [27,28], and instruction-level taint tracking [81–83]. To break the horizontal stovepipes (e.g., abstraction layers), cross-abstraction-layer semantics bridging technologies are introduced or developed into SKRM, to capture cross-layer (mapping, translation or causality) relationships in-between different levels of computer and information system semantics. For instance, as shown in Fig. 2, a logical dependency Attack Graph [91–93] is vertically inserted between the App/Service Layer and Operating System Layer, to enables causality representation and tracking between network service level pre-conditions (configuration and vulnerability information) and identification of successful exploits at the OS level. (3) Based on the above two breakthroughs, the multi-layer enterprise network SKRM model is formalized and evaluated as the integrator of isolated network situation knowledge. With a different perspective and granularity, each SKRM layer generates a graph that covers the entire network and thus integrates inter-compartment awareness of all the mission assets at that layer. The graphs are then interconnected with each other by cross-layer relationships (e.g., mapping, translation, and semantics bridging). The resulted graph stack represents SKRM in an integrated fashion, transforming isolated SA into a "big-picture-oriented" SA.

The following sections describe the SKRM model, the SKRM graph stack generation, and SKRM-enabled mission diagnosis.

2.2 SKRM Model

Detecting and preventing intrusions in cyber space is like "catching big fishes in the sea". Like fishermen, we need a well-knit "fishing net" to capture cyber attacks. Made of data, what will it be like? Our SKRM model, as illustrated in Fig. 2, serves as the "fishing net". It breaks the "isolation" in-between heterogenous data sources, and enables a "big picture" to deliver macroscopic perspective and holistic understanding.

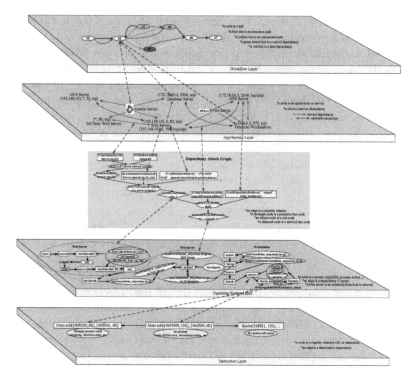

Fig. 2. The enterprise network Situation Knowledge Reference Model (SKRM) [73].

SKRM Overview and Features. SKRM seamlessly integrates four abstraction layers of cyber situation knowledge in an enterprise network: Workflow Layer, App/Service Layer, Operating System Layer and Instruction Layer, from top to bottom, with finer and finer granularities in technical details. The following is the summary of the SKRM overview and features from [73]:

- Each abstraction layer generates a graph, and each graph covers the entire enterprise network;
- Cross-layer relationships are captured. The individual graphs are interconnected to become a graph stack;

- The graph stack enables both inter-compartment diagnosis and cross-layer analysis;
- Each abstraction layer is a view of the same network from a different perspective and thus at a different granularity;
- Isolated perception that is gained at different layers/granularities is integrated into a more comprehensive, scalable system to support higher levels of SA, namely comprehension and projection.

SKRM Layers. The layers are abstracted from the explored literature based on the categorization of isolated situation knowledge, in terms of different levels in computer and information system semantics, as well as corresponding expertise. Specifically, workflow paths are powerful to model and manage the daily business/mission processes. Application or service dependencies are invaluable to localize any faults or problems in multi-service network environments, for the purpose of stability and efficiency. OS object (file or process) dependencies are useful to backward or forward track the intrusion propagation. Dynamic instruction taint tracking is helpful for fine-grained intrusion harm analysis.

Workflow Layer. Workflow is widely used to model and manage organization business processes [74]. A workflow is made up of several essential tasks in order to complete a business process, in which the tasks are sequenced in a specific order ensuring the correct dependency relationship between each other. Organization workflows are supposed to be consistent and reliable to ensure correct execution paths. If a workflow is compromised, the tasks or data in workflow may have been corrupted (perhaps based on malicious injection or modification), or the execution sequence in paths have been modified. Hence, we propose Workflow Layer as the top layer in SKRM to capture the business/mission processes within an enterprise. The Workflow Layer shown in Fig. 2 could be referred to as an example of 7 tasks.

Definition 1. *Workflow Layer* [73]
     The graph of Workflow Layer can be represented by a directed graph $G(V, E)$, where:

- V is the set of nodes (tasks);
- E is the set of directed edges (immediate precedence relations);
- If $(t_i, t_j) \in E$, then (t_i, t_j) is a directed edge pointed from task t_i to task t_j, and t_j should be executed subsequently to t_i. The directed edges derive the *data and control dependency* relationships among tasks;
- A workflow $G(V, E)$ has a start node with 0-indegree, and some end nodes with 0-outdegree. Any path from the start node to the end node is an *execution path.*

App/Service Layer. The functioning of workflows ultimately lies in the execution of tasks, which further depend on the proper execution of specific application software. Moreover, according to [47], the functionality, performance and reliability of a particular application may rely on multiple pre-requisite services,

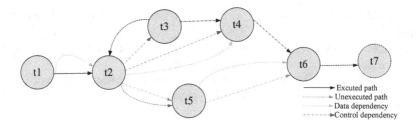

Fig. 3. The graph of Workflow Layer [73].

that are hosted in other relevant nodes in the network. Therefore, we propose an App/Service Layer in SKRM to capture the applications/services and their dependency relationships. The App/Service Layer shown in Fig. 2 is an example.

Definition 2. *App/Service Layer* [73]

The graph of App/Service Layer can be represented by a directed graph $G(V, E_1, E_2)$, where:

– V is the set of nodes (applications or services);
– E_1 is the set of uni-directional edges (dependencies), and E_2 is the set of bi-directional edges (network connections);
– Service nodes are denoted as a three-tuple (*ip, port, protocol*);
– If $(A_i, S_j) \in E_1$, then (A_i, S_j) is a *dependency* relation from application A_i to service S_j. If $(S_m, S_n) \in E_2$, then (S_m, S_n) is a *network connection* between service S_m to service S_n.

Operating System Layer. The further exploration is done inside specific hosts, after they are located to host application or services for the execution of workflows. As a result, we further introduce the Operating System Layer into SKRM, to build an OS-level dependency graph. The Operating System Layer of Fig. 2 illustrates an example.

Definition 3. *Operating System Layer* [73]

The dependency graph at the OS Layer can be specified by a directed graph $G(V, E)$, where:

– V is the set of nodes (system objects, mainly a process, a file or a socket inside a system);
– E is the set of directed edges which means immediate dependency relations;
– If $(N_A, N_B) \in E$, then node N_A is influencing N_B in a certain way which we can call as *dependency*, represented as edges in the graph.

Instruction Layer. Fine-grained intrusion impact diagnosis at the instruction layer may help find the missed intrusions at the process-file level [83]. Hence, an Instruction Layer is proposed in SKRM to specify and correlate the memory cells,

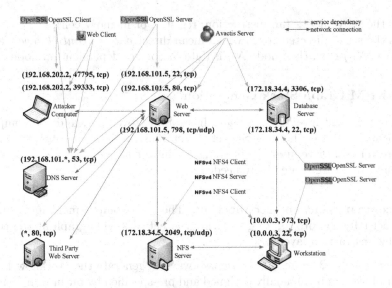

Fig. 4. The graph of App/Service Layer [73].

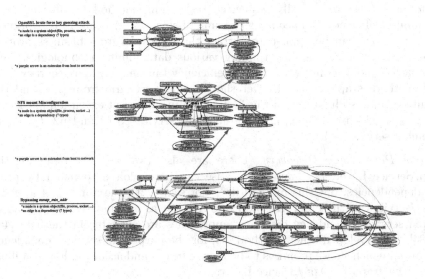

Fig. 5. The graph of Operating System Layer [73].

disk sectors, registers, kernel address space, and other devices [73]. As shown in
the Instruction Layer of Fig. 2, a graph at the instruction level can be generated
based on mapping each instruction flow to the corresponding system objects
[81,83]. Besides, the dynamic taint analysis semantics [82] could be applied here.

Definition 4. *Instruction Layer* [73]

A graph of the Instruction Layer can also be specified by a directed graph
$G(V, E)$, where:

- V is the set of nodes (an instruction, register, or memory cell);
- E is the set of directed edges which mean direct *data or control dependence*;
- If $(N_A, N_B) \in E$, then node N_B is data or control dependent on node N_A.

2.3 SKRM Graph Stack Generation

The above-defined layers are actually horizontal stovepipes, and the compartments (tasks, services, hosts, OS-level objects, instruction-level objects) on the layer are vertical stovepipes. To break them, inter-compartment and cross-layer interconnections are respectively needed.

Inter-compartment Interconnection. The inter-compartment interconnection is actually the process of generating the network-wide graph at the corresponding abstraction layer [73].

Workflow Design/Mining. There are two ways to generate the Workflow Layer: (1) Workflows can be manually designed and pre-specified by business managers, since a "defined" business outcome is what the workflow wants to achieve by performing a set of logically sequenced tasks. This method is suffering from the limited efficiency and accuracy of human beings; (2) Alternatively, workflow mining [75–78] can be applied to extract the workflows from business process actual execution log data by running various data mining technologies. This approach is more promising regarding efficiency (automatic) and accuracy. The first method is applied to the web-shop business scenario from [74], and the resulted graph is illustrated in Fig. 3, in which two different execution paths can be recognized - p1: $t_1 t_2 t_3 t_4 t_6 t_7$ (non-member service path) and p2: $t_1 t_2 t_5 t_6 t_7$ (member service path).

Service Dependency Discovery. There are also two ways to generate the App/Service Layer: (1) human expertise can be exploited to manually draw the dependencies, but this method does not scale with the number of applications/services in the enterprise network [47]; (2) as alternatives, several automated service dependency discovery approaches are available in the field [45–47,84]. We developed a new method [85] for the purpose of service dependency discovery, which shows promises to be more efficient and accurate. Figure 4 illustrates the graph for App/Service Layer.

Inter-host OS Level Dependency Tracking. Recent work [27] shows that system calls can be parsed to determine the dependency relation type between two OS level objects. Following such "dependency rules", OS object level dependency graph can be built from the system call audit logs for each host. Our insight goes further to extend the single-host OS object dependency graph to cover the whole network by incorporating the socket-based communications between remote programs. This is demonstrated to be very effective to reveal unknown attack traces [29]. Section 3 will elaborate on this breakthrough. Figure 5 illustrates the graph for Operating System Layer.

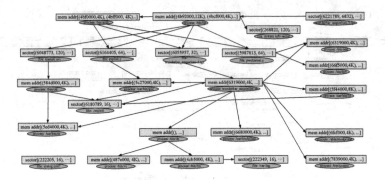

Fig. 6. The graph of Instruction Layer [73].

Instruction Level Taint Tracking. According to [83], the Instruction Layer could accommodate two parts of work: (1) fine-grained taint analysis can be applied to generate instruction flow dependency, which contains valuable binary information; (2) cross-layer infection diagnosis can be performed to bridge the "semantic gap" between Instruction Layer and Operating system Layer. Figure 6 illustrates the graph for Instruction Layer, in which the instruction-level objects (rectangle ones) are dynamically mapped with corresponding OS-level objects (ellipse ones).

Cross-Layer Interconnection. Cross-layer interconnection is to capture the cross-layer relationships, which then can be traversed from one SKRM layer to another, to gain new information and ultimately win holistic understanding of the whole scenario.

Cross-layer Semantics Bridging. Basically, semantics bridging (like mapping and translation) between two adjacent abstraction layers can be used to capture cross-layer relationships. For example, bi-directional mappings between the workflow tasks at Workflow Layer and the particular applications at the App/Service Layer can be made by mining their association from the network traces with workflow logs. The mappings between OS Layer objects and Instruction Layer objects can be done based on a reconstruction engine such as the one presented in [83]. Example mappings are illustrated in Fig. 2 denoted as purple bi-directional dotted lines between adjacent layers.

Attack Graph Representation and Generation. To interconnect the App/Service Layer and OS Layer, a dependency Attack Graph [92] could be vertically inserted between them, to capture causality relationship between App/Service Layer preconditions (network connection, machine configuration and vulnerability information) and OS Layer symptoms/patterns of successful exploits. Figure 7 illustrates the attack graph that we generated.

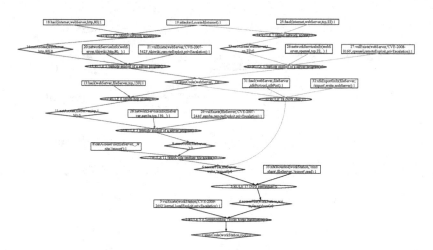

Fig. 7. The dependency Attack Graph [73]. (Color figure online)

Definition 5. *dependency Attack Graph* [73]
The dependency Attack Graph (AG) can be represented with a directed graph
$G(V, E)$, where:

- V is the set of nodes (*derivation nodes* denoted as ellipses, *primitive fact nodes* represented with rectangles and d*erived fact nodes* represented with diamonds);
- E is the set of directed edges which represent the *causality relationships* between nodes;
- One or more fact nodes could serve as the preconditions of a derivation node and cause it to take effect. One or more derivation nodes could further cause a derived fact node to become true.

The Attack Graph in Fig. 2 only illustrates a subset of Fig. 7, but it also illustrates the interconnection of the dependency Attack Graph with its adjacent two layers: (1) The App/Service Layer information (network connection, host configuration, scanned vulnerability) become the primitive nodes in Attack Graph, based on the Datalog representation for attack graph generation [92]; (2) the derived fact nodes in Attack Graph are mapped to the OS Layer intrusion symptoms (like intrusion pattern or signatures) based on network-wide OS level dependency tracking, which input is the OS level instances of host or service configuration. For example, process */usr/sbin/sshd* instantiates *sshd*, hence tracking it would reveal the repeated pattern of accessing sshd-related processes and files (i.e. *Node 14* in the dependency AG).

2.4   Case Study

We further performed a concrete case study in [73], based on the business/mission scenario adapted from [74], shown in Fig. 8a, to illustrate SKRM-based mission diagnosis in which SKRM serves as a key enabler of capabilities, like mission damage and impact assessment, asset identification and classification, etc. For this purpose, we put the scenario under a 3-step attack (*CVE-2008-0166*-OpenSSL brute force key guessing attack, NFS mount misconfiguration, *CVE-2009-2692*-bypassing *mmap_min_addr*), and several situation knowledge collectors are deployed in the scenario to acquire real data, including Nessus, MulVAL, Snort, Ntop, strace and our own developed ones [29].

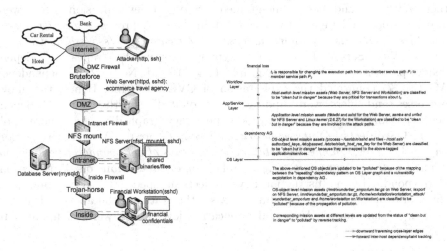

(a) The test-bed network and attack scenario.

(b) Mission asset identification and classification.

Fig. 8. Example SKRM-based mission diagnosis: the test-bed and enabled capability [73].

Capability: Mission Asset Identification and Classification As illustrates in Fig. 8b, top-down cross-layer SKRM diagnosis will enable capability that can identify and classify the mission assets. Starting from an obvious observation at the business level (like financial loss), mission asset identification and prioritization achieves at the identification and classification of host-switch level, application level and OS-object level mission critical assets into classes such as "polluted", "clean but in danger", and "clean and safe".

Specifically, after noticing the financial loss, the analysts suspected that attackers as non-members may have obtained member services via path p2, through analysis on the Workflow Layer (Fig. 3). As task t_2 is responsible for changing the execution path from p1 to p2, they tracked down the cross-layer edges from Workflow Layer to App/Service Layer, to perform particular inspection on task t_2. The critical host-switch level mission assets involved in transactions about t_2, *Web Server*, *NFS Server* and *Workstation*, were tagged into "clean but in danger" as they became the most possible attack goals. The analysts further tracked down the cross-layer edges from App/Service

Layer to dependency AG, and found four possible attack paths there: 23, 14, 6, 4, 1, 16, 14, 11, 9, 6, 4, 1, 16, 14, 6, 4, 1 and 23, 14, 11, 9, 6, 4, 1, which were highlighted with red, blue, purple and green colors respectively in Fig. 7. All the application level assets implicated by the attack paths were regarded as "clean but in danger": *tikiwiki* and *sshd* for the Web Server, *samba* and *unfsd* for NFS Server and *Linux kernel (2.6.27)* for the Workstation. The edges from the dependency AG to the OS Layer were further traversed, and hence fine-grained OS object level mission assets were also identified and tagged to "clean but in danger": process - */usr/sbin/sshd* and files - */root/.ssh/authorized_keys*, */etc/passwd*, */etc/ssh/ssh_host_rsa_key* for the Web Server. Later, the mapping between the "repeating" dependency pattern on OS Layer graph (Fig. 5) and Node 27 in dependency AG (Fig. 7) confirmed the exploitation of CVE-2008-0166. Hence, the above processes and filers were updated to "polluted". Further forward dependency tracking on the network-wide dependency graph discovered more "polluted" OS objects: */mnt/wunderbar_emporium.tar.gz* on Web Server, */export* on NFS Server, */home/workstation/workstation_attack/wunderbar_emporium*, */mnt/wunderbar_emporium.tar.gz*, and */home/workstation* on Workstation. Correspondingly, the Instruction Layer objects mapped to these system objects could also be tagged into "polluted". Also, the status of the above "clean but in danger" host-switch level and application level assets were all updated to "polluted".

2.5   Discussion and Conclusion

In summary, this section identifies the stovepipe problem for cyber situation awareness, and presents a formal SKRM model as the solution to break the stovepipes. The SKRM-based mission diagnosis case studies show that SKRM is a key enabler for capabilities like asset identification and classification.

More skipped case studies show that SKRM can enable other capabilities like mission damage and impact assessment, attack path determination and attack intent identification. It shows promising potentials to go beyond the purely intrusion detection or attack graph analysis. However, the current version of SKRM is still semi-automatic, needing additional work to become fully-automated and thoroughly evaluated in the scale of a real enterprise network.

3   Patrol: Revealing Zero-Day Attack Paths Through Network-Wide System Object Dependencies

3.1   Motivation

One of the stubborn research problems is the *zero-day attack* problem, which is also a result of the information asymmetry between the attackers and defenders. As a huge threat that may stealthily undermine the security infrastructure of enterprise networks, the vulnerabilities and exploits used to create the security holes are kept "zero-day" by the attackers, i.e. the occurrences and consequences of the vulnerability exploitations are totally without the awareness of the defenders. According to the Symantec researchers [86], a typical zero-day attack can remain undisclosed for 312 days on average.

Researchers from the security field make efforts to conquer this problem, with most of them focusing on the detection of zero-day vulnerability exploits. Such techniques include some anomaly detection [35–42] and specification-based detection [87,88] approaches. Based on profiling normal behavior and detecting deviations, they show promising capabilities to detect novel exploits. But, as a drawback, they usually suffer from high false positives.

One of the recent breakthroughs is made by our system named Patrol [29]. Inspired by the SKRM model, Patrol holds a big-picture vision investigating zero-day attacks in a path which we call *zero-day attack path*. Zero-day attack path is a novel observation from Parol that attackers have to go through an attack path before they finally reach their attack goal, and such an attack path often includes one or more zero-day exploits if not all. Specifically, due to the security infrastructure like firewall and IDS deployed in enterprise networks, attackers could not break into their target system directly with just one step. Instead, determined attackers patiently employ multiple-step attacks to compromise other intermediate hosts as stepping-stones. Basically, each compromise of one intermediate machine before the final target would be an exploitation of one vulnerability, no matter it is a disclosed one or a zero-day one. Thus, the path from the attacker to the final attack goal is a sequence of vulnerability exploits on compromised hosts. When such a sequence includes at least one zero-day exploit, it is a zero-day attack path.

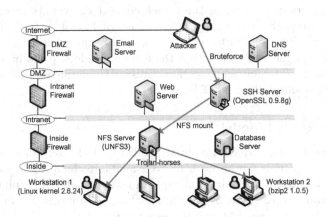

Fig. 9. An example attack scenario [29].

Figure 9 illustrates the example attack scenario from Patrol [29], which includes three steps of attacks: Step 1, a brute-force key guessing attack exploiting *CVE-2008-0166* on *SSH Server* to gain root privilege; Step 2, the NFS mount taking advantage the mis-configured export table on *NFS Server* to upload two crafted trojan-horse files, which contain exploit code of *CVE-2009-2692* and *CVE-2011-4089*, to other network machines through a public directory (*/exports*); Step 3, the mount and execution of the arbitrary code in uploaded trojan-horse files to create hidden channels. Hence, two attack paths exist: *p1{CVE-2008-0166, NFS misconfiguration, CVE-2009-2692}* and *p2{CVE-2008-0166, NFS misconfiguration, CVE-2011-4089}*. Patrol assumes the time back to *August 1, 2009*, then *CVE-2008-0166* becomes the only known vulnerability, and *p1* and *p2* both become zero-day attack paths.

Zero-day attack path is a bigger perspective to view the zero-day attack problem. It is also a new strategy to address this problem by leveraging the weakness of the attackers: it's almost impossible for the attackers to exploit only zero-day vulnerabilities along the path to reach their final target. As a result, zero-day attack paths usually include components corresponding to the exploits of known vulnerabilities, and commodity intrusion detection systems can raise alerts to help security administrators notice them. This may lead to the disclosure of the "zero-day" components in the attack path based on forward or backward tracking from the noticed parts along the path. In many cases identifying zero-day attack paths is substantially more feasible than detecting individual zero-day exploits.

The identification of zero-day attack paths is like chasing thieves from detected clues to reveal their stealthy route breaking into the victim properties, and Patrol is designed to implement this in the cyber world. Due to its "zero-day" (also known as "unknown") nature, the "zero-day attack path" problem is actually an instance of the cyber situation awareness problems, as it is essentially an effort to break the "information asymmetry" between the attackers and the defenders, i.e. revealing the attack context of exploits including zero-day ones on the path. Specifically, the findings of Patrol show us the system object level activities related to the infection and propagation processes, which greatly facilitates the analysis dig out the formerly hidden parts in attacks, i.e. zero-day exploits. The following sections present the approach, model, design, implementation and evaluation of Patrol.

3.2   Approach and Model

The literature is explored for potential solutions of the zero-day attack path problem. However, it is found out that no available technique can well address this problem due to its "zero-day" nature. For example, attack graph techniques [89–92] generate attack paths by correlating the exploitations of found vulnerabilities into attack sequences towards specific targets. The resulted attack path is inherently the model of the causality dependencies among the adjacent vulnerabilities. The benefit is that these techniques can be leveraged to show all potential attack paths that can walk the attacker to the victim machines. But, attack graph techniques also suffer from a big limitation: they are incapable of capturing unknown vulnerabilities and thus zero-day attack paths are not included in the resulted attack graph, i.e. the set of known attack paths.

Another candidate solution to the zero-day attack path problem is the alert correlation approaches, which were born to correlate isolated alerts to form potential attack paths. Whether it can expose zero-day attack paths depends on whether the alerts are raised to point out the exploitations of zero-day vulnerabilities. Only when techniques to detect zero-day exploits are employed, such as the ones mentioned above [35–88], zero-day attack paths could be possibly identified. The bad news is that the alerts which the correlation largely depends on would genetically inherit high false rates from such techniques. Moreover, the alert correlation technique itself suffers from inaccuracy as it's inherently an attempt to integrate possibly different contexts into a unified "story", which results in another fold of false rates in addition to the ones of zero-day exploit detection.

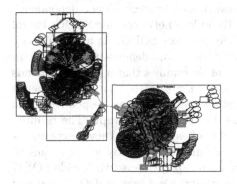
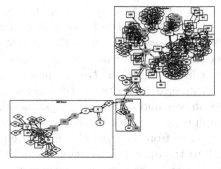

(a) An example 3-host SODG for the attack scenario in Fig. 9, with *1288* OS objects from *143120* system calls. The SIPPs hidden in it is highlighted in red.

(b) The red colored SIPPs hidden in (a), with *175* OS objects. The trigger node is highlighted in red color and other verified malicious nodes in grey.

Fig. 10. This figure is to show what the SODG and SIPPs are like. A box contains a per-host SODG, in which a rectangle denotes a process, a diamond denotes a socket, and an ellipse denotes a file. *They look unreadable because of the fine granularity at OS-level and the scale of network. Readers are not expected to understand the details.* A main merit of Patrol is that it can dig out SIPPs from the network-wide SODG [29]. (Color figure online)

To identify zero-day attack paths, Patrol employs a different *strategy*: "Instead of first collecting vulnerabilities or alerts and then correlating them into paths, we first try to build a superset graph and identify the suspicious intrusion propagation paths hidden in it as candidate zero-day attack paths, and then recognize the highly suspicious candidates among these paths" [29]. This decision is reached based on four *key insights*: "(1) As the only way for programs to interact with OS, system calls are found hard-to-avoid and attack neutral; (2) We find that a network-wide superset graph can be generated from system calls, and zero-day attack paths are showing themselves in it. This graph is also attack neutral. It exists no matter whether any vulnerability is exploited or not; (3) The superset graph is inherently a set of paths. We find a way to get its appropriate subsets as candidate zero-day attack paths. These paths actually and naturally correlate vulnerability exploitations, different from the logical correlation in attack graph; (4) The candidate zero-day attack paths expose unknown vulnerability exploitations along them, and thus can orientate us to recognize such exploitations. With these paths serving as network-wide attack context, the accuracy and performance of detecting unknown vulnerability exploitations can be better than the detection with only isolated per-host context" [29]. Interested readers are referred to Fig. 10 for an example of a superset graph (Fig. 10a) and the suspicious intrusion propagation paths (Fig. 10b) hidden in it.

By assuming that a network consists of Unix-like operating systems, and system objects are mainly classified into processes, files and sockets, Patrol proposes to build the superset graph, namely network-wide system object dependency graph (SODG), from system call traces. To build a network-wide SODG, Patrol first constructs SODG for each host, namely per-host SODG. As in Definition 6 [29], system calls are parsed to generate OS objects and dependency relations inbetween them. For example, system call *read* determines that a process depends on a file (denoted as $file \rightarrow process$), while *write* infers that a file depends on a process ($process \rightarrow file$). As nodes and directed edges respectively, the OS objects and dependency relations then form a directed graph. The resulted graph is the per-host SODG, which is capable of capturing unknown exploits, as it is built from system calls and system calls are the only way for programs to talk to the operating system. As in Definition 7 [29], the network-wide SODG can be constructed by recursively concatenating the per-host SODGs, when and only when there exists at least one directed edge in-between two nodes from two different SODGs. Figure 10a gives an example of a 3-host SODG. Definitions 6 and 7 are concretized versions of Definition 3.

Definition 6. *per-host System Object Dependency Graph* [29]
If the system call trace for the i-*th* host is denoted as Σ_i, then the per-host SODG for the host is a directed graph G(V_i, E_i), where:

- V_i is the set of nodes, and initialized to empty set $\varnothing$;
- E_i is the set of directed edges, and initialized to empty set $\varnothing$;
- If a system call $syscall \in \Sigma_i$, and *dep* is the dependency relation parsed from *syscall* according to dependency rules, where $dep \in \{(src \rightarrow sink), (src \leftarrow sink), (src \leftrightarrow sink)\}$, *src* and *sink* are OS objects (mainly a process, file or socket), then $V_i = V_i \cup \{src, sink\}, E_i = E_i \cup \{dep\}$.*dep* inherits timestamps *start* and *end* from *syscall*;
- If $(a \rightarrow b) \in E_i$ and $(b \rightarrow c) \in E_i$, then c transitively depends on a.

Definition 7. *network-wide System Object Dependency Graph* [29]
If the per-host SODG for the i-*th* host is denoted as $G(V_i, E_i)$, then the network-wide SODG can be denoted as $\cup G(V_i, E_i)$, where:

- $\cup G(V_2, E_2) = G(V_1, E_1) \cup G(V_2, E_2) = G(\cup V_2, \cup E_2)$, iff $\exists obj_1 \in V_1, obj_2 \in V_2$ and $dep_{1,2} \in \cup E_2$, where $dep_{1,2} \in \{obj_1 \leftarrow obj_2, obj_1 \rightarrow obj_2, obj_1 \leftrightarrow obj_2\}$. $\cup V_2$ denotes $V_1 \cup V_2$, and $\cup E_2$ denotes $E_1 \cup E_2$;
- $\cup G(V_i, E_i) = \cup G(V_{i-1}, E_{i-1})\} \cup G(V_i, E_i) = G(\cup V_i, \cup E_i)$, iff $\exists obj_{i-1} \in \cup V_{i-1}, obj_i \in V_i$ and $dep_{i-1,i} \in \cup E_i$, where $dep_{i-1,i} \in \{obj_{i-1} \leftarrow obj_i, obj_{i-1} \rightarrow obj_i, obj_{i-1} \leftrightarrow obj_i\}$. $\cup V_i$ denotes $V_1 \cup \cdots \cup V_i$, and $\cup E_i$ denotes $E_1 \cup \cdots \cup E_i$.

The network-wide SODG is by nature a set of paths, and if a zero-day attack path exists it will be one of the set. Patrol identifies suspicious intrusion propagation paths (SIPPs) in the network-wide SODG as candidate zero-day attack paths. As in Definition 8 [29], the SIPPs are a subgraph of SODG, in which all the objects either have directed edges from or to trigger nodes, where trigger nodes are those OS objects noticed by administrators to be involved in any alerts from deployed security sensors, such as Snort [17], Tripwire [34] or Patrol itself. Figure 10b shows an example of the SIPPs hidden in the 3-host SODG (Fig. 10a).

Definition 8. *Suspicious Intrusion Propagation Paths* (SIPPs) [29]
If the network-wide SODG is denoted as $\cup G(V_i, E_i)$, where $G(V_i, E_i)$ denotes the per-host SODG for the i-*th* host, then the SIPPs are a subgraph of $\cup G(V_i, E_i)$, denoted as $G(V', E')$, where:

- V' is the set of nodes, and $V' \subset \cup V_i$;
- E' is the set of directed edges, and $E' \subset \cup E_i$;
- V' is initialized to include *trigger nodes* only;
- For $\forall obj' \in V'$, if $\exists obj \in \cup V_i$ where $(obj \rightarrow obj') \in \cup E_i$ and $start(obj \rightarrow obj') \leq lat(obj')$, then $V' = V' \cup \{obj\}$ and $E' = E' \cup \{(obj \rightarrow obj')\}$. $lat(obj')$ maintains the *latest access time* to obj' by edges in E';
- For $\forall obj' \in V'$, if $\exists obj \in \cup V_i$ where $(obj' \rightarrow obj) \in \cup E_i$ and $end(obj' \rightarrow obj) \geq eat(obj')$, then $V' = V' \cup \{obj\}$ and $E' = E' \cup \{(obj' \rightarrow obj)\}$. $eat(obj')$ maintains the *earliest access time* to obj' by edges in E'.

It is worth noting that the SODG and SIPPs are both instantiations of the OS layer graph of the SKRM model (Fig. 2), as the SODG and SIPPs inherently capture the attacker's attack context or trace at OS level. The network-wide SODG can be unmanageable in size, while Patrol solves this problem by digging out its "suspicious" subgraph, i.e. the identified SIPPs, which is much smaller regarding size. Although smaller, the SIPPs captures almost all the zero-day attack paths, because the only possible way for a zero-day attack path to escape SIPPs is that attackers only exploit zero-day vulnerabilities along the path. This is extremely very rare and unlikely. As a result, a zero-day attack path will be inside the SIPPs as long as it exists. Patrol proposes a method, named shadow indicator checking, to recognize the highly suspicious candidate zero-day attack paths among the SIPPs.

3.3   System Design

Patrol uses a modular design for its system. Figure 11 illustrates its four major components, where only the first one works on the fly, and the other three are off-line to avoid any additional overhead imposed on individual hosts.

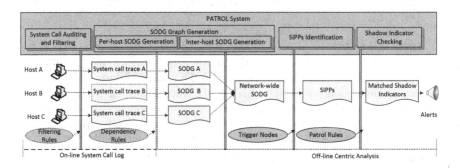

Fig. 11. System overview of Patrol [29].

System Call Auditing and Filtering. The first module is a runtime system call monitor, which is designed in Patrol to collect system call traces from each host. The system call auditing is expected to fulfill the following requirements: (1) It is supposed to audit all the "live" processes, rather than just some possible processes. The reason behind this is the impossibility to pre-determine which specific processes to audit, without the risk that system calls from other processes can be skipped with critical intrusion information. (2) Network-wide system call auditing is essential for recognizing any suspicious paths across the hosts, hence system call auditing should be performed network-wide. That is, all hosts should be in the list to be audited, and all the socket communications across hosts should be audited. (3) It's not accurate to identify system objects solely by their process IDs or file descriptor numbers, which may be revoked for later reuse by the operating system. Hence, other OS-aware information should be preserved for sufficiency to accurately identify OS objects. (4) Patrol is also interested in recording the time information of a system call being invoked or returned, as its algorithm later leverages temporal relationships to help determine whether a system call is involved in intrusion propagation.

The system call trace data is then sent from individual hosts to a central analysis machine. Before that, system calls need to be filtered to avoid any additional bandwidth or computation costs on data transfer and analysis. Filtering preprocessing is introduced into the system, applying some rules to prune highly redundant or possibly innocent system calls. Such pruning could speed up the graph generation and reduce the complexity of its resulted graphs. Currently, the filtering rules in Patrol are mainly applied towards the following system objects: (1) The dynamic linked library files like libc.so.* and libm.so.*, which are loaded each time an executable is run, causing a lot of redundancy; (2) Dummy objects like stdin/stdout and /dev/null; (3) objects about pseudo-terminal master and slave (/dev/ptmx and /dev/pts); (4) Objects related to log related like syslogd and /var/log/∗; (5) Objects related to system maintenance (apt-get and apt-config). In addition to these rules, Patrol allows users to specify more filtering rules to prune system calls, gaining more speed boosting of graph generation, but also at larger risk of filtering out non-innocent objects. Because of this trade-off, filtering preprocessing is implemented as options in Patrol. Besides, Patrol employs a tuning parameter called time window to adjust the frequency of sending system call logs to the analysis machine after filtering. It is defined to be the periodic time span during which system calls are logged [29]. Setting this para-meter is tricky, as too big a value could cause the system call data accumulative to have bigger latency on data transfer and analysis.

SODG Generation and Concatenation. Patrol system constructs per-host SODGs by parsing system calls from individual hosts. A system call is typ-ically interpreted into OS objects (process/file/socket) and their dependency relations. The OS objects become nodes in the SODGs and the dependency relations become directed edges in-between them. Such transformation is done according to some pre-defined dependency rules, such as the ones proposed in [27–29,94], in which system call names are usually used to determine depen-dency relation types, and system call arguments are used to uniquely recog-nize and name SODG nodes, as well as decide the edge directions. For exam-ple, system call "*sys_open, start:470880, end:494338, pid:6707, pname:scp, path-name:/mnt/trojan, inode:9453574*" from the Patrol dataset is transformed to (6707, scp) ← (/mnt/trojan, 9453574), where *pid* and *pname* are used to recog-nize the process, and *pathname* and *inode* are used to identify the file [29].

Per-host SODGs are concatenated together to build the network-wide SODG. This can be done because of the fact that hosts in a network need to interact (communicate) with each other, causing a per-host SODG to have directed edges to/from other per-host SODGs. As long as two nodes in two different per-host SODGs share one or more directed edges, they can be concatenated together with the shared edges serving as the glue. It is found out that the glue edges are usually caused by socket-based communications, as local programs often talk with remote programs through message passing, which could be reflected in system call *socketcall*. As a result, by identifying and paring the corresponding socket objects involved in this system call, the two separate per-host SODGs can be stitched together. For example, in Patrol's dataset, system call "*sys_accept, start:681154, end:681162, pid:4935, pname:sshd, srcaddr:172.18.34.10, src-port:36036, sinkaddr:192.168.101.5, sinkport:22*" results in a directed edge (172.18.34.10, 36036) → (192.168.101.5, 22), which glues together the per-host SODGs of *172.18.34.10* and *192.168.101.5* [29]. As pointed out by Definition 7, the network-wide SODG is built by recursively running the above gluing process. Starting from two per-host SODGs, they are first glued to a 2-host SODG, then a 3-host SODG by concatenating a 3rd per-host SODG, then a 4-host SODG by concatenating a 4th per-host SODG, and so on. The algorithm goes on recursively and ends up with no gluing edges left between any per-host SODG and the resulted network-wide SODG.

SIPPs Identification. The third module is designed to dig out SIPPs from the network-wide SODG, namely SIPPs identification. Benefiting from the network-wide SODG, Patrol extends the capability of intra-host forward or backward dependency tracking to go across the boundaries of individual hosts. Through inter-host dependency tracking from some seed nodes, Patrol can find all the network SODG objects that have direct or transitive dependency relations to/from them. When the seed nodes are the trigger nodes recognized and fed by security administrators, the resulted nodes and edges identified by Patrol form SIPPs by Definition 8. Trigger nodes are alerted by security sensors like Snort, Tripwire, etc., and noticed by security experts. For example, they could be "files that are deleted, added, or modified in unexpected ways, and processes that behave in an unusual or malicious manner" [29].

To identify SIPPs, Patrol may first perform backward tracking using trigger nodes as seeds, because trigger nodes may be not the start of an intrusion. In many cases the IDS systems suffer from detection latency, i.e. an alert could be delayed manifestation of the intrusion start. Backward tracking could be helpful to find the start [27], and then the start can be used to perform forward tracking. Specifically, the backward dependency tracking is leveraged to identify all the SODG objects that have direct or transitive directed edges to the trigger nodes (indicating that trigger nodes are affected by the up-stream objects), while the forward dependency tracking is to find the objects that have direct or transitive directed edges from the trigger nodes (indicating that trigger nodes affect the down-stream objects). Patrol implements both the backward and forward dependency tracking as breadth-first search (BFS) [95] algorithms, which was depicted in Definition 8.

Shadow Indicator Checking. Patrol further performs shadow indicator checking to identify highly suspicious candidate zero-day attack paths among the SIPPs, as SIPPs could still be complex. Shadow indicator checking is based on the concepts of vulnerability shadow and shadow indicator. These concepts are proposed based on the key observation that vulnerabilities share some common features. For example, 693 common weaknesses get enumerated in CWE [96], and 400 common attack patterns are classified by CAPEC [97]. The concept of vulnerability shadow is much in the same spirit, but it differs by characterizing exploitations of vulnerabilities at the OS lever, rather than directly characterizing vulnerabilities. Beyond the existence of the above-mentioned shared common features, this new characterization finds that the exploitations of some vulnerabilities often share similar characteristics in SODG as well. Moreover, the common SODG characteristics exist in a long time span, meaning that the characteristics extracted from previous exploitations of known vulnerabilities can be applied to detect exploitations of unknown vulnerabilities.

Definition 9. *Vulnerability Shadow* and *Shadow Indicator* [29]

A vulnerability shadow is a Cantor set denoted as $S = \{v \mid p(SODG(v))\}$, where:

- v is a known or unknown vulnerability, whose exploitation is part of the SODG represented as $SODG(v)$;
- p, the shadow indicator for S, is a boolean-valued set indicator function: $SODG(v) \rightarrow \{true, false\}$.$p$ can be a conjunction of several predicates, in a form like $p = p_1 \& p_2 \& \cdots \& p_n$ (n is a natural number), where for $\forall 1 \le i \le n$, p_i is predicating an attribute of a node or edge in $SODG(v)$, and $\&$ stands for *AND* operation in logic (p is true, iff p_i is true for $\forall 1 \le i \le n$);
- $v \in S$, iff $p(SODG(v)) = true$.

To take advantage of this insight, Patrol defines vulnerability shadow and shadow indication (Definition 9) [29], where vulnerability shadow is a set of known and unknown vulnerabilities, and shadow indicator is its set indication function. The indicator function is defined based on the common characteristics extracted from SODGs. Vulnerability shadow is actually the built set, using the indicator function to indicate membership of vulnerabilities in the set. As a result, exploitations of the vulnerabilities in the same vulnerability shadow all have the common SODG characteristics. Figure 12 illustrates an example vulnerability shadow *bypassing mmap_min_addr*, with *node.name = page_zero&node.indegree>0 &node.outdegree>0* as its shadow indicator [29]. The indicator was first observed in exploiting CVE-2009-1895 and CVE-2009-1897, and then can be used to recognize the exploitations of CVE-2009-2692, CVE-2009-2695, CVE-2009-2698, etc. Unknown vulnerabilities that do not have an official CVE ID yet could also be categorized into this shadow, as long as their exploitations can trigger the shadow indicator to become true.

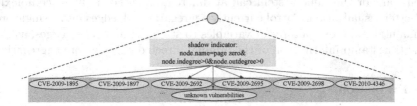

Fig. 12. A vulnerability shadow example: *bypassing mmap_min_addr* [29].

Shadow indicators are not welcomed by legitimate paths as they imply the occurrence of an exploitation. When shadow indicators are detected on a path inside the SIPPs, the path is very likely to be an attack path. If any of these indicators could not be mapped to the existing alerts from deployed vulnerability scanners or IDS systems, the attack path could highly possibly be a zero-day attack path, which will be reported by the system. Patrol employs rule-based checking to recognize the shadow indicators. For example, the rule to check the shadow indicator of bypsssing mmap_min_addr is *indicator page_zero (function: indegree>0&outdegree>0; msg: "bypassing mmap_min_addr")*.

3.4   Implementation

The implementation efforts for Patrol mainly falls into two parts: the online system call auditing and off-line data analysis.

System Call Auditing and OS-aware Reconstruction. The system call auditing is implemented through a loadable kernel module, which monitors 39 system calls for all the running processes. The monitoring is done by hooking: the module hooks interested system calls such as the socket-related ones (like *sys_accept* and *sys_sendto*) encapsulated in system call *socketcall*. Additional codes are placed in the hooks to record system call arguments and return values, or preserve the descriptor information of the OS kernel data structures accessed during the system calls, such as *task_struct* for the process objects and *files_struct* for the file objects. OS-aware information could be retrieved from these descriptors, including the process IDs, process names, absolute file paths and inode numbers. They are leveraged in Patrol for accurate OS object identification. Besides, time information is also recorded for each system call, such as its invoke and return time. The current version of resulted system call auditing supports Linux kernel versions 2.6.24 through 2.6.32.

Graph Representation and Edge Aggregation. The data analysis code is written in gawk code, that produces dot-compatible [98] output for graph representation. The graphs in Patrol are represented with adjacency matrix as a quick lookup is needed to decide whether there is already an existing edge between two nodes. With adjacency matrix, this query occupies only $O(1)$ time. Otherwise, it may take $O(|v|)$ or $O(|e|)$ time, where $|v|$ and $|e|$ respectively stands for the number of nodes and edges in a graph. A large number of edges may exist between each pair of SODG nodes, which are caused by different system calls or the same system call at different time. For reduced complexity and better visualization, Patrol currently aggregates such edges into a single one, and maintains data structures or variables to store the number of edges, as well as the timestamp information of the original directed edges before aggregation.

3.5   Evaluation

For the purpose of evaluating Patrol, it was extensively tested in a web-shop test-bed which was built to simulate the real-world enterprise network environment. As illustrated in Fig. 9, the test-bed network was deployed with various sensors like firewalls, Nessus [18], Oval [19], Snort, Wireshark [13], Ntop [14] and Tripwire. Based on such topology, the attack scenario in Fig. 9 was also implemented into the test environment. With the assumption that the time right now is tuned back to August 1, 2009 [29], the use of the published vulnerabilities in this attack scenario could help us emulate unknown vulnerabilities. This is done because of the lack of zero-day resources (a typical zero-day exploit could remain undisclosed for averagely 312 days [86]), while we have to produce zero-day attack paths and exploit unknown vulnerabilities for the evaluation of Patrol. Such emulation also benefits us because we can have access to the exploit code and other information of the emulated vulnerabilities for verification. The caution is that we need to carefully maintain the timelines of vulnerability shadows to ensure that no specific knowledge of the emulated vulnerabilities is pre-used.

Correctness. Among all the vulnerabilities in the attack scenario, only CVE-2008-0166 is the known one and only its exploit successfully triggered an alert "SSH potential brute force attack" from Snort. Hence, both attack paths *p1* and *p2*, described in Sect. 3.1, in the attack scenario became "zero-day". However, in contrast, Patrol successfully identified *p1* and *p2* at the OS level: Figs. 13 and 14 respectively illustrate *p1* and *p2* [29]. As *p2* and *p1* share the same Step 1 and Step 2, summarized in Sect. 3.1, Fig. 14 only shows Step 3 in *p2*.

Based on comparing the SODG nodes and edges of *p1* and *p2* with the intrusion knowledge extracted from the exploit code, the CVE entries in NVD [99] and the documentation of corresponding vulnerabilities, we verified the correctness of *p1* and *p2*. The malicious nodes in Figs. 13 and 14 were marked with grey color if verified. The nodes corresponding to the shadow indicators were also highlighted in red color. The results show that Patrol is capable of correctly capturing the malicious objects and their interactions during the intrusion break-in and propagations.

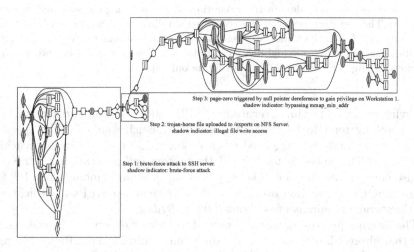

Step 3: page-zero triggered by null pointer dereference to gain privilege on Workstation 1.
shadow indicator: bypassing mmap_min_addr

Step 2: trojan-horse file uploaded to /exports on NFS Server.
shadow indicator: illegal file write access

Step 1: brute-force attack to SSH server.
shadow indicator: brute-force attack

Fig. 13. The zero-day attack path *p1* dug out from the SIPPs (Fig. 10b) by Patrol, capturing the 3-step attack in the attack scenario. The identified shadow indictors are highlighted in red color. The grey nodes are proved to be malicious during verification [29]. (Color figure online)

Efficiency. We also evaluated the efficiency of Patrol on data analysis, which mainly spends time on SODG generation, SIPPs identification and shadow indicator checking. The results show that "SODG generation dominates the time overhead, and its computation cost increases approximately quadratic with the

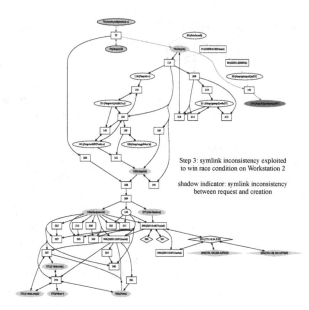

Step 3: symlink inconsistency exploited
to win race condition on Workstation 2

shadow indicator: symlink inconsistency
between request and creation

Fig. 14. Step 3 of the zero-day attack path *p2* identified by Patrol. The red and green dotted lines respectively denote the execution of the attack processes and innocent processes. The red lines replaced the requested symlink */tmp/ls* (*79*) with malicious code */tmp/evil* (*78*), which was later referenced by the innocent process *ls* (*115*). The identified shadow indictor is highlighted in red color. The grey nodes are proved to be malicious during verification [29]. (Color figure online)

time window size. The time overheads of SIPPs identification and shadow indicator checking tend to be linear and relatively much smaller". The speed of Patrol data analysis is maximized when time window size is *15* mins, reaching *6.498* KB/s. This speed is far beyond the system call generation *1.027* KB/s. We also noticed that the caused latency is about *2.37* min (among which 108.88 s spent on SODG generation overhead and 7.54 s spent on SIPPs identification), and the storage requirement is about *0.085 GB/day.*

The filtering processing was also proved to be very effective. The test results show that filtered data costs much less time than unfiltered data. Before filtering, the worst case overhead is the SODG generation for SSH Server, which takes about *30* min. The large overhead is mainly from the checking operations upon each existing object to avoid duplication when new objects are added. Taking this as an example, the SODG generation drops to less than *1* min after filtering. This is because a large number of these files are effectively pruned by filtering rules, from *15515* to *248*.

Performance Overhead. The benchmarks, LMBench [100] and UnixBen ch, were used to evaluate the online part of Patrol, the system call auditing module. According to LMBench outputs, which focus on the impact on individual core kernel system calls, the addon overhead is within *10%*. The worst case overhead is

52.7 % for *sys_stat* and 175% for *sys_fstat*, but the imposed overhead was just *0.3–0.4 microseconds* in both cases. According the UnixBench results, which focus on the slow-down of the whole system that orchestrates the above individual hooked system calls together, the performance overhead of Patrol is averagely *20.8%* for the whole system. Using kernel decompression and kernel compilation to measure the system performance of Patrol, the results show that the two intensive workloads respectively impose *15.93%* overhead and *20.34%* overhead on the system.

Scalability. Regarding scalability, we estimated Patrol's time and bandwidth overheads on an enterprise network equipped with 10000 hosts, 10 GB/s network bandwidth and a HPC cluster of 640 processor cores (20 processors with 32 cores per processor) [29]. Based on the above evaluation data, the Gustafsons law was used, when parallelization could be applied to reduce the overheads. The results show that the *bandwidth overhead* is about *10.029* MB/s, which only occupies less than *1%* of total bandwidth, taking the system call generation speed 1.027 KB/s. The *SODG generation time* for 10000 hosts' data collected in 1 time window (i.e. 15 mins) is estimated to be *28.35* min, taking single-host SODG generation overhead 108.88 s. The corresponding *SIPPs identification time* will be about *12.57* min, taking time overhead of single-host SIPPs identification 7.54 s and assuming at maximum 100 hosts directly or transitively depend on each other.

3.6 Limitation and Conclusion

Due to its potential design and implementation limitations, Patrol may not be able to handle all the situations. For example, when an attack path goes through a vulnerability which resides in kernel space, Patrol will lose its path-based trace since it could not go beyond the system call interface. Another situation is the advanced persistent attack which may be a long-term and cross-victim attack, Patrol may be able to capture the subsets of the intrusion propagation paths at different time spans, but would fail to correlate them

As an instance of the cyber situation awareness problems, this section presents a system named Patrol which tackles the "zero-day attack path" problem (one of the "information asymmetry" problems due to its zero-day nature). By building a network-wide system object dependency graph, identifying suspicious intrusion propagation paths in it, and recognizing shadow indicators on these paths, the system can dig out the zero-day attack paths at runtime.

4   Probabilistic Identification of Zero-Day Attack Paths

4.1   Motivation

The work of Patrol inspires us to view identifying zero-day attack paths as a way that is more feasible than identifying individual zero-day exploits. By constructing a System Object Dependency Graph (SODG), Patrol is able to reveal the zero-day attack paths at operating system level. Nonetheless, Patrol still has a limitation: the explosion in the number and size of zero-day attack path candidates. Considering the large number of intrusion detection points extracted from intrusion alerts, the tracking mechanism in Patrol can result in too many candidate zero-day attack paths. The number of false alerts can thus substantially increase the number of false positive path candidates. Moreover, the size of an individual candidate path can become too big as the forward and backward tracking preserves every tracking reachable object in an SODG. Therefore, recognizing real zero-day attack paths from the candidates becomes very difficult. Discerning the large number of paths is already overwhelming, and it further requires verification of numerous system objects.

4.2 Approach Overview

To address the explosion problem, we propose a probabilistic approach for zero-day attack path identification. The basic idea is to reduce the number and size of candidate zero-day attack paths by incorporating intrusion evidence collected from various information sources. The approach is composed of two steps. First, a system level dependency graph is established to capture the intrusion propagation. The dependency graph is System Object Instance Dependency Graph (SOIDG), rather than SODG used in Patrol. We will explain in a following section why SODG is not adopted directly. Second, a Bayesian network (BN) is built based on the SOIDG to leverage intrusion evidence. Given the evidence, an SOIDG-based BN is able to compute the probabilities of system object instances being infected. Connecting instances with high infection probabilities through dependency relations can form a path. This path is regarded as a candidate zero-day attack path. By mainly preserving instances with high infection probabilities, the SOIDG-based BN can substantially reduce the number and size of zero-day attack paths. The manual verification of zero-day attack paths thus becomes practical.

The feasibility of this approach is supported by the special attributes of the BN and SOIDG. The dependencies in SOIDG imply a type of cause-and-effect relations: an already infected instance of one object could cause the infection of an innocent instance of another object. We call this relation as *infection causality*, which is caused by a system call operation involving the two objects. For example, an infected process writing to an innocent file could get the file infected. Meanwhile, a BN is able to model cause-and-effect relations with a probabilistic graph. A BN can thus be constructed directly on top of SOIDG to model the infection causality relations.

4.3 Problems of Constructing Bayesian Network Based on SODG

As a type of system level dependency graph, the SODG is a potential candidate for being the base of constructing a Bayesian Network. It is able to capture the dependency relations among system objects, which can thus reflect the infection causalities. For instance, an innocent file may get infected if it depends on a already infected process (such dependency may be caused by the process writing to the file). Since BN models the causality relationship with a probabilistic graph, it seems that BN can be built directly on top of SODG.

Nevertheless, several features of SODG disqualify it from being the structure base of BN. To illustrate these features, we use the SODG shown in Fig. 15b, which is generated by parsing system calls in Fig. 15a.

First, the SODG cannot demonstrate the correct information flow if the time labels on edges are removed. Considering that BNs only take the graphical structure of SODGs but the time labels, the SODGs without time labels will result in incorrect infection causality relations in BN. For example, if the time labels in Fig. 15b are removed, the structure of SODG shows that *file 2* depends on *process B*, which further depends on *file 3*. The dependency relation implies that if *file 3* is infected, *file 2* is likely to get infected through the intermediate object *process B*. Nonetheless, the system log in Fig. 15a tells that *"process B reads file 3"* happens at time *t6*, which is after *"process B writes file 2"* at time *t4*. As a result, even if *file 3* gets infected, it won't affect the objects involved in prior system call operations. Therefore, reflecting the information flow in a correct way with solely graphical structure is critical for BN construction.

Second, SODG could possibly contain cycles. As shown in Fig. 15b, *file 1, process A*, and *process C* forms a cycle. Since BN is a type of acyclic graph, cycles in SODG are not allowed in BN.

Third, the number of parents for a node is not limited in SODG. If a system object depends on many other objects (e.g. a process reads many files), this object will get a large number of parents in the SODG. When a BN inherits the structure of an SODG, it has to assign the CPT tables for each node. Assigning CPT tables for a node with a large number of parents is very difficult and even impractical. If a node has n parents, and each parents has two possible states ("infected" and "uninfected"), the CPT table for the child node needs to specify 2^n numbers to demonstrate the infection causalities of the parent nodes to the child node.

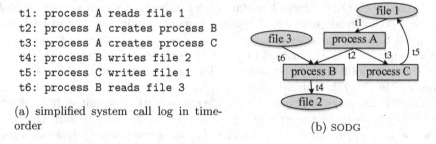

t1: process A reads file 1
t2: process A creates process B
t3: process A creates process C
t4: process B writes file 2
t5: process C writes file 1
t6: process B reads file 3

(a) simplified system call log in time-order

(b) SODG

Fig. 15. An SODG generated by parsing an example set of simplified system call log. The label on each edge shows the time associated with the corresponding system call.

4.4 System Object Instance Dependency Graph (SOIDG)

Since SODGs are inappropriate for being the base graphs of BNs, we propose a new type of operating system level dependency graph, namely *System Object Instance Dependency Graph (SOIDG)*. In SOIDG, each node is an instance of an object. Each instance is a "version" of the object at a specific time point. Different instances of the same object may have different infection status. The reason is that the infection status of an object could possibly change due to system call operations. An innocent object at time $t1$ may become infected at time $t2$, and thus the object's instance at $t1$ is "uninfected" while instance at $t2$ is "infected".

An SOIDG is generated according to the following rules. Given a dependency relation $src{\rightarrow}sink$ where src is the source object and $sink$ is the sink object, a new instance of src object is created only when src is a new object that has no instances existing in SOIDG. Compared to src, $sink$ should have new instance added into SOIDG whenever a dependency relation $src{\rightarrow}sink$ appears. The src and $sink$ objects are treated differently because the infection status of src is not affected by the relation $src \rightarrow sink$, while the infection status of $sink$ could possibly be influenced. A new instance should thus be created for $sink$ to reflect such influence.

The SOIDG addresses the problematic features existing in the SODG for BN construction. It is illustrated in Fig. 16, which is an SOIDG generated by parsing the same set of simplified system call log as in Fig. 15a.

First, an SOIDG can imply the correct information flow even without time information. In Fig. 16, the system call at time $t6$ is parsed as *file 3 instance 1*→*process B instance 2*, instead of *file 3*→*process B*. As a result, if *file 3* is infected, it only affects *instance 2* of *process B*, but no previous instances such as *process B instance 1*. Obviously *file 3* cannot infect *file 2* through *process B* neither. Hence, the mechanism of creating new instances ensures that only the infection status of new instances are affected by a new dependency relation, while the old instances remain untouched. The correct information flow can thus be represented with solely graphical structure of SOIDGs.

Second, the SOIDG doesn't contain cycles. Given a dependency $src \rightarrow sink$ and that $sink$ already exists in the graph, instead of pointing back to $sink$, src will point to a new instance of $sink$. This avoids creating cycles in the SOIDG. For example, in Fig. 16, instead of pointing back to *file 1 instance 1*, *process C instance 1* point to *file 1 instance 2*. The cycle among *file 1*, *process A* and *process C* in Fig. 15b is thus broken.

Third, the number of parents for a node in the SOIDG is limited. If an object $sink$ depends on n objects $src1$, $src\ 2$, ..., $src\ n$, $sink$ does not become the child nodes of these objects directly (otherwise $sink$ will get n parents). Instead, a new instance for $sink$ is created to serve as the child node each time a dependency relation happens. Hence, the n parents of $sink$ in the SODG are assigned to n instances of $sink$ as parents in the SOIDG. As a result, each node in an SOIDG can have two parents at most. One parent is a prior instance of the same object, and the other one is an instance of another object.

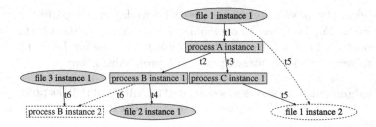

Fig. 16. An SOIDG generated by parsing the same set of simplified system call log as in Fig. 15a. The label on each edge shows the time associated with the corresponding system call operation. The dotted rectangle and ellipse are new instances of already existed objects. The solid edges and the dotted edges respectively denote the contact dependencies and the state transition dependencies.

4.5 SOIDG-Based Bayesian Networks and Zero-Day Attack Paths Identification

To construct SOIDG-based BN, the graphical topology of SOIDG is inherited directly in BN. In addition, the CPT table for each node has to be assigned. Assuming that each object instance has two possible infection states, "infected" and "uninfected", a CPT table specifies the strength of the infection causalities among object instances, such as how likely a child instance gets infected if the parent instance is already infected. After SOIDG-based BN is constructed, the next step is to incorporate evidence from a variety of information sources. Such evidence can be provided by human security admins, or by security sensors such as IDS. After probability inference, each node in the SOIDG gets a probability. It means that the BN can quantitatively compute the probabilities of each object instance being infected. Whenever a new piece of evidence is incorporated, the SOIDG-based BN will generate a new set of inferred probabilities. Generally speaking, the inferred results will get closer to real fact as more evidence is collected.

To reveal the zero-day attack paths from the SOIDG, nodes with high infection probabilities are preserved, as well as the intermediate nodes between these high-probability nodes. The preserved nodes and in-between edges form a path, which can be viewed as a candidate zero-day attack path. The candidate path is usually of manageable size and can be verified manually.

5   Conclusion

This chapter did a literature review for situation awareness (SA) concepts, and applied SA to the cyber field for enterprise network security diagnosis. The outcomes were reported as an integration framework that connects human beings with technologies' individual perspectives. A cyber SA model named SKRM was proposed to integrate these individual perspectives into a macroscopic framework. In addition, based on the SKRM's Operating System Layer, a runtime system named Patrol was presented to reveal zero-day attack paths in the enterprise network. Furthermore, to overcome the limitation of Patrol, this chapter also demonstrated the usage of Bayesian Networks, at the low level of Operating System, to reveal zero-day attack paths in a probabilistic way.

Acknowledgements. This work was supported by ARO W911NF-09-1-0525 (MURI), ARO W911NF-15-1-0576, NSF CNS-1422594, and NIETP CAE Cybersecurity Grant (BAA-003-15).

References

1. Dominguez, C.: Can SA be defined. Situation awareness: Papers and annotated bibliography, pp. 5–15 (1994)
2. Fracker, M.L.: A theory of situation assessment: implications for measuring situation awareness. In: Proceedings of the Human Factors and Ergonomics Society Annual Meeting, vol. 32. No. 2. SAGE Publications (1988)
3. Endsley, M.R.: Toward a theory of situation awareness in dynamic systems. Hum. Factors J. Hum. Factors Ergon. Soc. **37**(1), 32–64 (1995)
4. Salerno, J.J., Hinman, M.L., Boulware, D.M.: A situation awareness model applied to multiple domains. In: Defense and Security, pp. 65–74. International Society for Optics and Photonics (2005)
5. McGuinness, B., Foy, L.: A subjective measure of SA: the Crew Awareness Rating Scale (CARS). In: Proceedings of the First Human Performance, Situation Awareness, and Automation Conference, Savannah, Georgia (2000)
6. Alberts, D.S., Garstka, J.J., Hayes, R.E., Signori, D.A.: Understanding information age warfare. Assistant secretary of defense. (C3I/Command Control Research Program) Washington DC (2001)
7. Endsley, M.R.: Theoretical underpinnings of situation awareness: a critical review. In: Situation Awareness Analysis and Measurement, pp. 3–32 (2000)
8. Boyd, J.R.: The essence of winning and losing. Unpublished lecture notes (1996)
9. Witten, I.H., Frank, E.: Data Mining: Practical Machine Learning Tools and Techniques. Morgan Kaufmann, San Francisco (2005)
10. Tadda, G.P., Salerno, J.S.: Overview of cyber situation awareness. Cyber Situational Awareness **46**(1), 15–35 (2010)
11. Barford, P., Dacier, M., Dietterich, T.G., Fredrikson, M., Giffin, J., Jajodia, S., Jha, S., et al.: Cyber SA: situational awareness for cyber defense. In: Jajodia, S., et al. (eds.) Cyber Situational Awareness, pp. 3–13. Springer, US (2010)
12. Xiaoyan, J.D., Liu, P.: SKRM: Where security techniques talk to each other. In: 2013 IEEE International Multi-Disciplinary Conference on Cognitive Methods in Situation Awareness and Decision Support (CogSIMA), pp. 163–166. IEEE (2013)
13. Wireshark. Wireshark Foundation. http://www.wireshark.org
14. Ntop. http://www.ntop.org
15. Tcpdump/Libpcap. http://www.tcpdump.org/
16. The Bro Project. https://www.bro.org/
17. Snort. Sourcefire, Inc. http://www.snort.org
18. Nessus. Tenable Network Security. http://www.tenable.com
19. Oval. MITRE. http://oval.mitre.org
20. GFI LanGuard. GFI software. http://www.gfi.com/products-and-solutions/network-security-solutions/gfi-languard

21. QualysGuard. Qualys, Inc. http://www.gfi.com/products-and-solutions/network-security-solutions/gfi-languard
22. McAfee Foundstone. http://www.mcafee.com/us/services/mcafee-foundstone-practice.aspx
23. Lumeta IPsonar. http://www.lumeta.com/
24. SteelCentral NetCollector (formerly OPNET NetMapper). Riverbed Technology. http://www.riverbed.com/products/performance-management-control/network-performance-management/network-data-management.html
25. NMAP. https://nmap.org/
26. JANASSURE. Intelligent Automation, Inc. http://www.i-a-i.com/?core/cyber-security.html
27. King, S.T., Chen, P.M.: Backtracking intrusions. In: ACM SIGOPS Operating Systems Review (2003)
28. Xiong, X., Jia, X., Liu, P.: Shelf: preserving business continuity and availability in an intrusion recovery system. In: Computer Security Applications Conference (ACSAC) (2009)
29. Dai, J., Sun, X., Liu, P.: Patrol: revealing zero-day attack paths through network-wide system object dependencies. In: Crampton, J., Jajodia, S., Mayes, K. (eds.) ESORICS 2013. LNCS, vol. 8134, pp. 536–555. Springer, Heidelberg (2013). doi:10.1007/978-3-642-40203-6_30
30. Malwarebytes Anti-Exploit. https://www.malwarebytes.org/antiexploit/index.html
31. AVG AntiVirus. http://free.avg.com/us-en/homepage
32. McAfee AntiVirus. http://www.mcafee.com/us/
33. OSSEC. Trend Micro Security. http://www.ossec.net/
34. Tripwire. Tripwire, Inc. http://www.tripwire.com
35. Forrest, S., Hofmeyr, S.A., Somayaji, A., Longstaff, T.A.: A sense of self for unix processes. In: Proceedings of IEEE Symposium on Security and Privacy, pp. 120–128 (1996)
36. Lee, W., Stolfo, S.J., Chan, P.K.: Learning patterns from unix process execution traces for intrusion detection. In: AI Approaches to Fraud Detection and Risk Management (1997)
37. Kosoresow, A.P., Hofmeyer, S.A.: Intrusion detection via system call traces. IEEE Softw. 14, 35–42 (1997)
38. Hofmeyr, S.A., Forrest, S., Somayaji, A.: Intrusion detection using sequences of system calls. J. Comput. Secur. 6, 151–180 (1998)
39. Wagner, D., Dean, D.: Intrusion detection via static analysis. In: Proceedings of 2001 IEEE Symposium on Security and Privacy (S&P), pp. 156–168 (2001)
40. Kruegel, C., Mutz, D., Valeur, F., Vigna, G.: On the detection of anomalous system call arguments. In: Computer Security ESORICS (2003)
41. Tandon, G., Chan, P.: Learning rules from system call arguments and sequences for anomaly detection. In: ICDM DMSEC (2003)
42. Bhatkar, S., Chaturvedi, A., Sekar, R.: Dataflow anomaly detection. In: Proceedings of 2006 IEEE Symposium on Security and Privacy (S&P) (2006)
43. Debar, H., Wespi, A.: Aggregation and correlation of intrusion-detection alerts. In: Recent Advances in Intrusion Detection (RAID) (2001)
44. Valdes, A., Skinner, K.: Probabilistic alert correlation. In: Recent Advances in Intrusion Detection (RAID) (2001)
45. Bahl, P., et al.: Towards highly reliable enterprise network services via inference of multi-level dependencies. In: ACM SIGCOMM Computer Communication Review (2007)

46. Kandula, S., et al.: What's going on?: learning communication rules in edge networks. In: ACM SIGCOMM Computer Communication Review (2008)
47. Chen, X., et al.: Automating network application dependency discovery: experiences, limitations, and new solutions. In: Proceedings of the 8th USENIX Conference on Operating Systems Design and Implementation (2008)
48. ArcSight. HP Enterprise Security. http://www.hpenterprisesecurity.com/
49. NIRVANA. Intelligent Automation, Inc. http://www.i-a-i.com/?core/cyber-security.html
50. Barham, P., Donnelly, A., Isaacs, R., Mortier, R.: Using Magpie for request extraction and workload modelling. In: Proceedings of the 6th Conference on Symposium on Opearting Systems Design and Implementation, vol. 6 (2004)
51. Chen, Y.-Y.M., Accardi, A., Kiciman, E., Lloyd, J., Patterson, D., Fox, A., Brewer, E.: Path-based failure and evolution management. In: Proceeding of the International Symposium on Networked System Design and Implementation (NSDI) (2004)
52. Fonseca, R., Porter, G., Katz, R.H., Shenker, S., Stoica, I.: X-trace: a pervasive network tracing framework. In: USENIX Association Proceedings of the 4th USENIX Conference on Networked Systems Design and Implementation (2007)
53. Barham, P., Black, R., Goldszmidt, M., Isaacs, R., MacCormick, J., Mortier, R., Simma, A.: Constellation: automated discovery of service and host dependencies in networked systems. In: TechReport MSR-TR-2008-67 (2008)
54. King, S.T., Mao, Z.M., Lucchetti, D.G., Chen, P.M.: Enriching intrusion alerts through multi-host causality. In: NDSS (2005)
55. Zhai, Y., Ning, P., Xu, J.: Integrating IDS alert correlation and OS-Level dependency tracking. In: IEEE Intelligence and Security Informatics (2006)
56. Popa, L., Chun, B.-G., Stoica, I., Chandrashekar, J., Taft, N.: Macroscope: endpoint approach to networked application dependency discovery. In: ACM Proceedings of the 5th International Conference on Emerging Networking Experiments and Technologies (2009)
57. Keller, A., Blumenthal, U., Kar, G.: Classification and computation of dependencies for distributed management. In: Proceedings of Fifth IEEE Symposium on Computers and Communications (2000)
58. Bahl, P.V., Barham, P., Black, R., Chandra, R., Goldszmidt, M., Isaacs, R., Kandula, S., Li, L., MacCormick, J., Maltz, D., Mortier, R., Wawrzoniak, M., Zhang, M.: Discovering dependencies for network management. In: 5th ACM Workshop on Hot Topics in Networking (HotNets) (2006)
59. Dechouniotis, D., Dimitropoulos, X., Kind, A., Denazis, S.: Dependency detection using a fuzzy engine. In: Clemm, A., Granville, L.Z., Stadler, R. (eds.) DSOM 2007. LNCS, vol. 4785, pp. 110–121. Springer, Heidelberg (2007). doi:10.1007/978-3-540-75694-1_10
60. Natarajan, A., Ning, P., Liu, Y., Jajodia, S., Hutchinson, S.E.: NSDMiner: automated discovery of Network Service Dependencies. In: Proceeding of IEEE International Conference on Computer Communications (2012)
61. Peddycord III, B., Ning, P., Jajodia, S.: On the accurate identification of network service dependencies in distributed systems. In: USENIX Association Proceedings of the 26th International Conference on Large Installation System Administration: Strategies, Tools, and Techniques (2012)
62. Sheyner, O.M.: Scenario graphs and attack graphs. Ph.D. diss, US Air Force Research Laboratory (2004)
63. Sheyner, O., Wing, J.: Tools for generating and analyzing attack graphs. In: Formal Methods for Components and Objects (2004)

64. Jha, S., Sheyner, O., Wing, J.: Two formal analyses of attack graphs. In: Computer Security Foundations Workshop (2002)
65. Swiler, L.P., Phillips, C., Ellis, D., Chakerian, S.: Computer-attack graph generation tool. In: DARPA Information Survivability Conference & Exposition II (2001)
66. Noel, S., Jajodia, S.: Managing attack graph complexity through visual hierarchical aggregation. In: Proceedings of the 2004 ACM Workshop on Visualization and Data Mining for Computer Security (2004)
67. Jajodia, S., Noel, S.: Topological vulnerability analysis. In: Cyber Situational Awareness, pp. 139–154 (2010)
68. Noel, S., Elder, M., Jajodia, S., Kalapa, P., O'Hare, S., Prole, K.: Advances in Topological Vulnerability Analysis, pp. 124–129 (2009)
69. Jajodia, S., Noel, S., Kalapa, P., Albanese, M., Williams, J.: Cauldron: mission-centric cyber situational awareness with defense in depth. In: Military Communications Conference (MILCOM) (2011)
70. Noel, S., Jajodia, S., O'Berry, B., Jacobs, M.: Efficient minimum-cost network hardening via exploit dependency graphs. In: Proceedings of Annual Computer Security Applications Conference (ACSAC) (2003)
71. Wang, L., Jajodia, S., Singhal, A., Cheng, P., Noel, S.: k-Zero day safety: a network security metric for measuring the risk of unknown vulnerabilities. IEEE Trans. Dependable Secure Comput. 11(1), 30–44 (2014)
72. Albanese, M., Jajodia, S., Singhal, A., Wang, L.: An efficient approach to assessing the risk of zero-day vulnerabilities. In: SECRYPT (2013)
73. Dai, J., Sun, X., Liu, P.: Gaining big picture awareness through an interconnected cross-layer situation knowledge reference model. In: Proceedings of ASE/IEEE International Conference on Cyber Security (2012)
74. Yu, M., et al.: Self-healing workflow systems under attacks. In: Proceedings of 24th International Conference on Distributed Computing Systems (2004)
75. Agrawal, R., et al.: Mining process models from workflow logs. In: Advances in Database Technology-EDBT (1998)
76. De Medeiros, A., et al.: Workflow mining: current status and future directions. In: On The Move to Meaningful Internet Systems 2003: CoopIS, DOA, and ODBASE (2003)
77. Van Der Aalst, W.M.P., et al.: Workflow mining: a survey of issues and approaches. Data Knowl. Eng. 47(2), 237–267 (2003)
78. Gaaloul, W., et al.: Mining workflow patterns through event-data analysis. In: Applications and the Internet Workshops (2005)
79. Axelsson, S.: Intrusion detection systems: a survey and taxonomy. Technical report (2000)
80. Paxson, V.: Bro: a system for detecting network intruders in real-time. Comput. Netw. 31(23), 2435–2463 (1999)
81. Jiang, X., et al.: Stealthy malware detection and monitoring through VMM-based "out-of-the-box" semantic view reconstruction. ACM Trans. Inform. Syst. Secur. (TISSEC) (2010)
82. Newsome, J., Song, D.: Dynamic taint analysis for automatic detection, analysis, and signature generation of exploits on commodity software. In: Proceedings of the 12th Annual Network and Distributed System Security Symposium (2005)
83. Zhang, S., et al.: Cross-layer comprehensive intrusion harm analysis for production workload server systems. In: Proceedings of the 26th Annual Computer Security Applications Conferences (2010)

84. Czerwinski, S.E., et al.: An architecture for a secure service discovery service. In: Proceedings of the 5th Annual ACM/IEEE International Conference on Mobile Computing and Networking (1999)

85. Dai. J.: Gaining Big Picture Awareness in Enterprise Cyber Security Defense. Ph.D. Dissertation, College of IST, Penn State University, July 2014

86. Bilge, L., Dumitras, T.: An empirical study of zero-day attacks in the real world. In: Proceedings of the 2012 ACM Conference on Computer and Communications Security, pp. 833–844. ACM (2012)

87. Sekar, R., Gupta, A., Frullo, J., Shanbhag, T.: Specification-based anomaly detection: a new approach for detecting network intrusions. In: Proceedings of the 2002 ACM Conference on Computer and Communications Security (2002)

88. Ko, C., Ruschitzka, M., Levitt, K.: Execution monitoring of security-critical programs in distributed systems: a specification-based approach. In: Proceedings of 1997 IEEE Symposium on Security and Privacy (S&P) (1997)

89. Sheyner, O., Haines, J., Jha, S., Lippmann, R., Wing, J.M.: Automated generation and analysis of attack graphs. In: 2002 Symposium on Security and Privacy (S&P) (2002)

90. Jajodia, S., Noel, S., O'Berry, B.: Topological analysis of network attack vulnerability. In: Managing Cyber Threats: Issues, Approaches and Challanges, pp. 247–266 (2003)

91. Ou, X., Govindavajhala, S., Appel, A.W.: MulVAL: a logic-based network security analyzer. In: USENIX Security Symposium (2005)

92. Ou, X., Boyer, W.F., McQueen, M.A.: A scalable approach to attack graph generation. In: Proceedings of the 2006 ACM Conference on Computer and Communications Security (2006)

93. Sawilla, R., Ou, X.: Identifying critical attack assets in dependency attack graphs. In: Computer Security ESORICS (2006)

94. Goel, A., Po, K., Farhadi, K., Li, Z., de Lara, E.: The taser intrusion recovery system. In: ACM SIGOPS Operating Systems Review, vol. 39, no. 5, pp. 163–176. ACM (2005)

95. Knuth, D.E.: The Art Of Computer Programming (1997)

96. CWE. MITRE. http://cwe.mitre.org

97. CAPEC. MITRE. http://capec.mitre.org

98. Graphviz. http://www.graphviz.org

99. NVD. MITRE. http://nvd.nist.gov

100. McVoy, L.W., Staelin, C.: lmbench: portable tools for performance analysis. In: USENIX Annual Technical Conference, pp. 279–294 (1996)

101. Phillips, C., Swiler, L.P.: A graph-based system for network-vulnerability analysis. In: Proceedings of the 1998 Workshop on New Security Paradigms (1998)

102. Ramakrishnan, C.R., Sekar, R.: Model-based analysis of configuration vulnerabilities. J. Comput. Secur. 10(1/2), 189–209 (2002)

103. Ammann, P., Wijesekera, D., Kaushik, S.: Scalable, graph-based network vulnerability analysis. In: Proceedings of the 9th ACM Conference on Computer and Communications Security (CCS) (2002)

104. Ingols, K., Lippmann, R., Piwowarski, K.: Practical attack graph generation for network defense. In: Proceedings of 22nd Annual Computer Security Applications Conference (ACSAC) (2006)

105. Kruegel, C., Mutz, D., Robertson, W., Valeur, F.: Bayesian event classification for intrusion detection. In: 19nd Annual Computer Security Applications Conference (ACSAC) (2003)

106. Xie, P., Li, J., Ou, X., Liu, P., Levy, R.: Using Bayesian networks for cyber security analysis. In: Dependable Systems and Networks (DSN), IEEE/IFIP (2010)
107. Sun, X., Dai, J., Singhal, A., Liu, P.: Inferring the stealthy bridges between enterprise network islands in cloud using cross-layer Bayesian networks. In: 10th International Conference on Security and Privacy in Communication Networks (SecureComm) (2014)

Learning and Decision Making

Dynamics of Decision Making in Cyber Defense: Using Multi-agent Cognitive Modeling to Understand CyberWar

Cleotilde Gonzalez[1]([⊠]), Noam Ben-Asher[2], and Don Morrison[1]

[1] Dynamic Decision Making Laboratory, Carnegie Mellon University,
Pittsburgh, PA 15213, USA
coty@cmu.edu

[2] Computational and Information Sciences Directorate, U.S. Army Research Laboratory,
Adelphi, MD 20783, USA
noam@noamba.com

1 Introduction

Information technology is the center of gravity of everyday human activity. From the eyes of a citizen, a company, or a nation, successful every day activities need to be conducted while being aware of cyber security and protection, aiming to anticipate possible criminal activities that would damage our property (both physical and intellectual) and our privacy. Cyberwar has become an important threat to our national security, involving malicious activities across nation-wide organizations in offensive and defensive operations, and cyber-attacks are now part of everyday news.

Actors use computers and information networks to prevent, execute, or help others execute illegal electronic activities. Hackers or attackers are individuals who either independently or under the auspices and possible support of nation-state actors aim at damaging infrastructure and the information networks of important sections of the government, private companies and individuals. Cyber Analysts or defenders, are individuals often affiliated to an organization (government or private), aiming at protecting information systems and infrastructure against illegal intrusion and damage to their customers. End-users are the majority of individuals that use information technology for conducting their everyday activities in the hopes that defenders would help them to protect the security of their daily routine and their privacy. How successful are defenders at protecting end-users? Unfortunately, they are not very successful. Cybersecurity is an asymmetric, complex and dynamic situation in which attackers have advantages over defenders on knowledge, technology, and information. In many ways, like many other problems in our society (e.g., poverty, crime, drug abuse, etc.), we should address cybersecurity as a problem that will never be solved once and for all but needs to be managed successfully. Our goal should be to look for strategies to manage the problem in ways that reduce the costs, losses, and damage to our society.

In this chapter we contribute towards this goal by providing insights through simulations of cybersecurity scenarios using a multi-agent cognitive model framework. This framework which we call the CyberWar Game (Ben-Asher and Gonzalez 2014), builds on a robust learning model that has successfully captured the dynamics of decision

© Springer International Publishing AG 2017
P. Liu et al. (Eds.): Cyber Sitation Awareness, LNCS 10030, pp. 113–127, 2017.
DOI: 10.1007/978-3-319-61152-5_5

making from receiving feedback in experiential choice (Instance-Based Learning (IBL) model, see Gonzalez and Dutt 2011; Lejarraga et al. 2012; Gonzalez et al. 2015). The CyberWar Game scales up from models of individual behavior to address the dynamics of behavior in a network of attacker and defender actors. We adopt a simulation approach to explore what-if scenarios regarding the diversity of power and assets in a simulated society and the costs of cyber security defense. The main contributions of this research involves the extension of an IBL model to a multi-agent platform that captures network effects and the specific insights that simulation results provide regarding the dynamics of cyberwar.

1.1 Modeling Cognitively-Plausible Human Behavior

In the past years many breakthroughs have been made to improve cyber defense. Important innovative approaches and new technologies have been built to improve organizations' abilities to detect and prevent cyber attacks. However, human cognition and the role it plays in cyber defense have run behind the technological developments and this is an important gap in our ability to generate effective deterrence strategies (Gonzalez et al. 2015). Ultimately, it is humans that initiate a criminal activity, humans that make a choice to invest or not in cybersecuriy, they are the ones that monitor and may detect such criminal activity, and the ones that decide to take an unsafe path in their daily activities.

Recent efforts have attempted to address the challenges of understanding human factors in cyber defense, the computational representations of human situation awareness, and the integration of these efforts into existing cyber defense technology. For example, the notion that decision makers have a general-purpose mechanism whereby situation-decision-utility triplets are stored as chunks and later retrieved to generalize solutions to future decisions originates from instance-based learning theory (IBLT) (Gonzalez et al. 2003). IBLT is a theory of decisions from experience in dynamic tasks. A simple cognitive model, derived from IBLT, has recently been proposed for representing individual learning and for reproducing choice behavior in repeated binary choice tasks (Gonzalez and Dutt 2011; Lejarraga et al. 2012). The formalization of this model is presented in the next section. This model has shown to be a robust accounting of the choice and learning process in a large variety of tasks and environmental conditions (for a summary, see Gonzalez 2012). One of its strengths is that it offers a single learning mechanism to account for behavior observable in multiple paradigms and decision making tasks (Gonzalez 2012). However, Gonzalez and colleagues (2003) argue that the most important strength of IBLT is that it provides explanations of learning and decision making behavior in complex dynamic situations, such as cyber security.

Dutt et al. (2011) proposed an IBL model to study cyber SA. The model represented the cognitive processes of a cyber-security analyst who needs to monitor a computer network and detect malicious network events that constitute a simple island-hopping cyber attack. In this model, the memory of a simulated analyst was pre-populated with instances encoding knowledge of network events, including a set of attributes (e.g., IP address, whether the IDS issued an alert, etc.) that define a network event. An instance also included the analyst's decision regarding that specific combination of attributes, meaning whether the analyst decided that the event (i.e., set of attributes and their values) described malicious network activity or not. Finally, an instance also stored the outcome of that decision, indicating whether the event actually represented a malicious network activity or not. Controlling the representation of the analyst's memory provided the ability to manipulate situation awareness by adjusting the amount and type of instances stored in memory and represent malicious network activity. For example, the memory of a very selective analyst had 75% malicious instances and 25% non-malicious instances, while a less selective analyst's memory had 25% malicious instances and 75% non-malicious instances. When making a decision about whether a new network event is part of a malicious network activity or not, the model retrieved similar instances from memory according to the cognitive judgment mechanisms. Through the process of judging, making a decision and receiving feedback, the modeled analyst accumulated evidence that can indicate if there is an ongoing cyber attack. The risk tolerance parameter of the model governed this accumulation process. The number of malicious network events that the model detected was constantly compared to the analyst's risk tolerance, and once the number of malicious events was equal to or higher than the risk tolerance, the modeled analyst declared that there is an ongoing cyber attack. Thus, risk tolerance served as a threshold for evidence accumulation and risk taking.

The results from simulating different cyber analysts demonstrated that both the risk tolerance level and the past experiences of the analyst affect the analyst's cyber SA, with the effect of experiences (in memory) being slightly more impacting than risk tolerance. This work also highlighted the importance of modeling the adversary's behavior, by comparing the influence of impatient and patient attacker strategies on the performance of the defender. Patient attacker strategy and longer delays between the threat incursions on the network can challenge the security analyst and decrease her ability to detect threats. Thus, the cognitive model was capable of capturing the phenomenon that temporally distributed attacks attack patterns are more challenging than others to the simulated security cyber analyst.

Many efforts have been invested into expanding the mechanisms offered by this IBL model to multi-agent situations, scaling up the IBL models of individuals to addressing conflicts and social dilemmas such as the Prisoner's Dilemma (Gonzalez et al. 2015) and the Chicken, coordination Game (Oltramari et al. 2013). Stackelberg games and other game theoretic approaches have been used to study decision making in cyber security (Abbasi et al., 2016; Alpcan and Basar 2011; Grossklags et al. 2008; Lye and Wing 2005; Manshaei et al. 2013; Moisan and Gonzalez 2015; Roy et al. 2010). However, most of these efforts are limited to either static game models or games with perfect or complete information (Roy et al. 2010). To some extent, these assumptions misrepresent the reality of the network security context where situations are highly dynamic and the decision maker must rely on imperfect and incomplete information.

To overcome this, recent studies that apply game theory to security attempt to account for the bounded rationality of human actors, especially human adversaries (Abbasi et al. 2016; Pita et al. 2012). However, this and other game-theoretic approaches still do not fully address the cognitive mechanisms like memory and learning that drive the human decision making processes and can provide a first-principled predictive account of human performance, including both capabilities and suboptimal biases. Also, scaling up cognitively-plausible models to security scenarios with more than two agents is still a challenge (Gonzalez 2012). Since the predominant focus of developing multi-agent simulations has been for studying social interactions, the assumptions made about individual cognition has been very rudimentary (Sun 2006). In what follows we present our efforts to address these challenges by developing a framework of multiple human-like agents, leveraging findings from cognitive and social sciences.

2   CyberWar Game: Building Multi-agent Models from Cognitively-Plausible Models of Individuals

Conceptually, cyber warfare is an extension of the traditional attacker-defender concept to multiple agents (individuals, state-sponsored organizations, or nations) simultaneously executing offensive and defensive operations through computer networks. Recently, there has been an increasing interest in multi-agent models of social conflict that share some similarities with cyber warfare (Hazon et al. 2011). In parallel, there are attempts to study cyber attacks and cyber warfare through multi agent-based modeling (e.g., Kotenko 2005, 2007) that often represent strategic agents designed to execute an optimal strategy, rather than to learn and adapt strategies from experience. The CyberWar Game reported here builds on previous efforts (Ben-Asher and Gonzalez, 2015; Hazon et al. 2011; Juvina et al. 2011) to define multi-agent frameworks that capture some of the essential characteristics of the cyber world and aspects of adaptive decision makers.

The CyberWar Game takes place in a fully connected network of n agents over the course of R rounds. Each agent has two attributes, Power (P) and Assets (A) and can take three possible actions (j) (Attack, Defend, Nothing) against any another agent. Power represents the agent's cyber security infrastructure as well as possible vulnerabilities which are a reflection of the agent's investment in cyber security, what Juvina et al. (2011) called "outcome power". Thus, power influences the agent's ability to defend against attacks from other agents and the ability to execute successful attacks against the other agents. Assets are the agent's property (e.g., confidential information, physical resources) that needs to be protected from other agents. Assets are also required for the agent's ongoing operation. As such, the agent has to spend assets when attacking or defending, similarly changes in assets have direct influence on the power of the agent. At each round r, decisions occur simultaneously between each of all possible pairs of agents in the society $n(n-1)$. Note that each agent makes n-1 decisions in each round against each of the other agents. This means that all decisions are made and resolved in the context of the agents' Power and Assets as of the end of the previous round.

Attacks can be more or less damaging, defined by the ferocity of attack, f, $0 \leq f \leq 1$. This is a proportion of the assets stolen from the agent being attacked. Severe attacks will have a high f value (e.g., >.5), whereas weak attacks will have a low f value (e.g., <.5). Also, every battle entails costs for the participating agents. There is a cost of attack (C) and a cost of defense (D) while doing Nothing has a cost of zero. C, $0 \leq C \leq 1$ and D, $0 \leq D \leq 1$ are a proportion assets the agent has to spend to execute an action.

Each Attack or Defend action has an impact measured by Win_{ab}, a proportion that is a function of the Power of the agent executing the action (a) over the total power of the two agents involved in a battle, a and b:

$$Win_{ab} = \frac{P_a}{P_a + P_b}. \text{ Note that } 0 \leq Win_{ab} \leq 1.$$

At each round r, an agent a, decides to take an action j against a target agent b (where a <> b). An agent can take an Attack or Defend action against another or be attacked and defended from other agent, if and only if the agent's assets are greater than zero. A Nothing action can be taken regardless of the agent's assets.

The outcomes x_{ab} and x_{ba} of the actions taken by a pair of agents in round r are defined as follows:

		Agent b		
		Attack	Defend	Nothing
Attack	$x_{ab} =$	$Win_{ab} * f * A_b - C * A_a$ $- Win_{ba} * f * A_a$	$Win_{ab} * f * A_b - C * A_a$	$Win_{ab} * f * A_b$ $- C * A_a$
	$x_{ba} =$	$Win_{ba} * f * A_a - C * A_b$ $- Win_{ab} * f * A_b$	$Win_{ba} * A_b - D * A_b$ $- Win_{ab} * f * A_b$	$- Win_{ba} * f * A_b$
Defend	$x_{ab} =$	$Win_{ab} * A_a - D * A_a$ $- Win_{ba} * f * A_a$	$Win_{ab} * A_a - D * A_a$	$Win_{ab} * A_a - D$ $* A_a$
	$x_{ba} =$	$Win_{ba} * f * A_a - C * A_b$	$Win_{ba} * A_b - D * A_b$	0
Nothing	$x_{ab} =$	$- Win_{ab} * f * A_a$	0	0
	$x_{ba} =$	$Win_{ba} * f * A_a - C * A_b$	$Win_{ba} * A_b - D * A_b$	0

(Agent a labels the rows Attack / Defend / Nothing)

All agents in the network are given initial Assets A^0 and Power P^0 values greater than zero at round r = 0. The values of Assets and Power for each agent are updated according to the sum of all the outcomes in each round. The assets in round r + 1 for each agent a are calculated as the sum of the current round's assets plus the sum of agent a's outcomes in round r from all the Attack, Defend, and Nothing actions against other agents.

$$A_a^{r+1} = A_a^r + \sum_{b=1}^{b=n-1} x_{ab} \tag{1}$$

Therefore, assets change dynamically during the game as a result of each agent's actions and the actions of each of the other agents. At any given round, if the new assets for r + 1 are negative, $A_a^{r+1} < 0$, they are set to zero, and thus the agent cannot attack, it cannot defend, it cannot be attacked and it cannot be defended from. So that it becomes a still agent and the only option is to stay inactive (do Nothing) for the rest of the game.

Power of an agent a in round r + 1 is changed as a function of the proportion of change in assets from the current to the next round $\left(\dfrac{A_a^{r+1} - A_a^r}{A_a^r} \right)$. If there is no change in Assets ($A_a^{r+1} = A_a^r$), power in the new round will stay the same as in the current round ($P_a^{r+1} = P_a^r$). If an agent has increased its net Assets ($A_a^{r+1} > A_a^r$), its power in round r + 1 will increase, and if it has lost Assets ($A_a^{r+1} < A_a^r$), its power in round r + 1 will decrease:

$$P_a^{r+1} = P_a^r + P_a^r * \left(\frac{A_a^{r+1} - A_a^r}{A_a^r} \right) \tag{2}$$

3   Making Decisions in the CyberWar Game: Instance-Based Learning Model

We extended the IBL model of binary choice (Gonzalez and Dutt 2011; Lejarraga et al. 2012) to allow each agent to take three possible actions against each of the other possible agents available in the society (n – 1). That is, we created a multi-agent framework with the characteristics of the CyberWar Game described above, where each agent is an IBL cognitive agent, maintaining the learning and decision mechanisms of the IBL model (Gonzalez and Dutt 2011; Lejarraga et al. 2012).

An IBL agent is boundedly-rational. That is, an IBL agent aims at maximizing its outcomes but it is bounded by cognitive constraints such as memory, recency, and frequency effects, and the agent's ability to retrieve such information. An instance is a unique combination of attributes (Situation), Action (Decision), and Outcome (Utility), called an SDU in IBLT (Gonzalez et al. 2003). In the CyberWar Game each agent is an IBL model with its own separate memory, and with the same mechanisms, goals, and cognitive characteristics, but that may vary according the particular settings of Power and Assets and the dynamics of the game.

At round r = 0 an instance is created to represent each of the possible actions that each agent may take against each of the other agents. These instances are created with an initial value of assets A_a^0 and power P_a^0 and a default outcome x_{ab}^0 (these are called prepopulated instances, see Lejarraga et al. 2012). Because the default outcome value is the same for all agents and all possible actions, all agents make a random choice.

Each instance i in the IBL model has a value of Activation which represents how readily available the information is from memory (Anderson and Lebiere 1998). The Activation equation used in the current model is an extension from that reported in past research (e.g., Gonzalez and Dutt 2011; Lejarraga et al. 2012) by adding a Partial Matching component form Anderson and Lebiere (1998). Thus, activation is a sum of three components: Base-level, partial matching, and noise.

$$A_i = \ln \sum_{r_p \in \, obs} \left(r - r_p \right)^{-d} + \sum_{\alpha \, \in \, sit} P(M_\alpha - 1) + \sigma \ln \left(\frac{1 - \gamma_{i,r}}{\gamma_{i,r}} \right) \tag{3}$$

3.1   Base Level

In $\ln \sum_{r,\in obs} (r - r_p)^{-d} r_p$ is the time (round number) in which this instance has been observed, d, decay, is a non-negative free parameters of IBL. Thus base-level represents the frequency and recency activation. This component is higher for instances that have been observed more frequently, and it is also higher for instances that have been observed recently, decaying with the passage of time.

3.2   Partial Matching

$\sum_{\alpha \in sit} P(M_\alpha - 1)$ is the sum over the attributes (α) of the situation, P is the mismatch penalty, a non-negative free variable; and M_α is the similarity of attribute α in the instance to the corresponding attribute of the Situation-Decision being considered as part of this step's decision making process. Each M_α is defined such that $0 \le M_\alpha \le 1$, where a value of 1 means a perfect match, identical or equivalent values; and 0 means a complete mismatch. For intermediate values, the closer to 1 the more similar the attribute values are considered. Note that the partial matching component of the activation is always zero or negative, because it is a mismatch penalty applied to the activation. When all attributes match perfectly, there is no penalty. As more attributes fail to match perfectly, and as the mismatches become more pronounced, there is more of a penalty, reducing the activation value of the instance. In the case of the CyberWar Game the Situation includes four attributes: the assets held at this round by the agent, the power held at this round by the agent, the assets held at this round by the agent's opponent for which it is determining an action, and the power held at this round by the agent's opponent. From the definition of the game, all four of these values are non-negative, real numbers. The same quadratic similarity function is used for each. If α_a and α_b are two values of an attribute, their similarity is given by:

$$
M_\alpha = \begin{cases} \left(1 - \dfrac{\alpha_b - \alpha_a}{\alpha_b}\right)^2 & if\, \alpha_a < \alpha_b \\[2mm] 1 & if\, \alpha_a = \alpha_b \\[2mm] \left(1 - \dfrac{\alpha_a - \alpha_b}{\alpha_a}\right)^2 & if\, \alpha_a > \alpha_b \end{cases} \tag{4}
$$

Thus, for the CyberWar Game the partial matching sums over four values of M_α.

3.3   Noise

Noise, $\sigma \ln \left(\dfrac{1 - \gamma_{i,r}}{\gamma_{i,r}} \right)$, is a component that adds variability to the activation value. σ is a free parameter of IBL, and $\gamma_{i,r}$ is a random draw from a uniform distribution bounded between 0 and 1 for each outcome and trial.

Once the activations of all relevant instances are known, a probability of retrieval of an instance is computed:

$$P_i = \frac{e^{\frac{A_i}{\tau}}}{\sum_{j \in K_0} e^{\frac{A_j}{\tau}}} \tag{5}$$

Where K_O is the set of all instances for an Action (Decision) o, and τ is random noise defined as $\tau = \sigma \sqrt{2}$, where σ is the same free parameter as in the activation Eq. 4, above.

From the probability of retrieval and the outcome of each Action (Decision) o, a Blended Value (BV) can be computed. For the CyberWar Game there are three possible decisions: attack, defend, or nothing (if either the agent or its opponent has no assets, there is only one possible decision, nothing). The values of x_{ab} (or x_{ba}) computer in the CyberWar Game are stored as outcomes (utilities) in the instances of the IBL model (U_i), and the BV of a decision is:

$$BV_o = \sum_{i \in K_o} P_i U_i \tag{6}$$

At any round, the Action (decision) with the largest BV is selected.

4   CyberWar Game: Questions and Simulation Results

The CyberWar Game proposed above has great potential for answering many relevant questions of interest to cybersecurity, given that it is built on computational agents that have shown to robustly represent human choice. A goal of the current research is to uncover the dynamics of societies in which the agents vary in their Power and Assets and in which the cost of attack increases. We use a simulation approach in which multiple societies of N agents engage in R battles (rounds), and we observe in which situations are attacks more common and what leads to more defensive actions or inactivity of the agents. The goal is to uncover how the attributes of CyberWar game (e.g., power, assets, costs of attack and defense) may lead to more aggression (Attack actions), protection (Defense actions) or inactivity (do Nothing actions) of the agents, and to determine the consequences of such dynamics.

For this purpose we take an approach in which we experimentally manipulate the attributes in various societies and compare results against a society in "equilibrium" (i.e., Control condition) in which all agents are equal: all agents have the same starting

Power and Assets, and the cost of attack (C) and defense (D) are the same for all agents, and in which all attacks are of equal ferocity ($f = 0.2$). We then manipulate the different attributes of the agents and the CyberWar game, while other attributes stay the same as in the control condition.

In the data reported next, we ran equal societies of 12 agents across 30 repeated rounds. The control condition included agents that had the same initial amount of assets and equivalent initial power (50 initial assets, 50 initial power), and where $C = D = 0.2$. That is all agents in the society were initially the same, and the costs of attack and defend were 20% of the amount of assets available at any given round. Results from this condition in comparison to other experimental conditions are presented next.

4.1 Agents' Diversity and Their Influence on the Dynamics of Choice

Results from the control condition in which the society was homogenous (same assets and power) and the costs of attack and defense were equal, were compared to three types of heterogeneous societies: (a) a society in which half of the agents started rich (assets = 90) and half of the agents started poor (assets = 10) but all had the same power (power = 50); (b) a society in which half of the agents started powerful (power = 90) and half of the agents started weak (power = 10) with the same assets (assets = 50); and (c) a society that was most diverse where initial attributes varied in four groups: rich and powerful (90–90), rich and weak (90–10), poor and powerful (10–90) and poor and weak (10–10). In these three comparison groups we defined the costs to be the same as in the control condition $C = D = 0.2$.

Figure 1 shows the average proportion of choices over the course of 30 rounds, for the control condition and the three comparison groups. From the definition of the Cyberwar game, an agent can Attack or Defend against another agent only when its assets are greater than zero and this agent is forced to do nothing when its assets are less or equal to zero. Thus, Fig. 1 also shows the proportion of "force-nothing" actions per round (the interpretation of these are ignored from this point on). As observed in the control condition, the attack, defend, and nothing actions of the agents decrease over the course of the 30 rounds of battle. The most common type of action the agents take is to defend their assets (25,863 decisions of this type), followed by doing nothing (6,523) and lastly attack (3,772). Defending assets is also the more profitable action, as it is a way in which agents can grow their assets by investing in defense while doing business as usual. Attacking even though it is the least common action is the second most profitable, as it involves growing the agent's own assets by stealing the assets of others.

According to the manipulation of agents in the society, we observe that as a society becomes more diverse (agents of different types defined by assets and/or power define the society), there is a faster decrease in the total number of actions. This might suggests that diverse societies get involved faster in a self-destructing war. However, defending continues to be most common as well as the most profitable action.

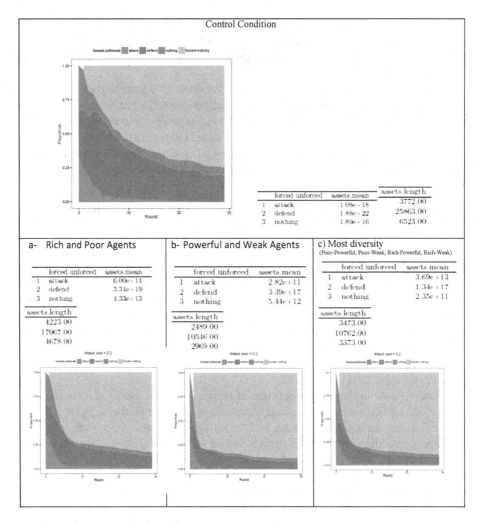

Fig. 1. Overall proportion of actions of each time over the course of 30 rounds in the control condition (top panel) against three experimental conditions that manipulate the initial assets and power of the agents in the society.

4.2 Decreasing the Cost of Going to War

The results from the simulation above assume that the cost of attack and the cost of defense are the same. In naturalistic situations, they are quite different. The costs of defense have increased greatly, while for unsophisticated adversaries it is relatively inexpensive to execute an attack. This section presents results from simulations in the heterogeneous societies defined above but in which the cost of attack is ¼ of the cost of defense (C = 0.05, and D = 0.2).

Figure 2 (left panel) shows the average proportion of choices of different types over the course of 30 rounds, for the three heterogeneous societies (same as above) when

C = D = 0.2; and Fig. 2 (right panel) shows the corresponding proportions when C = 0.05, and D = 0.02. A general observation is that the total number of actions increases when the cost of attack is lower. There is a counter intuitive prediction here. In general, attacking becomes more attractive, but less so than one would expect. Decreasing the cost of attacks does increase the proportion of attacks, but has a much stronger effect on the increased proportion of defend actions. Also, despite the decrease in the cost of attack, the end state of the society is better (compared to the higher attack costs) in terms of the number of active agents (i.e., lower proportion of forced actions). Thus, defending continues to be most common as well as the most profitable action, independently of the cost of attack.

4.3 How Do Different Types of Agents React to a Lower Cost of Attack?

A question emerging from the manipulation of societies and the cost of attack presented refers to the dynamics of different types of agents in these societies and costs. Can we predict the future of agents based on their initial power and assets status and their membership in a society?

Figure 3 shows the average proportion of choices separately for the four groups of agents formed in the most diverse society, where agents start: poor and powerful, poor and weak, rich and powerful, and rich and weak. The left panel shows the results in the condition in which the cost of attack is high (C = 0.2) and the right panel shows the results in the situation in which the cost of attack in low (C = 0.05). The general observation is that for survival, it is more important to start powerful than to start rich. Agents that start weak are active only for a few rounds while powerful agents survive over the course of the 30 rounds. For all types of actions the amount of assets is larger for the poor-powerful and the rich-powerful agents, compared to the weak agents. Furthermore the powerful agents clearly defend more than they attack or do nothing regardless of their initial assets, and in turn, the powerful agents end up with the largest amount of assets during the defense actions.

5 Discussion

Cyberwar is not an abstract speculation. The threat, potential and actual damage to U.S. military and commercial networks by other agents (individuals, governments, states) is real. Yet, we know very little regarding the potential motivations, strategies, and effects of cyber-attacks across nations, states and organizations, and how our cyber defensive operations may approach and prevent international cyber-attacks.

In this research we aim at contributing to a better understanding of potential activities and dynamics of cyber-attack and defense actions by using drawing on insights from a socio-cognitive computational approach. We study societies of heterogeneous agents that are powerful or weak, wealthy or poor; societies in which agents exhibit human boundedly rational characteristics of decision making. We propose a new research framework which we call the CyberWar Game, which presents a description of the dynamics of a world in which agents take actions to attack other agents and steal their

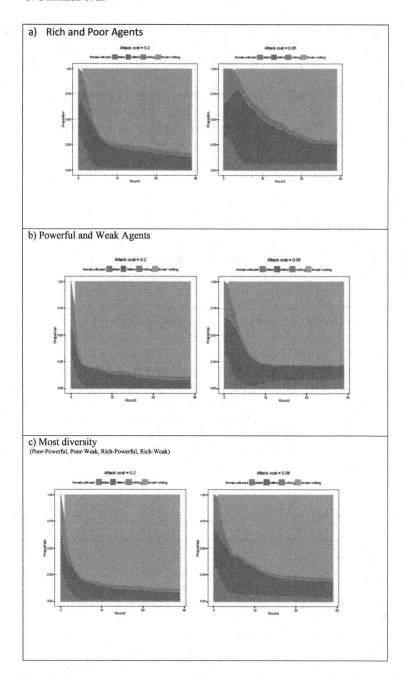

Fig. 2. Overall proportion of actions of each time over the course of 30 rounds in the three conditions with heterogeneous societies, comparing a situation in which the cost of attack is high (left panel) and the cost of attack is low (right panel).

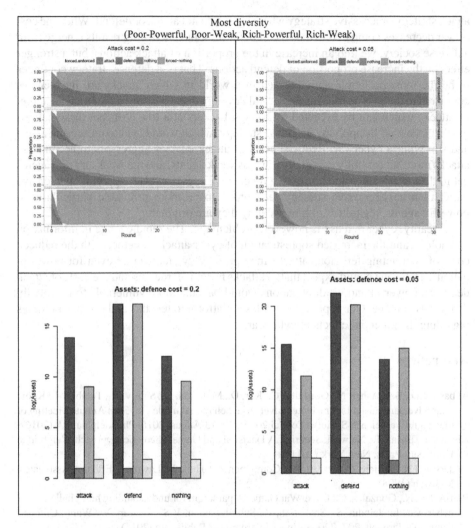

Fig. 3. Overall proportion of actions for four groups of agents (Poor-Powerful, Poor-Weak, Rich-Powerful, Rich-Weak) in the most diverse society over the course of 30 rounds, comparing a situation in which the cost of attack is high (left panel) and the cost of attack is low (right panel).

assets, defend their own assets, or stay still and do nothing. In contrast to other agent-based networks, our research expands models of cognition which often focus on individual-level effects, and investigate how networks of agents that are boundedly-rational behave in various societies that produce diverse motivations for the actions these agents can take.

Our simulation results suggest that agents in a diverse society where agents differ in power and resources are more prone to engage in self-destructing activities and quickly evolve to make a limited number of agents rich and powerful. However, a defense strategy is one that warrants the preservation of resources compared to an aggressive attack strategy or a passive strategy where agents do not attack or defend. When the cost of war decreases compared to the cost of defense, some interesting results emerge from a diverse society, we find an increase in the proportion of attack actions, but a stronger effect on the increase proportion of defend actions. That is, a defense strategy continues to be the most profitable activity even in a world in which attacks are inexpensive compared to defense costs. Thus, powerful developed and wealthy nations are the target of attacks which can be executed by foreign hackers at a low cost, but these nations would be best off by applying a defense strategy, which would lead to preserving assets and surviving a cyberwar. Reduced costs of attack enables aggressors to accomplish attacks more successfully especially towards weak agents, and the weak and rich agents get to disappear rather quickly from a diverse society. However, applying a defensive rather than an aggressive strategy may prove to be more profitable particularly to powerful agents, regardless of how wealthy they are originally.

In reality, cyber defense is however, problematic. The rapid change in information technology and the increased sophistication of cyber attacks together with the reduced costs of conducting ferocious attacks may prove very challenging even for powerful nations. Thus, one would expect that as attacks become ferocious and the costs of attack decrease, powerful and wealthy nations would become more vulnerable to potentially dangerous damage. Our approach provides a platform to test this and other hypotheses regarding the potential effects of cyberwar.

References

Abbasi, Y.D., Ben-Asher, N., Gonzalez, C., Kar, D., Morrison, D., Sintov, N., Tambe, M.: Know your adversary: insights for a better adversarial behavioral model. In: 38th Annual Meeting of the Cognitive Science Society (CogSci 2016), 10–13 August 2016, Philadelphia, PA (2016)

Alpcan, T., Basar, T.: Network Security: A Decision and Game-Theoretic Approach. Cambridge University Press, New York (2011)

Anderson, J.R., Lebiere, C.: The Atomic Components of Thought. Lawrence Erlbaum Associates, Mahwah (1998)

Ben-Asher, N., Gonzalez, C.: CyberWar Game: A paradigm for understanding new challenges of cyber war. In: Jajodia, S., Shakarian, P., Subrahmanian, V.S., Swarup, V., Wang, C. (eds.) Cyber Warfare, pp. 207–220. Springer International Publishing (2015)

Dutt, V., Ahn, Y., Gonzalez, C.: Cyber situation awareness: modeling the security analyst in a cyberattack scenario through instance-based learning. In: 25th Annual WG 11.3 Conference on Data and Applications Security and Privacy (DBSec 2011). Richmond, Virginia, USA, 11–13 July 2011

Gonzalez, C.: From individual decisions from experience to behavioral game theory: lessons for cybersecurity. Invited panelist to perspectives from cognitive engineering on cyber security. In: Cooke, N., et al. (eds.) Proceedings of the Human Factors and Ergonomics Society 56th Annual Meeting, (HFES 2012), Boston, MA, 22–26 October 2012, pp. 268–271. Human Factors and Ergonomics Society (2012)

Gonzalez, C., Ben-Asher, N., Martin, J., Dutt, V.: A cognitive model of dynamic cooperation with varied interdependency information. Cogn. Sci. **39**, 457–495 (2015)

Gonzalez, C., Ben-Asher, N., Oltramari, A., Lebiere, C.: Cognition andtechnology. In: Kott, A., Wang, C., Erbacher, R. (eds.) Cyber Defense and SituationAwareness, pp. 93–117 (2014)

Gonzalez, C., Dutt, V.: A generic dynamic control task for behavioral research and education. Comput. Hum. Behav. **27**, 1904–1914 (2011)

Gonzalez, C., Lerch, F.J., Lebiere, C.: Instance-based learning in dynamic decision making. Cogn. Sci. **27**, 591–635 (2003)

Grossklags, J., Christin, N., Chuang, J.: Secure or insure? A game-theoretic analysis of information security games. In: 17th International Conference on World Wide Web. ACM, New York, (2008)

Hazon, N., Chakraborty, N., Sycara, K.: Game theoretic modeling and computational analysis of n-player conflicts over resources. In: 2011 IEEE Third International Conference on Privacy, Security, Risk and Trust (PASSAT) and 2011 IEEE Third Inernational Conference on Social Computing (SocialCom), pp. 380–387. IEEE (2011)

Juvina, I., et al.: Intergroup prisoner's dilemma with intragroup power dynamics. Games **2**, 21–51 (2011)

Kotenko, I.: Agent-based modeling and simulation of cyber-warfare between malefactors and security agents in Internet. In: 19th European Simulation Multiconference Simulation in wider Europe (2005)

Kotenko, I.: Multi-agent modelling and simulation of cyber-attacks and cyber-defense for homeland security. In: 4th IEEE Workshop on Intelligent Data Acquisition and Advanced Computing Systems: Technology and Applications, IDAACS 2007, pp. 614–619. IEEE (2007)

Lejarraga, T., Dutt, V., Gonzalez, C.: Instance-based learning: a general model of repeated binary. J. Behav. Decis. Mak. **25**(2), 143–153 (2012)

Lye, K.-W., Wing, J.M.: Game strategies in network security. Int. J. Inf. Secur. **4**(1–2), 71–86 (2005)

Manshaei, M.H., Zhu, Q., Alpcan, T., Başar, T., Hubaux, J.P.: Game theory meets network security and privacy. ACM Comput. Surv. (CSUR) **45**(3), 25 (2013)

Moisan, F., Gonzalez, C.: Learning Defense Strategies in an Asymmetric Security Game (2015)

Oltramari, A., Lebiere, C., Ben-Asher, N., Juvina, I., Gonzalez, C.: Modeling strategic dynamics under alternative information conditions. In: 12th International Conference on Cognitive Modeling (ICCM 2013), Carleton University, Ottawa, Canada, 11–14 July 2013 (2013)

Pita, J., John, R., Maheswaran, R., Tambe, M., Yang, R., Kraus, S.: A robust approach to addressing human adversaries in security games. In: Proceedings of the 11th International Conference on Autonomous Agents and Multiagent Systems, vol. 3, pp. 1297–1298. International Foundation for Autonomous Agents and Multiagent Systems, Richland, SC (2012)

Roy, S., Ellis, C., Shiva, S., Dasgupta, D., Shandilya, V., Wu, Q.: A survey of game theory as applied to network security. In: 2010 43rd Hawaii International Conference on System Sciences (HICSS), pp. 1–10. IEEE (2010)

Sun, R.: Cognition and multi-agent interaction: From cognitive modeling to social simulation. Cambridge University Press, New York (2006)

Studying Analysts' Data Triage Operations in Cyber Defense Situational Analysis

Chen Zhong[3]([✉]), John Yen[1], Peng Liu[1], Rob F. Erbacher[2],
Christopher Garneau[2], and Bo Chen[4]

[1] College of Information Sciences and Technology,
Pennsylvania State University, State College, USA
{jyen,pliu,bxc30g}@ist.psu.edu
[2] Army Research Lab, Adelphi, USA
{robert.f.erbacher.civ,christopher.j.garneau.civ}@mail.mil
[3] Indiana University Kokomo, Kokomo, USA
chzhong@iuk.edu
[4] University of Memphis, Memphis, USA
bchen2@memphis.edu

Abstract. Cyber defense analysts are playing a critical role in Security Operations Centers (SOCs) to make sense of the immense amount of network monitoring data for detecting and responding to cyber attacks, including large-scale cyber attack campaigns involving advanced persistent threats. The network data continuously generated by multiple cyber defense systems, which may contain many false alerts, are overwhelming to the analysts. Analysts often need to make quick decisions/responses in a very short time based on their awareness of the situation at that moment. Data triage is the first and the most fundamental step performed routinely by the analysts — it filters a massive network monitoring data to identify known malicious events. Due to the high noise-to-signal ratio of network monitoring data, this steps accounts for a very significant portion of the time and attention of intrusion detection analysts. Therefore, a smart human-machine system that improves the performance of data triage operation in SOC is highly desirable. In this chapter, we describe a human-centered smart data triage system that leverages the cognitive trace of intrusion detection analysts. Our approach is based on a dynamic cyber-human system that integrates three dimensions: cyber defense analysts, network monitoring data, and attack activities. The approach leverages recorded analytic processes of intrusion detection analysts, which we refer to as "cognitive traces". These traces of the analysts capture the examples of malicious events detected from the network monitoring data. Such traces from senior analysts provide a powerful opportunity for training junior analysts in performing data triage operations. To realize this potential, we also developed a smart retrieval framework that automatically retrieves traces of other senior analysts based on their similarity to the events already identified by a junior analyst. The traces from analysts, as demonstrated by a case study, also enable us to better understand their analytic processes in a systematic, yet minimum-reactive way. We summarize this chapter by discussing limitations of the proposed framework and the directions of future research regarding improving the data triage operations of cyber defense analysts.

© Springer International Publishing AG 2017
P. Liu et al. (Eds.): Cyber Sitation Awareness, LNCS 10030, pp. 128–169, 2017.
DOI: 10.1007/978-3-319-61152-5_6

1   Introduction

As organizations rely more and more on their networks to support daily activities or business, they have an increasing need for defending their networks against all types of cyber attacks [1]. Therefore, many organizations (e.g., financial companies, government and military departments) have decided to set up their own Security Operations Centers (SOCs), which are customized human-in-the-loop cyber defense systems.

SOCs collect data from both internal network and external intelligent sources. Most networks nowadays are equipped with sensors monitoring network traffic and detect cyber attacks. These sensors include network and host intrusion detection/prevention system (IDS/IPS), firewall monitoring and logging, vulnerability assessment, and security information and event management (SIEM) products. Given the monitoring data, a SOC usually relies heavily on the human analysts to make sense of these data to achieve cyber situational awareness (i.e., Cyber SA). More specifically, the following questions need to be answered: Whether a network is under attack? How does the attack happen? What will attackers do next?

Most data are collected from the sensors (e.g., IDS alerts and firewall logs) at a rapid pace as well as in massive volume. It requires analysts to conduct a series of analysis to achieve the Cyber SA. Existing cognitive task analysis studies in cyber defense situational analysis have demonstrated that analysts perform various types of analysis. D'Amico and Whitley described six broad analysis roles of computer network defense (CND) analysts: triage analysis, escalation analysis, correlation analysis, threat analysis, incident response and forensic analysis [2]. Data triage is the first and the most fundamental stage in Cyber SA analysis, because it provides a basis for closer inspection for further analysis to finally generate attack incident reports. An incident report provides the basis for incident response, threat analysis, forensic analysis, and other cyber defense operations, both at the tactical level and at the strategic level. Due to the rapid influx of network monitoring data from sensors, analysts usually need to make quick decisions/responses within a very short period, for instance, filtering the incoming data to identify indicators for suspicious events, weeding out false alerts, generating hypotheses regarding malicious events, and investigating data from different sensors regarding the suspicious events.

Cyber SA data triage presents multiple challenges to the analysts in today's SOCs. First, because the network data continuously generated by multiple cyber defense systems are overwhelming and may contain many false alerts, analysts need to apply their domain expertise and experience to make high quality decisions regarding which parts of the network data are worth further analysis and what are suspected malicious events to report as an incident. Moreover, analysts have to perform data triage under time pressure. Quick decisions are necessary because early detection of a cyber attack can not only reduce the negative impacts of the attack, but also can disrupt the chains of cyber attack to prevent them from reaching their original attack target. Finally, data triage process in a SOC needed to be performed continuously 24/7 by analysts are grouped to cover different periods through work shifts; transferring the knowledge gained by one shift of analysts (e.g., suspected but not yet confirmed malicious events; attack behaviors observed, etc.) to the next shift is the third challenge of the data triage process.

A critical factor for determining the success of a SOC in tackling those challenges is the effectiveness of the cyber defense analysts' cognitive processes in performing data analysis tasks. The detailed cognitive process of data triage analysts rather complex and yet not well understood. The understanding of the cognitive process of analysts is further complicated by the fact that different analysts, even given the same set of sensor data, often demonstrate different cognitive processes due to their use of different strategies and their preferences for the use of existing tools available in SOC. An improved understanding of the analysts' cognitive process for data triage can provide several critical benefits for enhancing the effectiveness of SOC. It can enhance the accountability of decision making, improving the training of analysts, developing better cognitive aids and collaboration supports to address the three challenges described above.

Several cognitive task analysis (CTA) studies have been conducted to provide valuable insights about the high-level processes of analysts such as their roles and the workflows [2,3], their cognitive demands [4], and their performance in Cyber SA data analysis [5]. However, analysts' fine-grained cognitive activities in data triage remain unclear [6]. Understanding the fine-grained cognitive process of an analyst is the basis for developing automation tools to facilitate data triage. The fine-grained cognitive process of a senior analyst also offers the opportunity to allow other junior analysts to leverage it to improve their own analysis.

Therefore, the goal of our research is to capture, analyze, and leverage the fine-grained data triage processes of analysts so that the data triage performance of SOC can be significantly improved. More specifically, our study is attempted to answer the following research questions:

- R1: What are the unique characteristics of data triage in Cyber SA? Can we formally define the data triage process in this context?
- R2: What are the key components in analysts' cognitive processes and how to represent analysts' cognitive processes in Cyber SA data triage?
- R3: How to track analysts' data triage processes?
- R4: How to enhance analysts' data triage in Cyber SA by leveraging the captured data triage processes?

To address these questions, we first related the results of the existing CTA studies to the theories in sensemaking and decision making and pointed out the unique characteristics of data triage in Cyber SA (Sect. 2). Based on our understanding, data triage is defined as a dynamic human-cyber system including Cyber SA data, incidents, "world knowledge", analysts and analysts data triage operations and mental model (which will be explained in detail in the following sections). The analysts' cognitive processes in data triage is mainly the interaction between analysts and the Cyber SA data. We first introduced a conceptual model that identifies the key components in analysts' cognitive processes. The conceptual model enables us to define data triage operation as the atoms in analysts' cognitive processes. Based on such definition of data triage operation, an operation trace representation is used to represent the analysts' cognitive process in a fine-grained way.

Based on the trace representation, human-computer interactive toolkit is designed and implemented to capture cyber defense analysts' operation traces when they are performing cyber analysis tasks. This toolkit is not an intended outcome of the research to assist analysts with their work but used as a tool to capture the subjects' cognitive process in our experiment. To collect traces of analysts' cognitive process in data triage, the experiment has been designed with a set of network data sources and an underlying attack scenario. 30 professional cyber defense analysts were recruited to perform cyber defense situational analysis in our experiment using the operation-auditing toolkit. The toolkit recorded each analyst's operations in a trace file in a non-intrusive way. Given the traces of analysts' operations, we investigated the data-triage-related operations by conducting graph analysis. To leverage the captured operation traces, a context-based retrieval system was developed which can provide novice analysts with step-by-step guidance. The system manages the captured operation traces of expert analysts and retrieves the relevant data triage operations based on an analyst's current analysis context.

This chapter is organized as follows. In Sect. 2, we describe the major characteristics of data triage in Cyber SA. Based on our understanding of the characteristics, we define data triage in Sect. 3, which is a dynamic Cyber-Human System (CHS) containing six major components: (1) the attack activities happening in the network, and (2) the massive and rapidly changing network monitoring data, and (3) a set of reported incidents created to report suspicious attack kill chains, and (4) a set of "world knowledge", and (5) analysts' mental models, and (6) data triage operations performed for data triage. Focusing on the human analysts, we further define the data triage operations in Sect. 4. As the first step towards achieving our research goal, a minimum-reactive method for capturing analysts' fine-grained data triage operations is proposed in Sect. 5. Drawing on the definition of data triage operations, a trace representation is proposed to represent a data triage process. An interactive toolkit is developed to record analysts' operations when they are performing data triage. We conducted a laboratory experiment with professional analysts involved and recorded the traces of their data triage processes in accomplishing a simulated cyber defense situational analysis task. A case study is conducted as the first-step evaluation of the collected traces, which is described in Sect. 6. As the first attempt to leverage the captured traces, we developed a retrieval system to provide novice analysts with step-by-step guidance by suggesting the relevant captured traces of senior analysts' previous performance, which is described in Sect. 7. After that, we relate our work to the relevant theories, methodologies and techniques in Sect. 8. The data analysis in Cyber SA is a fledgling yet promising field, with a lot of research questions remaining unanswered. We thus discuss the research directions in Sect. 9.

2   Characteristics of Data Triage in Cyber Situational Awareness

2.1   Data Analysis Driven by Cyber Situational Awareness

The jobs of cyber defense analysts are conceptualized differently across organizations, which leads to diversity in expectations, tasks and responsibilities assigned to the analysts of different levels [2, 44]. However, they are all driven by the goal of gaining cyber situational awareness [2, 8, 9].

The notion of cyber situational awareness is rooted in situational awareness. Endsley defined situational awareness as a process of three main phases: (1) "the perception of the elements in the environment with a volume of time and space", (2) "the comprehension of their meaning", and (3) "the projection of their status in the near future" [10]. The situational awareness in the field of cyber defense covers the phases of perception, comprehension, and projection. More specifically, it includes the perception of current network situation (e.g., identifying the suspicious network activities and attack types), the awareness of the attack impact, the awareness of how an attack evolves and behaves, the awareness of why and how the attack happens, the awareness of how trustworthy of the collected information items are, and whether a decision made based on these information items is good or not, and how effective is the potential of assessment for future threats [8].

The concept of situational awareness is referred by the Recognition Primed Decision (RPD) model proposed by Klein as "the expert decision makers evaluate a situation and match that situation to a situation previously encountered". Boyd's OODA loop is a similar term, which is applied in military operations, described it as the decision process of Observe, Orient, Decide, and Act [11]. Making sense of monitoring data is the key for situation awareness. Pirolli and Card [12] proposed a sense making loop model containing a foraging loop and a sense making loop based on the results of cognitive task analysis of intelligence analysis. Both the foraging loop and the sense making loop are iterative: the foraging loop focuses on how an analyst performs information seeking, and the sense making loop focuses on how the analyst's mental model is developed in this process. This nested loop structure is "an integration of bottom-up processes and top-down processes" [12]. According to Pirolli and Card, the bottom-up processes are processes from theory to data, such as searching and filtering, reading and extracting, schematizing, building cases and telling story. The top-down processes are processes from data to theory, in which analysts re-evaluate, search for support, search for evidence, search for relations and search for information [12].

The sense making model also points out that the data analysis process is an iterative process where raw data are transformed into useful information and new observations adjust analysts' mental model. Therefore, the data analysis process is driven by the analysts' goal of increasing understanding of the potential cyber threats.

2.2   Massive and Rapidly Changing Data

Aimed at gaining cyber situational awareness, multiple sensors are deployed in a network to monitor various network activities. Bass first pointed out that the data collected from multiple sensors which are used as input into intrusion detection systems are heterogeneous. The data may consist of "numerous distributed packet sniffers, system log-files, SNMP traps and queries, signature-based ID systems, user profile databases, system messages, threat databases and operator commands" [13]. Besides the data collected by computer/network sensors, other important sources also come from the data generated by human intelligence, including the data of SIEM systems (e.g., threat databases), data from external sources (e.g., external attack or threat reports) and data collected from social media (e.g., Facebook and Twitter) [14]. The heterogeneous data vary significantly in types and formats, including quantitative and qualitative data (types), structured, semi-structured, and non-structured data (formats). In addition, the Cyber SA data change continuously over time together with the attack threats [15]. This is due to the highly dynamic nature of cyber security environment, which mainly comes from the uncertain network activities and the changing of attackers' behaviors and exploitation techniques [8]. As a result, the cyber defense analysts are faced with massive and rapidly changing data.

D'Amico et al. described the process of how computer network defense (CND) analysts transform raw data into situational awareness, in which raw data are gradually transformed into interesting activities, suspicious activities, events, incidents and intrusion sets [2]. D'Amico pointed out that the raw data are filtered and gradually transformed into information through different stages of analysis, including triage analysis, escalation analysis, correlation analysis, threat analysis, and incident response analysis [12]. Triage analysis is the first stage that filters the raw input data by weeding out the false alerts or the reports of normal network activities. The triage results will be used in the following escalation and correlation analysis by analysts to gain further awareness of the attack activities, methods and targets. The related data are grouped and transformed into sets of intrusion incidents. Threat and incident response analysis are beyond the basic network connection data analysis but a higher-level data analysis, which mainly relies on various types of intelligence/insights to perform prediction and attack forecasting [2].

2.3   Human-in-the-Loop Data Triage

Due to cognitive limitation of humans, it seems challenging for cyber defense analysts to transform the raw data which are massive and rapidly changing over time to intrusion sets. After realizing the need of cyber defense analysts, many studies have been conducted to investigate how analysts perform data analysis and how the data analysis process can be improved. A security expert has been recognized as an important role in network intrusion detection [16]. To aid cyber defense analysts to make sense of large amount of data, various visualization tools haven been developed to visualize different network data to assist analysts in the tasks of monitoring, analysis, response, pre-development and future development [7].

Although human analysts have very limited working memory and computational capability compared with computers, human brains are much better at interpreting data, comprehending situations, generating hypotheses, and making decisions in a flexible manner. Gaining much experience in the "on-the-job" training, senior analysts usually can perform data triage more efficiently than novice analysts [17,18]. Therefore, it is always beneficial to study how analysts perform the data triage to elicit the experts' expertise.

Cognitive task analysis (CTA) studies have been used by researchers to study the cognitive processes of cyber defense analysts in cyber situational awareness. The CTA study of intrusion detection experts conducted by the Air Force enabled the researchers to identify the cognitive requirements for network intrusion detection which are essential to successful intrusion detection [16]. Focusing on the computer network defense (CND) analysts, D'Amico et al. studied the roles of analysts and the workflow of data analysis, and identified the cognitive requirements for improving CND visualization techniques [2]. A further investigation of network analysts' workflow was conducted through a multi-phase CTA study with a focus on the analysts' needs for visualization, which provides the details of analysts' tasks, concerns and goals [4].

Existing CTA studies in Cyber SA show that triage analysis is the fundamental step for the further analysis as the first examination of data [2]. Most analysts in SOCs are conducting triage analysis and making decisions under time pressure and working in shifts to guarantee a 24/7 coverage. Therefore, it's worth to pay special attention to the triage analysis.

2.4   Reporting Incidents for Incident Response

The result of data triage is the basis for further analysis (e.g., threat analysis, forensic analysis, etc.), according to D'Amico and Whitley's data transition model [2]. An incident is defined as "a violation or imminent threat of violation of computer security policies, acceptable use policies, or standard security practices" [19]. The output of a data triage process is a set of incident reports, each of which usually contains the following information [20–22]:

- Status (whether the report is complete or incomplete)
- Reporter
- Incident type (e.g., Account compromise, Denial-of-Service, Malicious code, Misuse of systems, Reconnaissance, spam, phishing, scams, 0-day attack, unauthorized access, etc.)
- Source IP (where the attack packets came from)
- Incident scope (e.g., which machines have been affected)
- Incident time line
- Incident description (e.g., explain how and why this attack incident happened)
- Evidence data (i.e., which data sources, alert, flow, connection, or payload provide evidence for the incident)

- Remediation actions (e.g., recommendations)
- Correlated incidents

In the process of data analysis, analysts need to quickly estimate the network events reported in data. Incident reports are generated to report the abnormalities. If the analysts suspect that some incidents belong to a same attack chain, they may further specify the relationships between the incidents. The generated incident reports will be further refined in further analysis processes in which the incidents will be further investigated in detail or from a broader community scope.

3 Definition of Data Triage in Cyber Situational Awareness

Considering the unique characteristics of data triage in Cyber SA, it's worthwhile to define this data triage process in a formal way. The formal definition described in this section identifies the key constructs of data triage process, which are the basis for the further study at a fine-grained level.

3.1 Data Triage: A Dynamic Cyber-Human System

Figure 1 shows an example of data triage process. Several data sources collected over time are presented to an analyst sequentially. Each data item indicates a network event, which reports either a malicious or a normal network event. The malicious events may belong to different attack chains. Provided with the data sources, an analyst performs a sequence of data triage operations (which will be described in detail in this section) to narrow down the searching scope to a smaller subset of interest. These triage operations are conducted based on their existing observation of the network events and their domain knowledge and experience. As a result, the analyst reports his/her hypotheses about the possible attack chains in incident reports or revises the existing incident reports accordingly.

Given a network, an analyst's data triage process is a dynamic Cyber-Human System (CHS) evolving over time. This dynamic CHS composes of (1) the attack activities happening in the network, and (2) the massive and rapidly changing monitoring data collected from multiple sources, and (3) a set of reported incidents and the inferred temporal and casual relationships into attack kill chains, and (4) a set of "world knowledge" (e.g., the intelligence about the attacks and the mission to protect the network), and (5) the mental model of the analyst that consists of the hypotheses about the possible attacks happening in the network, and (6) the data triage operations performed by the analysts who gradually filter the data indicating suspicious network events.

We define data triage through defining each "state of the CHS". Assume an analyst is performing data triage of a network. At a certain point of analysis time t, a state of data analysis process can be defined by a tuple,

$$S(t) = (t', \mathcal{D}(t')_t, \mathcal{A}(t')_t, \mathcal{I}_t, \mathcal{K}_t, \mathcal{H}_t, \mathcal{O}_t),$$

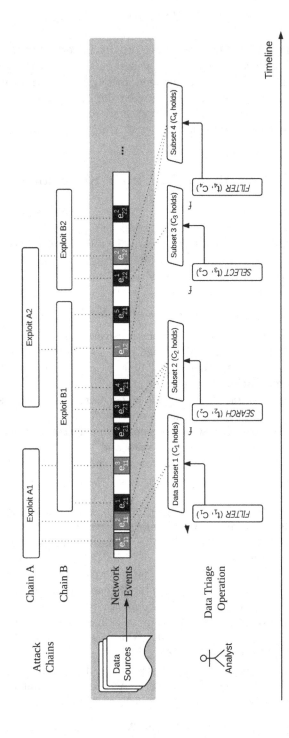

Fig. 1. A data triage process involves an analyst gradually filtering the data sources to detect the suspicious network events and link them according to the possible attack chains.

where

- t is the current time of analysis system.
- t' is the time when the network events occurred.
- $\mathcal{D}(t')_t$ is the data sources to be analyzed at time t, which can be generalized to a sequence of network events occurred at time t'.
- $\mathcal{A}(t')_t$ is the attack chains to be discovered at time t, which may leave evidence in $\mathcal{D}(t')_t$.
- $\mathcal{I}_t = (\{e(t')_t\}, R_{e(t')_t})$ is a set of incidents detected at time t. $\{e(t')_t\}$ is a set of suspicious network events occurred at time t' which is analyzed at time t, and $R_{e(t')_t}$ consists of the temporal and causal relationships among the events in $\{e(t')_t\}$.
- $\mathcal{K}_t$ is the analyst's domain knowledge about the network and attacks at time t, as well as the experience knowledge of data analysis.
- $\mathcal{H}_t = (\{h_t\}, R_{h_t})$ is the analyst's mental model at time t. $\{h_t\}$ is a set of the analyst's hypotheses about possible attacks. R_{h_t} contains the relationships between the hypotheses in $\{h_t\}$ which are determined by the analyst at time t.
- $\mathcal{O}_t$ is a set of data triage operations conducted by the time t, which are explained in Sect. 4.

This definition indicates that the data triage, as a CHS, changes from one state to another over time. In this CHS, the data sources $(\mathcal{D}(t')_t)$ collected by the sensors report the events in the network, which are determined by the network activities and the attackers' behaviors $(\mathcal{A}(t')_t)$ in the physical world. The time t' refers to the occurring time of network events in the data sources $\mathcal{D}(t')_t$, which is different from the CHS time t. The analyst interacts with the collected data $(\mathcal{D}(t')_t)$ with the aim of detecting the evidence of $\mathcal{A}(t')_t$. By performing the data triage operations $(\mathcal{O}_t)$, the analyst gradually filters the suspicious network events and generates hypotheses about the possible attack chains based on his/her observations, and in return updates his/her mental model $(\mathcal{H}_t)$. Based on the updated mental model, the analyst will be able to report the identified attack incidents $(\mathcal{I}_t)$. Meanwhile, the detected incidents may further deepen the analyst's domain knowledge and experience knowledge $(\mathcal{K}_t)$.

3.2   Data Triage Input: Massive and Rapidly Changing Data Sources

Figure 2 illustrates the massive and rapidly changing data sources in Cyber SA. We show the categories of data in six different dimensions (which can be further extended). We describe the categories as follows.

- The data can be categorized based on the sensors from which they are collected. The common data sources include alerts of intrusion detection systems (IDS) alerts, firewall logs, traffic packages, vulnerability reports, network configurations, server logs, system security reports and anti-virus reports.
- In terms of data format, the data can be categorized into structured, semi-structured, and non-structured data.

- In terms of the level of monitoring scale, the data can be divided into the activities of network, host, database, application, and directory.
- In terms of accessibility, internal data refer to the data which can be directly accessed by the analysts within a SOC, while external data refer to the data outside the SOC which will be available by request only.
- In terms of general type, the data include both qualitative and quantitative data.
- According to whether the data are time-sensitive or not (i.e., timing), the data can be divided into stable and streaming data. Stable data are relatively fixed and not necessarily changing over time, e.g., network configurations and vulnerability reports. Streaming data refer to the data sources which are continuously collected throughout the run of the network, such as IDS alerts and firewall logs. The large volume and time sensitive features of the streaming data bring significant challenges for data triage. We thus focus on streaming data.

Most of the streaming data are well-formed but may have different formats across various sources. The common part of streaming data sources is that they can be viewed as a sequence of data entries in temporal order considering that they are collected over time. A data entry can be an alert, a report or a log item.

The Cyber SA raw data report the network events perceived by the monitoring sensors (including human intelligence). From the view point of Cyber SA data analysis, we define the unit of analysis as a network event. A network event can be specified by one or more data entries from different data sources. For example, an IDS alert and an entry in firewall log correspond to a same network event. We define network event as follows.

Definition 1. *Given a network, a **network event** e is a multi-tuple that specifies the characteristics of a connection activity happened in the network,*

$$e = <occurTime, detectTime, eventType, attackType_{prior},$$
$$srcIP, srcPort, dstIP, dstPort, prot, sensor, severity, conf, msg>$$

Where $occurTime$ is the occurrence time of the event; $detectTime$ is the earliest timestamp of the event being detected; $eventType$ is the type of network connection (e.g., built, teardown and deny); $attackType_{prior}$ is a prior knowledge from the sensor/agent who detected this event that specifies the type of the attack to which the event longs; by default, $attackType_{prior}$ is null; $srcIP$ and $srcPort$ are the IP address and port of the source of the network connection, respectively; $dstIP$ and $dstPort$ are the IP address and port of the target, respectively; $prot$ is the network protocol; $sensor$ refers to the sensors who detected this event; $severity$ and $conf$ specify the level of severity and confidence of the event, respectively; msg specifies other important characteristics of the event, determined by the sensor.

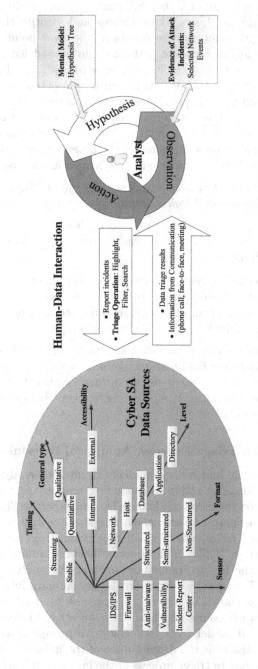

Fig. 2. The architecture of analysts interacting with the massive and rapidly changing Cyber SA data.

3.3   Data Triage Output: Incidents in Attack Chains

Data triage, as the first stage of Cyber SA data analysis, performs a number of functions: (1) coordinate diverse data sources and identify the noteworthy network events, and (2) connect these events in the view point of multi-step attack to support intelligent response. Attack chain is modeled as a sequence of network state changes upon exploits over exposure [23,24]. In the context of Cyber SA data analysis, an attack chain can be presented by a sequence of network events reported by multiple (heterogeneous) sensors.

As data generated from different sources may indicate different network activities, human analysts need to detect the true "signals" from them and "connect the dots" to gain high-level understanding of the potential network attacks. We define the relationships between two events are defined as follows.

Definition 2. *Let e_i, e_j be two network events. We define "happen-before" and "is-a-pre-step" the temporal and logic relationships between e_i and e_j as*

- *happen-before(e_i, e_j): e_i.occurTime $<$ e_j.occurTime.*
- *is-a-pre-step(e_i, e_j): e_i and e_j are in a same attack chain and e_i is a previous step of e_j in the attack chain.*

The expected outcome of cyber defense situational analysis is the network security incident reports which describe the suspicious network events and their relationships. The instance of an attack chain is defined as a network incident. A formal definition of network incident is given below.

Definition 3. *An attack incident is defined as a tuple, $<att, E, R>$, where att is an attack identifier which specifies an attack chain; $E = (e_1, \ldots, e_n)$ is a sequence of network events occurred to carry on the attack chain att. $R = \{happen\text{-}before(e_i, e_j), is\text{-}a\text{-}pre\text{-}step(e_i, e_j)\}$, refer to the temporal or logical relationships between two events $e_i \cdot$ and e_j in E.*

3.4   Human in Data Triage Process: Analytical Reasoning Processes

To accomplish data triage and report incidents of interest, analysts perform a series of information foraging activities, including reading, searching, filtering and extracting, based on their domain knowledge and expertise [3]. This process is called analytical reasoning process, which refers to "central to the analysts' task of applying human judgments to reach conclusions from a combination of evidence and assumptions" [25]. The interaction between a human analyst and the collected data is the key to understanding how the analyst accomplishes the data triage task. Therefore, we focus on the human-data interaction in the data triage process, as shown in Fig. 2. This process produces two products: (1) the identified network events and how they are related to each other, and (2) the analysts' mental model. Analysts' cognitive process involving actions, observations and hypotheses is the driving force of the interaction.

We study the human data triage process at the in-between level of the macro-level cognitive task analysis study and the micro-level behavior statistical analysis regarding the unit of analysis. The macro-level CTA usually focuses on the human task performance, cognitive load (e.g., short-term memory), thoughts, and cognitive bias, e.g., the study of the situational awareness analysts' jobs and cognitive needs [2–4], and the study of the Cyber SA measurements [26,27]. These studies usually involve interviews, observations, verbal protocols and questionnaires, in which the cognitive assessment procedure has an impact on the analysts' behaviors being assessed (as "reactivive recording" methods in [28]. On the contrary, the micro-level behavior statistical analysis usually uses the data from nonreactive recording, which may involve automatic keystroke logging [29,30], eye tracking [29,31] or even brain-level EEG/fMRI recording [32].

The in-between level analysis is mainly motivated by the disadvantages of both the macro-level and micro-level cognitive study in the field of Cyber SA. On one hand, it's difficult to conduct macro-level study of Cyber SA data analysis. The cyber defense analysts are sensitive to interruptions, considering the fact that they are working under pressure and fully concentrated on the tasks. Therefore, the reactive behavior recording methods could influence analysts' task performance. Besides, verbalizing the key aspects of the thought process is also difficult for analysts because some thoughts are "so automated as a result of their prior knowledge and/or training" [33]). In addition, analysts may not have time for interviews considering the 24/7 security operations. Another practical limitation faced by Cyber SA researchers is that the access to an organisation's network and professionals is quit limited due to confidential concerns. Therefore, it's necessary to incorporate automatic recording to capture the key aspects in data triage process. One the other hand, one major limitation of the micro-level study is that, there could be many important behaviors which can't be captured, or can't be recovered in the following reflective analysis due to the lack of the analysts' situated confirmation/interpretation [28].

To deal with the problem, we study the human cognitive process in Cyber SA data triage at an in-between level that links the key cognitive components in data triage to automatic operation recording to achieve better understanding of the data triage process in Cyber SA. Analysts' operations include filtering out the false positive alerts and identifying the data of interest, and they are guided by the analysts' hypotheses about possible attacks. Meanwhile, analysts' hypotheses are generated based on analysts' current observations of the suspicious data. In this way, the raw data sources are gradually transformed into the evidence of attack incidents, and meanwhile the analysts gain their Cyber SA by generating hypotheses about the attack incidents. Next, we introduce a conceptual model of analysts' analytical reasoning process in data triage, which serves as a basis for the in-between fine-grained analysis.

The AOH Model of Analysts' Analytical Reasoning Processes. An analyst's cognitive process involves activities of information foraging and sensemaking [12]. These activities can be covered in an Action-Observation-Hypothesis model (AOH model) [35,45], as shown on the left side of Fig. 2. There are three key cognitive constructs in the AOH model: *action*, *observation*, and *hypothesis*. An *action* refer to an operation conducted by the analyst to filter and correlate network data; an *observation* refers to the data that are viewed as suspicous network events by the analyst; and a *hypothesis* is the analyst's hypothesis about the potential attack incident. The instances of *action*, *observation* and *hypothesis* are called "**AOH Objects**" [34,35].

The AOH objects iterate and form reasoning cycles: an analyst takes an *action* which leads to a new *observation*; with the this *observation*, the analyst can generate new *hypotheses* about the potential attack incidents; in order to investigate a new *hypothesis*, the analyst conducts further *action* in order to gain more *observations* [6,34]. The relationships between *action*, *observation* and *hypothesis* are defined as follows.

Definition 4. *Let a_i be an instance of* action, *o_j be an instance of* observation, *and h_k be an instance of* hypothesis, *we can define three types of relationships:*

- *$results(a_i, o_j)$: Conducting the action a_i results in the observation o_j.*
- *$triggers(o_j, h_k)$: Hypothesis h_k is generated based on the observation o_j.*
- *$motivates(h_k, a_j)$: Conducting a_i is motivated to further investigate hypothesis h_k.*

The relationships between the AOH objects can be represented in tree structures, called **AOH-Trees**. An example of AOH-Trees is shown in Fig. 3. The nodes are the AOH objects and the links are the relationships between the AOH objects. Based on the AOH-Trees, **Hypotheses-Trees (H-Trees)** are constructed to represent the mental activities in an analyst's cognitive process of data triage. In a H-Tree, the nodes are *hypotheses* only and an edge between two nodes represents a *leads-to* relationship between the two *hypotheses*. The following is the definition of the *leads-to* relationship.

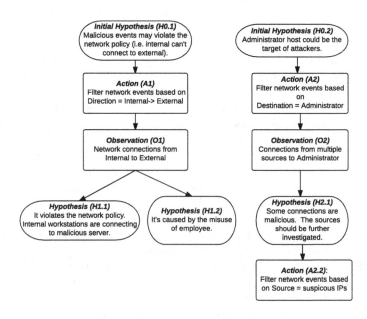

Fig. 3. AOH-Trees that represents the relationships between AOH Objects

Definition 5. *Let h_i and h_j be two hypothesis, an edge pointing from h_i to h_j represents the relationship leads-to(h_i, h_j). The relationship holds iff a_p, o_q, that motivates(h_i, a_p) and results(a_p, o_q) and triggers(o_q, h_j)*

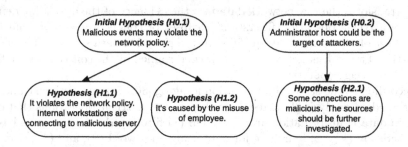

Fig. 4. The H-Trees corresponding to the AOH Trees in Fig. 3

Figure 4 is an example of the H-Trees extracted from the AOH-Trees of Fig. 3(a). H-Trees is used to represent an analyst' mental model in the Cyber SA data analysis process because it represents all the hypotheses and their relationships maintained by an analyst.

4   Analysts' Operations in Data Triage

Tasks in Triage (corresponding to triage analysis and some part of escalation analysis mentioned in [2]):

- Detect the suspicious network connection events: identify suspicious network connection (weeding out the false positives)
- Connect the suspicious network connection events: link the network connections according to potential attack path
- Organize the suspicious network connection event in sequence: generate incident reports based on the detected network connection event sequence to meet the needs of further investigation

Data triage operations refer to the *action* instances conducted by an analyst in accomplishing a data triage task. The analyst's mental model determines what triage operations to perform. It also explains the *motivates*(h_k, a_j) relationship: a *hypothesis* may motivate analysts to perform a new *action* for closer investigation. The outcome of a data triage operation is a set of network events of interest, which the analyst may find useful to enrich the evidence of a certain attack incident. It explains the *results*(a_i, o_j) relationship: an *action* leads to an *observation*.

Analysts interact with the network data sources by conducting operations to manipulate and analyze the data. A data triage operation may impact two aspects: (1) the data transformation and (2) the mental model transformation. We explain each of them in detail in the following.

4.1   Data Triage Operation Related to Data Transformation

Conducting triage operations enables analysts to identify a subset of network data that indicate suspicious network events (i.e., an *observation*), which may increase the situational awareness of attack incidents. Therefore, the triage operations transform the raw network data into the evidence of the attack incidents. Each data triage operation filters out a subset of connection events from the original set of network events specified in the provided data sources. The characteristics of the subset network events are determined by the constraint specified in the data triage operation.

According to the study of information foraging [36, 37] and existing studies of Cyber SA data analysis [4], three major types of data triage operations that can result in data transformation are identified: (1) filtering the data sources based on a condition (F), (2) searching for data using a keyword (S), and (3) selecting a collection of data with common characteristics of network events (H). They can be defined as follows.

- $FILTER(D_{input}, D_{output}, C)$: Filtering the input dataset (D_{input}) based on a condition (C) and resulting in a subset (D_{output}).
- $SEARCH(D_{input}, D_{output}, C)$: Searching a keyword (C) in a dataset (D_{input}) and resulting in a subset (D_{output}).
- $SELECT(D_{input}, D_{output}, C)$: Select a data subset ($D_{output}$) of an input dataset ($D_{input}$), the network events of subset (D_{output}) that have a common characteristic (C) to become the network events of interest.

4.2   Data Triage Operation Related to Analysts' Mental Model

An analyst may gain new *Observations* by performing a data triage operation related to the data transformation. The new *Observations* may (1) trigger the analyst's new *hypotheses* or (2) confirm/invalidate his/her previous *hypotheses*. In either case, the corresponding H-Trees (representing the analyst's mental model) will be modified. Therefore, conducting triage operations enables analysts to update their mental model. We can further define the data triage operations of the creation and modification of new *Observations* and *hypotheses*.

- $NEW\_HYPO(h, O)$: Generate a *hypothesis* h in the context of *observation O*.
- $MODIFY(h, v_1, v_2)$: Modify the content of a *hypothesis* h from v_1 to v_2.
- $CONFIRMDENY(h, TF)$: Confirm or deny a *hypothesis* h.

Once an analyst's mental model (i.e., H-Trees) has a hypothesis updated, the analyst may conduct further triage operations to gain more evidence to confirm the updated hypothesis. In this case, the following triage operation is determined by the analyst's mental model. The constraint of the triage operation indicates in which aspect the analyst is interested of the network data.

4.3   Trace Representation

Trace is defined to represent an analyst's analytical reasoning process in data triage.

Definition 6.

$$\mathcal{T} = (\mathcal{G}_{AOH}, \mathcal{G}_H, \mathcal{S}_{op})$$

where

- *$\mathcal{G}_{AOH}$ is the AOH-Trees, which is a heterogeneous network involving the analysts' actions (i.e., performing the data triage operations related to data transformation), observations of events of interest, and hypotheses. The edges are the causal relationships between the AOH objects which are identified by the analyst.*
- *$\mathcal{G}_H$ is the corresponding H-Trees, containing merely the analyst's hypotheses about possible malicious network events and attack chains. H-Trees represents the analyst's mental model.*
- *$\mathcal{S}_{op}$ is a sequence of data triage operations $(p_1, ..., p_n)$ in time order. $\forall p_i (1 \leq i \leq n)$, p_i is a tuple $(t_i, (op)_i(I, C_i))$, where t_i is the timestamp, and "$(op)_i(I, C_i)$ is the operation on a cognitive activity I under context C_i. I is an action, observation or hypothesis, C_i is a set of connections between I with the existing actions, observations and hypotheses." [35]*

5   Minimum-Reactive Method for Capturing Analysts' Fine-Grained Data Triage Operations

A data triage process involves complex human cognitive process. We've listed several potential benefits of gaining better understanding of human cognitive process. A necessary step to achieve this goal is to capture the analysts' **fine-grained** cognitive processes in data triage. There are three main challenges in developing such a capture method.

- (C1) The method should capture the fine-grained information of analysts' cognitive processes in data triage. Starting from the existing understanding of data triage process, we focus on the fine-grained level of understanding because it is the basis for carefully studying the rationale and strategies underlying analysts' data triage operations and leveraging them to improve intelligent systems. The fine-grained cognitive process refers to a detailed representation of data triage in which analysts' actions of data filtering, observations of suspicious events, and analysts' hypotheses about possible attack chains are explicitly described.
- (C2) The method should be minimum reactive. Reactivity refers to the influence of the process of observing analysts' analysis on their behaviors being observed [28]. Cyber defense analysts are working under extremely high time pressure regarding the rapidly changing cyber environment, and maintaining a working memory is critical to identify the relationships between recognized network events. Any distraction caused by the capture method could affect their performance on the cyber analysis task.

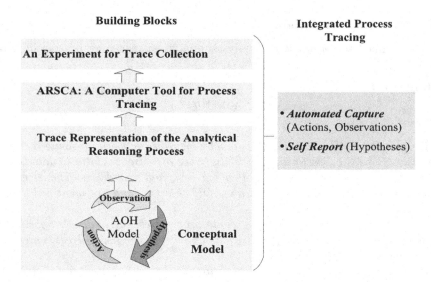

Fig. 5. The framework of the minimum-reactive method for capturing the analysts' fine-grained data triage operations [35]

– (C3) Collecting traces of cyber defense analysts' data triage process faces the real-world challenges regarding the accessibility to the analysts and the organizations' concern about confidential information leakage.

We introduce a computer-aided method to track the fine-grained data triage process which integrates both automatic capturing and situated self-reports. This method contains three main components: (1) a representation of analysts' cognitive process in data triage, (2) a computer tool that tracks various analysts' operations while they are performing data triage tasks, and (3) an experiment in which professional analysts were recruited to accomplish a simulated cyber defense situational analysis task with their operations being tracked [35]. Figure 5 shows the framework of the method. The representation, described in Sect. 4.3, can handle the first challenge (C1) of the capture method. Next, we mainly handle C2 and C3.

5.1   ARSCA: A Computer Tool for Tracing Data Triage Operations

To handle the second challenge (C2), a computer tool, named ARSCA, is developed to be used in the experiment to record an analyst's data triage operations based on the pre-defined representation in a non-intrusive way. To guarantee the non-intrusiveness, this tool is designed following several rationales [35]:

– Using this tool should not affect analysts' normal practice in data triage.
– The tool should not add too much extra workload to analysts.
– This tool should be easy to learn and use.

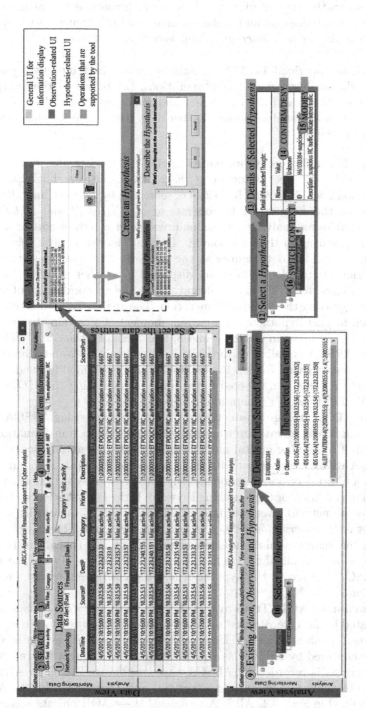

Fig. 6. Main components of the ARSCA user interface (in Data View and Analysis View) [35]

Figure 6 shows the user interface of ARSCA which contains two main views: (1) Data View which displays all the data sources, and (2) Analysis View which displays the existing *action, observation* and *hypothesis* instances and their relationships.

The functions provided in ARSCA can be categorized into two groups: (1) enabling the analyst's data triage operations, (2) recording the analyst's data triage operations, and (3) visualizing and managing the AOH-Trees and H-Trees created by the analyst during his/her data triage process. More details are described in [38].

- **Enabling Data Triage Operations.** ARSCA supports the data triage operations defined in Sect. 4, including SEARCH, FILTER, and SELECT. In Fig. 6, Region 2 and 3 provide functions of searching by keyword and filtering by condition, thus supporting the operations of *SEARCH* and *FILTER*. Region 4 enables an analyst to make inquiries about a certain port or a specific term appearing in the data sources. Region 5 lets an analyst select the entries in a provided data source as the network events of interest. Once selected, the selected data entries are displayed in another window (Region 6) for the analyst to review and confirm them as the network events of interest, thus supporting the *SELECT* operation. The analyst using this tool can write down his/her hypotheses at a current moment of a certain observation. This function is shown in Region 7 and 8, which enables the *NEW_HYPO* operation. ARSCA visualizes the analyst' existing hypotheses and enables the analyst to modify them. Region 13 enables the analyst to modify the description and truth value of a selected hypothesis, thus enabling the *MODIFY* and *CONFIRM/DENY* operation.
- **Recording Data Triage Operations.** Once the analyst using ARSCA performs a data triage operation (either those related to data transformation or those related to refining mental model), this operation is automatically captured by ARSCA together with its timestamp. For example, if the analyst conducts a filtering or searching operation, ARSCA will record the time and the filtering condition or the searching keyword. If the analyst selects a subset of data as the network events of interest, ARSCA will automatically record the subset as an *observation* defined in Sect. 3.4 (Region 5). If a new thought occurs in the analyst's mind, he/she can write down this thought in Region 8, with Region 7 displaying the selected suspicious data as the current context. ARSCA will record the hypothesis and its relationship to the relevant observation.
- **Visualization of AOH-Trees and H-Trees.** An analyst's data triage operation related to data transformation is automatically captured by ARSCA as the *Actions*; a subset of data selected as suspicious network events is automatically captured by ARSCA as an *observation*; any thought written down by the analysts is recorded by ARSCA as a *hypothesis*. Therefore, ARSCA captures the analyst's *Actions, Observations,* and *hypotheses,* that is, AOH objects defined in Sect. 3.4. ARSCA visualized these AOH objects according to their relationships, thus visualizing the AOH-Trees in Region 10 in Fig. 6:

an *action* appears together (as a node) with an *observation* indicates the *action* led to this *observation*; a *hypothesis* nested in an *observation* means the analyst created the *hypothesis* based on the *observation*; an *action* nested in an *hypothesis* indicates the *hypothesis* motivated the analyst to perform this *action* for further investigation.

A node in the visualized AOH-Trees (Region 10) is either a node representing a pair of an *action* and its corresponding *observation* or representing a *hypothesis*. The analyst can view the details of the node of *action* and *observation* pair by selecting the node in Region 10, and then ARSCA will display in Region 11 the data entries that are selected in the *action* as the *observation* of suspicious network events.

Table 1. An example of a sequence data triage operations recorded by ARSCA

#	Data Triage Operation
1	<Item Timestamp="05/24 13:24:15"> FILTER (SELECT * FROM Task2Firewall WHERE Protocol = 'TCP', Task2Firewall) </Item>
2	<Item Timestamp = "05/24 13:25:29"> SELECT (FIREWALL-[4/5/2012 10:15:00 PM]-[Built]-[TCP] (172.23.240.254, 10.32.5.59), FIREWALL-[4/5/2012 10:15:00 PM]-[Built]-[TCP] (172.23.30.220, 10.32.0.100)) </Item>
3	<Item Timestamp = "05/24 13:34:41"> NEW_HYPO (H_(3524121) H_(44524411) "this is a thought") </Item>

Once the analyst finishes a task, ARSCA outputs the AOH-Trees, H-Trees, and the sequence of data triage operations performed by the analyst in time order. These files are written in XML format. A portion of XML file showing the data triage operation sequence is displayed in Table 1. This example shows that the analyst first performed a FILTER operation with the condition "protocol = TCP", and then selected the two data entries in the filtered data set (i.e., the second SELECT operation). Based on the observation, the analyst wrote down a thought (i.e., the NEW_HYPO operation).

5.2   Experiment: Collecting Data Triage Operation Traces

Traces need to be collected when analysts are performing cyber security data analysis. There are several real-world challenges (C3 as mentioned): (1) An organization does not want outside researchers to interview their workers (e.g., CND analysts) nor to access to their internal network. (2) Most analysts work in a 24/7 work shift with a very tight time schedule, so they do not have enough time to participate interviews. Otherwise, the normal security practice in the organization will be interrupted [35].

To tackle these concerns, we design a laboratory experiment with a simulated Cyber SA data analysis task. Neither the data sources nor the network topology reveal any information of the real-world setting of an organization's network, thus eliminating the organizations' concerns about privacy and confidentiality. In addition, this experiment is designed to be time-efficient for analysts by leveraging ARSCA in data collection. It means analysts do not need to make extra efforts on reporting or summarizing their analysis behaviors (e.g., interviews, verbal protocols), except for writing down some thoughts to benefit their own analysis process in the task (which is not mandatory in the experiment). Next, we describe the detailed experimental design.

Experimental Design. The real-world concerns are very important factors to be considered in our experimental design in order to conduct a successful experiment. These factors are as follows.

- We should be able to gain the sense of the analysts' domain knowledge and expertise, as well as their physical and mental status at the time of the experiment, because these are important factors that may influence an analyst's task performance.
- The analysts should be trained to get familiar with the experiment environment to make sure that their performance in the experiment is close to theirs in the real-world job setting.
- The experiment conductor may not have the opportunity to face-to-face communicate with the recruited analysts if the analyst identifies are also treat security in an organization.
- We'd better assume cyber defense analysts (event experts) are not good at or can not afford enough time and energy expressing the critical thoughts in their minds.
- We should be able to control the experiment time in a period which is acceptable for cyber defense analysts.
- We need to collect analysts' comments and conclusions after they finish the analysis task to have a good sense of their task performance. Besides, they can also server as a valuable reference or explanation from the analysts themselves when we review the traces collected in the experiment.
- The experiment data need to be stored explicitly in a format that is easy for the organization to review them before passing them to the researchers.

Based on the above constraints, the experiment is designed with four main stages: (S1) pre-task questionnaire (5 min), which inquires the information of the analyst's domain knowledge and expertise and their physical and mental status, (S2) tutorial session (20 min), which trains the analyst to use the experimental environment to perform data analysis, (S3) data triage task (at most 60 min), in which the analyst works on a Cyber SA data analysis task together with ARSCA, and (S4) post-task questionnaire (15 min), which contains both open-ended and close-ended questions asking about the analyst's findings and conclusion about the possible cyber attack chains [35].

Stage 1: Pre-task Questionnaire. A pre-task questionnaire taking 5 min is the first stage. The first part of the pre-task questionnaire includes the demographic questions about age, gender, ethnicity, and native language. The second part of questions asks about the domain knowledge and expertise of the analyst. It includes the work title, working years, five five-point Likert scale rating questions about the knowledge in cyber security, two questions about security expertise (familiarity with security techniques and security certificates), and familiarity with VAST challenges 2012 data (which is used in the simulated cyber analysis task), and the two five-point Likert scale rating questions about the analyst's current mental and physical status.

Stage 2: Tutorial Session. The tutorial session is designed to eliminate the influence of the analyst's familiarity of the experiment environment on his/her performance in the task. Five short videos are provided in this tutorial session to go through a mock-up task using ARSCA in the experiment environment. After finishing all the videos, each analyst needs to pass a quiz (i.e., a list of practical questions). Otherwise, he/she needs to go back to the tutorial material again to get correct answers to all the quiz questions.

Stage 3: Data Triage Task. We first provide the analyst with a task introduction document, in which we describe the network configuration and the role and responsibility of the analyst in this task. Besides, the introduction documents also describe the data sources provided to the analyst in this task and explain the meaning of the fields of the data. After going through the introduction document, the analyst can start analyzing the provided data sources in his/her own way. Meanwhile, ARSCA works together with the analyst so it can record every data triage operations conducted by the analyst in the task. The task will be described in detail together with the data sources in the following sections.

Stage 4: Post-task Questionnaire. After finishing the task, the analyst needs to take a post-task questionnaire. The first part of the post-task questionnaire is open-ended questions, which are coded as "IMP_OBS", "FD_OBS", "IMP_HPY", and "EVTS". They are described in Table 2. "IMP_OBS" and "FD_OBS" ask the analyst about the most important observations. "IMP_HYP" asks about the most important hypothesis. "EVTS" asks the analyst to "connect the dots" by providing a storyline of the possible attack chains [35].

The second part of post-task questionnaire includes four rating questions using a five-point Likert scale asking about the analysts' opinion on the experiment setting and their task performance. These questions are shown in Table 3, coded as "Task_Com", "SET_CFT", "EXP_RFL", and "CONC".

Table 2. The four open-ended questions in the post-task questionnaire.

Code	Question
IMP_OBS	"Reflecting back, what are the 3 most important evidences that you observed in the data that contributed to your conclusion?"
FD_OBS	"Please explain how you find the above evidences"
IMP_HPY	"Reflecting back, what are the 3 most important thoughts in your mind that contributed to your conclusion?"
EVTS	"Based on your analysis, please create one or more narratives that describe the events on the network (i.e., tell the storyline of the potential events)"

Table 3. The four rating questions about experiment setting and task performance [38].

Code	Question
A five-point Likert Scale: Strongly Disagree (1) Disagree (2) Neutral (3) Agree (4) Strongly Agree (5)	
TASK_CMP	Ask whether the task is of reasonable complexity. "The task is of reasonable complexity regarding the analysis activities it involves (e.g., data exploration, thinking reasoning, making decisions)"
SET_CFT	Ask whether they feel comfortable with the experiment setup. "I felt comfortable with the setup of the experiment (e.g., the provided software tool and physical environment), and my performance is not hindered by the experiment setup"
EXP_RFL	Ask how much capability/expertise is leveraged. "My capability/expertise of cyber analysis is fully leveraged and is reflected in accomplishing the task"
CONC	Ask how concentrated in accomplishing the task. "I'm fully concentrated on accomplishing the task"

Recruitment. With this experimental design, we successfully obtained the IRB approval and recruited 30 professional analysts from Army Research Lab and collected the traces of their data triage process. These analysts have various domain expertise at different levels. In additional to the professional analysts, we also recruited the doctoral student specialized in cyber security. Although they are not professionals, they were chosen because they have sufficient domain knowledge and experience in cyber defense situational analysis.

Simulated Cyber Defense Situational Analysis Task. We asked the participants to accomplish a Cyber SA data analysis task which is to report the suspicious network events underlying a set of data sources. We selected cyber analytics task of VAST Challenge 2012 Mini Challenge2 [39] and tailored our task out of it. The reason why we chose this data set is because its quality is close to the real-world problem regarding its size and noise-to-signal ratio (containing 23,711,341 firewall logs and 35,948 IDS alerts) [40]. Besides, a description of the underlying cyber attack scenario is associated with the data set as the sample answer for the challenge. This cyber attack scenario is a multi-step attack which took place with 40 h on an organization's network containing approximately 5000 hosts.

Although this data set provided by VAST challenge has a high quality, we can not directly use it in our experiment because it is impossible for the participants to go through them in the experiment time (at most 60 min). Therefore, we need tailor it into a small chunk of data. Given the attack scenario, we select a 10-minute time window out of the total 40-hour time period in which three types of critical malicious network events were happening and left evidence in the data sources. The three types of network events include (1) IRC communication between the internal workstations and the external Command and Control (C&C) servers, (2) denied file exfiltration attempts using FTP protocols, and (3) successful file exfiltration using SSH protocols. The data sources corresponding to this 10-minute attack time-window were finally extracted as the data set used in our task, which contains 239 IDS alerts and 115, 524 firewall logs.

We need to evaluate this task from two aspects. First of all, we should ensure it's suitable for participants to complete within the required experiment time. Moreover, the task should be of reasonable complexity regarding the difficulty of detecting the malicious network events relevant to the attack. The task was evaluated through a pilot study in which an senior analyst was asked to detect the suspicious network events by analyzing the task data set in the experiment setting. The pilot study also help us refine the training materials used in the tutorial session to make the experiment run smoother.

6   A Case Study of the Captured Data Triage Process

The traces collected from the experiment enable us to evaluate the capturing method. A case study is conducted to analyze the collected traces of analysts' data triage operations, which gives us a better understanding of the analysts' cognitive processes captured in the traces. The case study focuses on interpreting the sequences of analysts' operations in temporal order. The unit of analysis is the operation associated with a timestamp.

6.1   Qualitative Trace Analysis Method

The first step of analyzing a trace is to interpret the hypotheses which are typed down by the analyst in his/her analysis. For example, a participant wrote, "Websites are communicating with financial servers. They are communicating over what appears to be IRC which is commonly used by malware." We can know that the participant has the domain knowledge that "IRC can be used by malware" and he/she generated this hypothesis based on this knowledge. However, the information explicitly recorded in the trace can't completely reveal the analyst's cognitive process. Therefore, the next step is to infer the cognitive activities that are not explicitly recorded in the trace (i.e., the implicit information). These activities can usually be inferred from the traces.

Figure 7 shows an example of a partial trace. The partial trace contains a sequence of operations in the simplified representation. It shows that the analyst first browsed the IDS alerts at time t_1, and then selected a set of alerts of

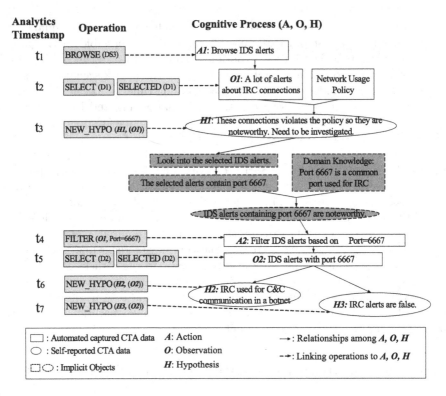

Fig. 7. An analyst's operation sequence is interpreted by the underlying AOH objects and their logic relationships [35]

IRC connections and confirmed them as an observation (i.e., O1). Based on the observation O1, the analyst generated a new hypothesis (H1) about policy violation. The network policy is marked explicit because it is mentioned in the hypothesis H1. The analyst then filtered the IDS alerts based on "Port=6667". We notice that some network events using port "6667" also appeared in the observation O1. So we can infer that the analyst conducted filtering based on this condition because he/she thought the IDS alerts with port "6667" were worthy of further investigation. The reason why he suspected these alerts could be that he has the domain knowledge that port "6667" is a common port used by malicious C&C communication. Therefore, we created the implicit objects between the NEW_HYPO operation and the FILTER operation which explains why P1 conducted the filtering after generating the hypothesis. We analyzed the 30 traces in the same way and found three cases of different analytical reasoning processes, which are discussed in detail as follows.

6.2   Case 1: "Gradually Narrowing Down"

Figure 8 shows the cognitive processes recovered from an analyst's trace. The analyst first performed a *FILTER* operation on the network events in IDS alerts at t_1 and observed a set of network connections from external IPs to internal IPs (O1). He thought this set of network events were highly suspicious (H1) so that he performed another *FILTER* operation at t_4 to further narrow down his search space by adding another condition "DstPort = 6667" to the filtering condition used in *FILTER* at t_1. In this way, the analyst detected a set of malicious network events that indicates malicious IRC communication from several Command & Control (C&C) servers to a group of internal workstations. This case indicates the analyst gradually filtered out the irrelevant data to narrow down the search space to locate the key evidence. This is the most common strategies used by the analysts in the experiment.

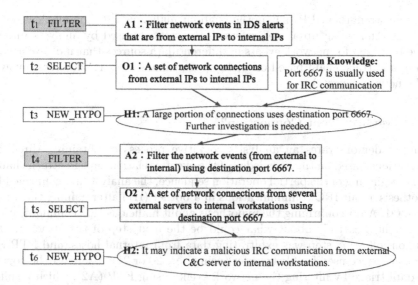

Fig. 8. A case of an analyst detecting suspicious network events by "gradually narrowing down" [35]

6.3   Case 2: "Following a Cue"

Figure 9 is a follow-up of the analyst's analytical reasoning process in Fig. 7, which indicates a "following a cue" data triage strategy. According to our discussion of the case in Fig. 7, he generated a hypothesis (H2) about malicious IRC communication in a botnet. Starting from H2, Fig. 9 shows that P1 filtered the network events recorded in firewall logs based on a same condition "SrcPort = 6667" to search for more details that support H2. It resulted in a set of network connections between a same set of internal IPs using source port 6667, and

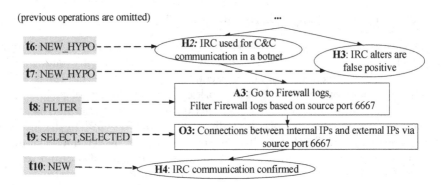

Fig. 9. A case of an analyst locating suspicious network events by "following a cue" [35]

therefore strengthened P1's hypothesis about malicious IRC communication. In this case, "following up a cue" refers to the strategy used by analysts in data triage to search for network events in different data sources that indicate a same step in an attack chain based on a clue (e.g., same set of IP addresses involved in the network events).

6.4 Case 3: "Event Connection"

Figure 10 demonstrates an analyst's cognitive process of obtaining three key observations based on the knowledge of the events' relationships in attack chains. At the beginning of the partial operation sequence, the analyst first confirmed his hypothesis about IRC communications in a botnet (H1) after gaining the observation O1. After confirming the hypothesis about malicious IRC communication, he thought creatively about what could be the next step of the attacker. One common following step was exfiltrating data from internal hosts, and FTP is a common service used for file transfer (using port 20 or 21). Therefore, he continued data triage by filtering the network events using FTP (A2), which resulted in the observation O2. O2 let him know that there were indeed malicious FTP attempts but were failed. He expected those bots would choose another way, and decided to search for the connections using SSH (using port 22). He filtered the firewall logs based on "port = 22" ($FILTER$ at t_6), and found that three SSH connections were successfully built between internal IP addresses and external IP addresses. So he generated a hypothesis that the bots exfiltrate data to outside C&C servers using SSH.

According to our understanding of the analyst's cognitive process, we can infer that he is familiar with the common attack chains and has the domain knowledge of the services used for Command & Control communication and data exfiltration. Thinking about the related events in an attack chain enabled him performed data triage in a very efficient way, which reflects his expertise gained from long-term on-the-job training.

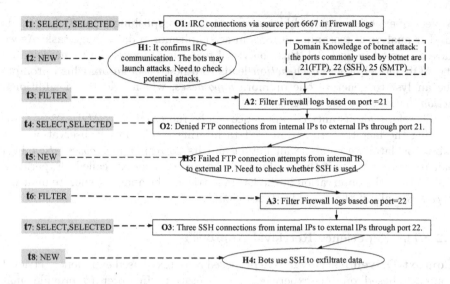

Fig. 10. A case of an analyst "proceeding from one event to its related events" [35]

Our preliminary trace analysis results show that it is possible to understand the analysts' cognitive processes of data triage through analyzing the collected traces. The traces contain the information of the key cognitive activities and the domain knowledge of analysts when they were performing a data triage task. Besides, the automatically captured information and the self-reports confirm and complement each other in the collected traces.

7   Data Triage Cognitive Trace Retrieval

The preliminary trace analysis has demonstrated that the captured traces of analysts' cognitive processes imply the strategies they used in the task and experience knowledge. In the real-world cyber defense analysis tasks, it's hence highly desirable to provide junior analysts some guidance based on the experience of expert analysts. Motivated by this need, we have developed a data triage support system that generates recommendations for an analyst based on similar data triage experience of other (e.g., senior) analysts. A key enabler of the system is a similarity-based retrieval of data triage traces, which is represented using the framework described in Sect. 3.4. This representation enables us to have a flexible and general way to represent the context of data triage, and to design a retrieval algorithm based on the similarity between these contexts.

7.1   Experience Representation Based on AOH Model

To build an experience retrieval system, the first step is to define the concept of "experience" in Cyber SA data triage. We model the experience as follows.

A piece of experience gained by an analyst in accomplishing a particular task is his/her analytical reasoning process in accomplishing a data triage task. As we have discussed in Sect. 3.4, this analytical reasoning process can be modeled by the AOH model, where each *action* leads to a new *observation*, which prompts the analyst to generate one or more *hypotheses*, which lead to an additional *action*, hence the cycle continues.

Therefore, an instance of experience can be represented by AOH-Trees. Considering the fact that an action of data filtering results in an observation of a subset of data, we combine an *action* and its corresponding *observation* in a pair to represent a unit that making up the current context, called "Experience Unit" (EU); the observation in the EU may trigger the analyst generate multiple *hypotheses* about the possible attack chains.

7.2   The Experience Retrieval Approach

Context-Driven Retrieval. We proposed a context-based experience retrieval approach based on the experience representation. In order to provide analysts with relevant experience instances as reference, the approach retrieves the matched experience instances from experience base based on the current context of data triage. Any update of the current context (i.e., gaining more observations) will trigger the updates of the matching results. The "context" of current process of data triage is defined by the "**EUpath**" in the AOH-Trees. "EUpath" is a list of EUs in the unique path from the root of the E-Trees to the current hypothesis of an analyst.

According to the definition of "context" of experience, the goal of the retrieval approach is to search the experience base for EU-paths that are similar to the current context and to generate a ranked list of EU-paths based on their degree of similarity to the current context. The similarity between EU-paths below is defined as follows.

Let P be an EU-path and P_C be the current context, the similarity is denoted as $Sim(P, P_C)$. Each EU-path is a set of EUs, therefore we use **Jaccard Similarity** to compute $Sim(P, P_C)$ [34]:

$$Sim(P, P_C) = \frac{|P \cap P_C|}{|P \cup P_C|} \tag{1}$$

We mainly consider the events in the *observation* of EU. Therefore, we have

$$Sim(P, P_C) = \frac{|P \cap P_C|}{|P \cup P_C|} = \frac{|Obs_P \cap Obs_{P_C}|}{|Obs_P \cup Obs_{P_C}|}$$
$$Obs_P = \{obs_x | obs_x = \{e_x\}, obs_x \in P\},$$
$$Obs_{P_C} = \{obs_y | obs_y = \{e_y\}, obs_y \in P_C\} \tag{2}$$

where *obs* refers to an *observation* instance and e refers to an network connection event. An *observation obs* contains a set of events.

Therefore, the similarity between two paths depends on the similarities between the network connection events contained in these two paths. The similarity between events are defined as follows. Let e_x, e_y be the events in two *observation*, the similarity between them, denoted as $f(e_x, e_y)$, is determined by matching the field values of their data sources. The matching includes:

- **Base Matching (BM).** BM refers to the minimum matching criteria, that is, if BM of e_x and e_y is violated, $f(e_x, e_y)$ equals to 0. One basic BM criterion is that e_x and e_y should correspond to the same data source. Experts can define other BM criteria by identifying the attributes of network connection events that must have the same value.
- **Weighted Matching (WM).** Once BM is satisfied, WM is used to calculate the degree of matching. Each individual ttribute of event is assigned a weight (based on domain knowledge). Given e_x and e_y, the WM score equals to

$$\sum w_i * Match(attr_i(e_x), attr_i(e_y)),$$

where the function $Match$ comparing the two attribute values (equals to 1 if they are equal, otherwise equals to 0).

Experience Retrieval System. The framework of the experience retrieval approach is shown in Fig. 11. It includes three main components, the experience base, an indexing module, and a similarity-based ranking module. The experience base contains the experience instances extracted from expert analysts' data triage traces.

The experience instances are indexed based on the network events that are contained in the *observation* of these experience instances. Given an experience

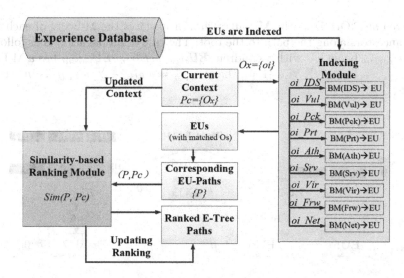

Fig. 11. The architecture of the context-driven similarity-based retrieval system [34]

instance, the indexing module maps the BM attribute values of the network events in this instances to the EUs that contain these events. The indexing will be updated once a new experience instance is added in the experience base. In this way, the system can quickly retrieve the relevant EUs given the events contained in the EUs in the current context.

The system retrieves relevant experience instances from the experience database based on the current context of the analyst's data triage process. Given the current context P_C, the system first extracts all the BM attributes from the EUs of P_C, and then identifies all the matched EUs in the experience base. With the matched EUs, the candidate EU-paths can be identified by searching for EU-paths which contain at least one matched EU.

The candidate EU-paths needs to be further ranked based on the level of similarities between these EU-paths and the current EU-path (i.e., current context).

The **Match Propagation (MP)** algorithm was proposed to efficiently rank the EU-paths based on the similarity between the EU-paths with the current context.

The MP algorithm can be described based on the structure of AOH-Trees [34].

- An EU could have several children.
- An EU has a parent.
- An EU is assigned a matching scores (**M-Score**) based on the similarity between the *observation* in this EU and the *observation* in the current context (initially 0).
- If an EU has children, this EU is assigned a list of M-Scores containing the M-Scores of its children (initially 0). We called the list "Subtree M-Score List (M-List)".

Given an AOH-Tree, the MP algorithm propagates the M-Score of each EU to its ancestors along the path to the root. The rule of propagation is as follows. Let EU_{parent} be an EU with n children, $EU_{c1}, \ldots, EU_{cn}$. EU_{parent} has a M-List: $\{w_{TEU_{c1}}, \ldots, w_{TEU_{cn}}\}$. $\forall i \in [1, n]$, the $w_{TEU_{ci}} = w_{EU_{ci}} + \sum w_{TEU_j}$ is in EU_{ci}'s M-List.

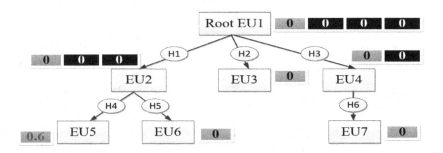

Fig. 12. An AOH-Tree to be ranked [34]

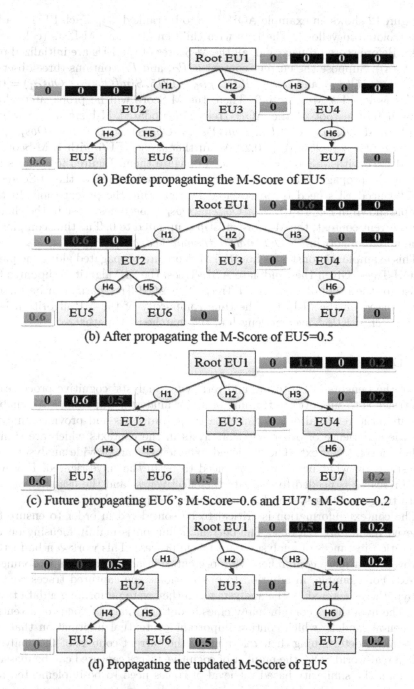

(a) Before propagating the M-Score of EU5

(b) After propagating the M-Score of EU5=0.5

(c) Future propagating EU6's M-Score=0.6 and EU7's M-Score=0.2

(d) Propagating the updated M-Score of EU5

Fig. 13. M-Score propagation [34]

Figure 12 shows an example AOH-Tree to be ranked [34]. Each EU has a M-Score (colored in yellow). The EUs with children also have M-Lists (colored in black). Before score propagation, all the M-Scores of the EUs are initialized to 0 (Fig. 13(a)). Suppose the current context is P_C, and P_C contains three observations, Obs_{C1}, Obs_{C2}, and Obs_{C3}. If $Obs_{EU5} \in EU5, Sim(Obs_{EU5}, Obs_{C1}) = 0.6$, EU-5 is assigned a M-Score 0.6. Then, the M-Score will be propagated along the path to the root of the AOH-Tree. The updated M-Lists are shown in Fig. 13(b). If $Obs_{EU6} \in EU6, Sim(Obs_{EU6}, Obs_{C1}) = 0.5$, and $Obs_{EU7} \in EU7, Sim(Obs_{EU7}, Obs_{C2}) = 0.2$. We further assign EU6 with a M-Score = 0.5 and EU7 with M-Score = 0.2, and propagate them. Figure 13(c) shows the result of the propagation. Once the current context is changed, the M-Scores of the influenced EUs need to be updated by repeating the propagation. In this example shown in Fig. 13(d), $Sim(Obs_{EU5}, Obs_{C1})$ becomes 0 due to the change of the current context, the M-Score of EU5 is updated to 0. The time complexity of the update algorithm is $O(Length of the matched path)$.

This example demonstrates how the M-Score are propagated along the paths in AOH-Trees. Given the candidate AOH-Trees, the MP algorithm updates the M-Lists of the roots of these AOH-Trees. The AOH-Tree paths can be further ranked based on the M-Lists. The time complexity of the MP algorithm is O (# of matched EUs * average length of the matched EU-paths).

7.3 Discussion

One of the benefits of capturing and retrieving analysts' cognitive processes of data triage is to support the training of junior analysts. Our framework enables the automatic retrieval of relevant data triage processes and provides analysts with the experience of other senior analysts in the contexts which are similar to their current context. The retrieved experiences can provide analysts some suggestions on what network events need to be further investigated. However, future research is needed to evaluate the effectiveness and the usability of such a data triage training system for junior cyber defense analysts.

The context information is critical to be considered in order to ensure the retrieved results are relevant. The current definition is mainly focusing on the observation instances of analysts' data triage process. This work can be further improved by a more comprehensive representation and associated reasoning of context. For example, in addition to observations, the captured traces contain the hypotheses entered by the analysts when they were performing a data triage task. The hypotheses contain many clues about the analysts' focus of attention and mental models, which contain important contextual information that can be useful for determining their relevance to the current context of the analyst.

In a real-world SOC, the number of cognitive traces captured can be massive. Therefore, the similarity-based retrieval of traces need to be implemented and evaluated in a scalable programming model and computing infrastructure such as Spark and Hadoop Distributed File System (HDFS).

8   Related Work

The study of data triage in Cyber SA is starting up from the existing findings and methods in several relevant research fields. In terms of the theoretical basis, the study is rooted in the filed of information foraging and data fusion. In terms of the human-in-the-loop nature, the studies of cognitive task analysis in Cyber SA or relevant fields provide very important starting point for our study. In terms of the ultimate goal of improving cyber defense analysts' performance, a brunch of visual analytics methods and intelligent systems have been proposed and developed to assist analysts in their jobs.

8.1   Information Foraging and Data Fusion

The data in Cyber SA are usually massive and change rapidly over time, as described in Sect. 2.2. The data collected from multiple sources are heterogeneous, and thus both information foraging and data fusion are necessary for analysts to detect the "true signals" of attacks by combining the information from multiple data sources. Bass described data fusion by mapping the OODA decision-support processes into different level of abstractions to gain cyber situational awareness [13]. Table 4 is a comparison between the OODA model and the AOH model (described in Sect. 3.4). It shows that we specifically focus on the iterative process in which the analysts perform filtering, searching, and selection actions on the large volume of data, select observations of interests, describe their hypotheses, which can lead to additional observations. These activities correspond to the "observation", "orientation", "decision" constructs in the OODA model.

Many data fusion model and methods have been evolving to enhance the process of data analysis in Cyber SA, considering the fact that the network data come from multiple sources. Joint Directors Laboratories (JDL) Data Fusion Working Group developed a model for data fusion process which is general across multiple fields. The process model takes the sources of "information at a variety of levels, ranging from sensor data to a prior information from databases to human input". This model breaks the data fusion process into five components: source pre-processing, object refinement, situation refinement, threat refinement, and process refinement. Data fusion algorithms and techniques can be categorized into these JDL components. Lan et al. proposed a framework that uses a data fusion method based on the Dempster-Shafer (D-S) evidence theory to gain cyber situational awareness [42].

Researchers have recognized the needs for a model that specifies how data fusion can be successfully applied to enhance Cyber SA [46]. The application of data fusion can contribute to intrusion detection [41], situational awareness [46], higher-level multi-step cybre attack tracking and projection [47].

The foraging loop in the sense making model corresponds to the data analysis process in cyber situational awareness. According to Pirolli and Card's sensemaking model, there is a tradeoff in the foraging loop among exploration ("increasing

Table 4. OODA model and the AOH model [34]

OODA	AOH	Description
Observation	Observation	The observation in OODA refers to the raw information which is presented before analysts' involvement. This data is captured in the Observation component in A-O-H model
Orientation		Orientation in OODA is "fusing information to build situational awareness)" [48]. This essentially incorporates the observation and through hypothesis cycles
	Action	The action performed to explore the monitoring data, to prove or disprove each hypothesis. These actions will result in new observations
	Observation	The observation of some interesting data resulted from actions. The collection of data may trigger analysts' new hypotheses
	Hypothesis	The thoughts generated based on the current observation. It could be an interpretation of current situation, questions in mind, or attempt to future actions
Decision	Hypothesis	The results of analyzing all hypotheses will result in a final decision. This is essentially the confirmed hypotheses of the A-O-H model
Action		Occurs after analysts' analytical reasoning processes and is thus not within the scope of the A-O-H model

the span of new information items into the analysis process"), enrichment ("narrowing the set of items to produce higher-precision sets of data"), and exploitation ("thorough reading of documents, extraction of information, generation of inferences, noticing of patterns, etc") [12]. Considering that most analysis jobs in cyber security is information-intensive, cyber defense analysts need their working environment to enable information foraging and simultaneous investigation [43].

8.2 Cognitive Task Analysis in Cyber SA

Cognitive Task Analysis (CTA) is a traditional method for studying human working processes. Some researchers with the access to the cyber defense analysts have conducted several CTA studies using various techniques, such as observation and interviews. Most of these studies focused on macro-level descriptions of cyber security analytics (e.g., the stages of data filtering and the roles of analysts [2–4]), had have gained some valuable insights into the analysts' cognitive processes. However, few have attended on the fine-grained cognitive activities due to several real-world difficulties in conducting CTA studies in cyber security. For instance, CTA studies can be too time-consuming as analysts, who have to rotate through day shift and night shift on a 24/7 schedule (24 h a day, 7 days a week) may have little time to participate in interviews. Besides, data triage tasks are memory-intensive and require vigorous concentration so that it is hard for analysts to give complete and accurate reports on their cognitive processes with a commonly-used think-aloud protocol.

8.3 Intelligent System for Cyber Data Analysis

The challenges of analysts in cyber data analysts come from the human's limited cognitive capability in processing large data and maintaining working memory and various cognitive bias (e.g., a common bias happened in data analysis is confirmation bias. Motivated to address these challenges, many researchers have developed various methods and technologies that come from artificial intelligence (AI) and human-computer interaction (HCI). Big data analysis is also powerful to solve the data analysis challenges in cyber situational awareness [14].

Case-Based Reasoning (CBR) is a family of approaches that uses "cases" to represent knowledge to solve new problems and reach to a conclusion or solution by conducting formal inference or information retrieval [49]. Cases can be structured, semi-structured or unstructured. The proposed context-based experience retrieval system uses both positive and negative "cases" of captured analysts' data triage traces. The negative cases (i.e., unsuccessful experience) can help analysts to avoid wasting time on investigating the irrelevant network events.

Besides of the automatic agents, the analysts' data processing capabilities can be enhanced by better interactive interfaces. Visual aids have been shown useful for sense making processes. Many visual analytics systems have been developed to present the multivariate nature of the data in cyber space to help analysts discover interesting patterns. Four main visualization approaches are very useful to display and manipulate the large amount of data: (1) "overview+detail, which uses a spatial separation between focused and contextual views"; (2) "zooming, which uses a temporal separation"; (3) "focus+context, which minimizes the seam between views by displaying the focus within the context"; and (4) "cue-based techniques which selectively highlight or suppress items within the information space" [50]. In additional to visual analytics, human-computer interaction system can help analysts maintain alternative hypotheses, overcome other cognitive limitations and avoid cognitive bias

9 Research Directions in the Future

Our work focuses on the data triage operations performed by the analysts, which lies in between the macro-level cognitive task analysis study and the micro-level neural study. The current results of the preliminary trace analysis have shown that the collected traces contain valuable information about the key cognitive activities of analysts. It can provide important implications for both levels in return. On one hand, the traces demonstrate the strategies and expertise knowledge used by the analysts during data triage, which can help researchers identify the analysts' cognitive needs and bias. On the other hand, traces serve as an important information source that helps explain the patterns found in neural data of much smaller granularity (e.g., EEG/fMRI data).

In our study of capturing analysts' cognitive processes, we observed a trade-off between CTA data collection (i.e. capturing traces) and CTA data analysis (i.e. analyzing traces). Considering the tight time schedule of cyber defense analysts, we try to minimize analysts' work load in our CTA data collection study. However, more efforts made on trace analysis are needed as the interpretation of the operations in traces is also a complex cognitive process. Fortunately, based on our preliminary trace analysis, we have observed some common patterns of sequential operations in traces. Therefore, it is highly likely to generate some guidelines or a procedure, even an automated tool for trace analysis.

Our study of the trace retrieval indicates that the collected traces provide an opportunity to provide novice analysts with the personalized guidance. Besides, the cognitive activities captured in traces can contribute to analyst training as another important measure for assessing analysts performance and learning outcome. Moreover, the formal representation of the data triage operations in traces enables us to develop automated methods to discover patterns among the analysts' behavior.

Acknowledgements. This work was supported by ARO W911NF-09-1-0525 (MURI), ARO W911NF-15-1-0576, NSF CNS-1422594, and NIETP CAE Cybersecurity Grant (BAA-003-15).

References

1. Security Operations: Building a Successful SOC, Hewlett-Packard Development Company, hp.com/go/sioc (2013)
2. D'Amico, A., Whitley, K.: The real work of computer network defense analysts. In: Goodall, J.R., Conti, G., Ma, K.-L. (eds.) VizSEC 2007, pp. 19–37. Springer, Heidelberg (2008)
3. D'Amico, A., Whitley, K., Tesone, D., O'Brien, B., Roth, E.: Achieving cyber defense situational awareness: a cognitive task analysis of information assurance analysts. In: Proceedings of the Human Factors and Ergonomics Society Annual Meeting, vol. 49, no. 3, pp. 229–233. SAGE Publications (2005)
4. Erbacher, R.F., Frincke, D.A., Wong, P.C., Moody, S., Fink, G.: A multi-phase network situational awareness cognitive task analysis. Inf. Vis. **9**(3), 204–219 (2010)
5. Granåsen, M., Dennis, A.: Measuring team effectiveness in cyber-defense exercises: a cross-disciplinary case study. Cogn. Technol. Work **18**(1), 1–23 (2015)
6. Yen, J., Erbacher, R.F., Zhong, C., Liu, P.: Cognitive process. In: Kott, A., Wang, C., Erbacher, R.F. (eds.) Cyber Defense and Situational Awareness. AIS, vol. 62, pp. 119–144. Springer, Cham (2014). doi:10.1007/978-3-319-11391-3_7
7. Etoty, R.E., Erbacher, R.F.: A survey of visualization tools assessed for anomaly-based intrusion detection analysis. No. ARL-TR-6891. Army Research Lab Adelphi MD Computational and Information Sciences Directorate (2014)
8. Barford, P., et al.: Cyber SA: situational awareness for cyber defense. In: Jajodia, S., Liu, P., Swarup, V., Wang, C. (eds.) Cyber Situational Awareness, vol. 46, pp. 3–13. Springer, US (2010)

9. Dutt, V., Ahn, Y.-S., Gonzalez, C.: Cyber situation awareness: modeling the security analyst in a cyber-attack scenario through instance-based learning. In: Li, Y. (ed.) DBSec 2011. LNCS, vol. 6818, pp. 280–292. Springer, Heidelberg (2011). doi:10.1007/978-3-642-22348-8_24

10. Endsley, M.R.: Toward a theory of situation awareness in dynamic systems. Hum. Factors J. Hum. Factors Ergon. Soc. **37**(1), 32–64 (1995)

11. Boyd, J.R.: The Essence of Winning and Losing (1996). Unpublished lecture notes

12. Pirolli, P., Card, S.: The sensemaking process and leverage points for analyst technology as identified through cognitive task analysis. In: Proceedings of International Conference on Intelligence Analysis, vol. 5, pp. 2–4 (2005)

13. Bass, T.: Intrusion detection systems and multisensor data fusion. Commun. ACM **43**(4), 99–105 (2000)

14. Mahmood, T., Afzal, U.: Security analytics: Big Data analytics for cybersecurity: a review of trends, techniques and tools. In: 2nd National Conference on Information Assurance (NCIA), pp. 129–134. IEEE (2013)

15. Zuech, R., Khoshgoftaar, T.M., Wald, R.: Intrusion detection and big heterogeneous data: a survey. J. Big Data **2**(1), 1–41 (2015)

16. Biros, D.P., Eppich, T.: THEME: security-human element key to intrusion detection. Signal-Fairfax **55**(12), 31–34 (2001)

17. Ericsson, K.A., Lehmann, A.C.: Expert and exceptional performance: evidence of maximal adaptation to task constraints. Annu. Rev. Psychol. **47**(1), 273–305 (1996)

18. Chen, P.C., Liu, P., Yen, J., Mullen, T.: Experience-based cyber situation recognition using relaxable logic patterns. In: IEEE International Multi-Disciplinary Conference on Cognitive Methods in Situation Awareness and Decision Support (CogSIMA), pp. 243–250. IEEE (2012)

19. Grance, T., Kent, K., Kim, B.: Computer security incident handling guide. NIST Spec. Publ. **800**, 61 (2004)

20. Information Security: Agencies Need to Improve Cyber Incident Response Practices. GAO-14-354, 30 April 2014. Publicly Released: May 30, 2014

21. Freiling, F.C., Schwittay, B.: A common process model for incident response and computer forensics. IMF **7**, 19–40 (2007)

22. Prosise, C., Mandia, K., Pepe, M.: Incident Response & Computer Forensics. McGraw-Hill/Osborne, New York (2003)

23. Dawkins, J., Hale, J.: A systematic approach to multi-stage network attack analysis. In: Second IEEE International Information Assurance Workshop, Proceedings, pp. 48–56. IEEE (2004)

24. Jha, S., Sheyner, O., Jeannette, M.W.: Minimization and reliability analyses of attack graphs. No. CMU-CS-02-109. Carnegie-Mellon Univ. Pittsburgh PA School of Computer Science (2002)

25. Thomas, J.J., Cook, K.A.: The science of analytical reasoning. In: Illuminating the Path: The Research and Development Agenda for Visual Analytics, pp. 32–68 (2005)

26. Mancuso, V.F., Minotra, D., Giacobe, N., McNeese, M., Tyworth, M.: idsNETS: an experimental platform to study situation awareness for intrusion detection analysts. In: IEEE International Multi-Disciplinary Conference on Cognitive Methods in Situation Awareness and Decision Support (CogSIMA), pp. 73–79. IEEE (2012)

27. Giacobe, N.A.: Measuring the effectiveness of visual analytics and data fusion techniques on situation awareness in cyber-security. PhD diss., The Pennsylvania State University (2013)

28. Poling, A., Methot, L.L., LeSage, M.G.: Fundamentals of Behavior Analytic Research. Springer Science & Business Media, US (2013)
29. Lee, F.J., Anderson, J.R.: Does learning a complex task have to be complex? A study in learning decomposition. Cogn. Psychol. **42**(3), 267–316 (2001)
30. Kukreja, U., Stevenson, W.E., Ritter, F.E.: RUI: recording user input from interfaces under Windows and Mac OS X. Behav. Res. Methods **38**(4), 656–659 (2006)
31. Allopenna, P.D., Magnuson, J.S., Tanenhaus, M.K.: Tracking the time course of spoken word recognition using eye movements: evidence for continuous mapping models. J. Mem. Lang. **38**(4), 419–439 (1998)
32. Rabinovich, M.I., Huerta, R., Varona, P., Afraimovich, V.S.: Transient cognitive dynamics, metastability, and decision making. PLoS Comput. Biol. **4**(5), e1000072 (2008)
33. Tom, P., Santtila, P., Bosco, D.: The ability of human judges to link crimes using behavioral information: current knowledge and unresolved issues. In: Crime Linkage: Theory, Research, and Practice. CRC Press, p. 268 (2014)
34. Zhong, C., Samuel, D., Yen, J., Liu, P., Erbacher, R., Hutchinson, S., Etoty, R., Cam, H., Glodek, W.: RankAOH: context-driven similarity-based retrieval of experiences in cyber analysis. In: IEEE International Inter-Disciplinary Conference on Cognitive Methods in Situation Awareness and Decision Support (CogSIMA), pp. 230–236. IEEE (2014)
35. Zhong, C., Yen, J., Liu, P., Erbacher, R., Etoty, R., Garneau, C.: An integrated computer-aided cognitive task analysis method for tracing cyber-attack analysis processes. In: Proceedings of the 2015 Symposium and Bootcamp on the Science of Security, p. 9. ACM (2015)
36. Pirolli, P.: Information Foraging Theory: Adaptive Interaction with Information. Oxford University Press (2007)
37. Pirolli, P., Card, S.: Information foraging. Psychol. Rev. **106**(4), 643 (1999)
38. Zhong, C., Yen, J., Liu, P., Erbacher, R., Etoty, R., Garneau, C.: ARSCA: a computer tool for tracing the cognitive processes of cyber-attack analysis. In: IEEE International Inter-Disciplinary Conference on Cognitive Methods in Situation Awareness and Decision Support (CogSIMA), pp. 165–171. IEEE (2015)
39. "VAST Challenge 2012 Mini-Challenge 2", Visual Analytics Community (2012)
40. Scholtz, J., Whiting, M.A., Plaisant, C., Grinstein, G.: A reflection on seven years of the VAST challenge. In: Proceedings of the 2012 BELIV Workshop: Beyond Time and Errors-Novel Evaluation Methods for Visualization, p. 13. ACM (2012)
41. Bass, T.: Multisensor data fusion for next generation distributed intrusion detection systems, pp. 24–27 (1999)
42. Lan, F., Chunlei, W., Guoqing, M.: A framework for network security situation awareness based on knowledge discovery. In: 2nd international conference on Computer Engineering and Technology (ICCET), vol. 1, pp. V1–226. IEEE (2010)
43. Fink, G.A., North, C.L., Endert, A., Rose, S.: Visualizing cyber security: usable workspaces. In: 6th International Workshop on Visualization for Cyber Security, VizSec 2009, pp. 45–56. IEEE (2009)
44. McClain, J., Silva, A., Emmanuel, G., Anderson, B., Nauer, K., Abbott, R., Forsythe, C.: Human Performance Factors in Cyber Security Forensic Analysis (2015)
45. Zhong, C., Kirubakaran, D.S., Yen, J., Liu, P., Hutchinson, S., Cam, H.: How to use experience in cyber analysis: an analytical reasoning support system. In: IEEE International Conference on Intelligence and Security Informatics (ISI), pp. 263–265. IEEE (2013)

46. Giacobe, N.A.: Application of the JDL data fusion process model for cyber security. In: SPIE Defense, Security, and Sensing, p. 77100R. International Society for Optics and Photonics (2010)
47. Yang, S.J., Stotz, A., Holsopple, J., Sudit, M., Kuhl, M.: High level information fusion for tracking and projection of multistage cyber attacks. Inf. Fusion **10**(1), 107–121 (2009)
48. Vandenberghe, G.: Visually assessing possible courses of action for a computer network incursion. In: SANS Institute, InfoSec Reading Room (2007)
49. Aamodt, A., Plaza, E.: Case-based reasoning: foundational issues, methodological variations, and system approaches. AI Commun. **7**(1), 39–59 (1994)
50. Cockburn, A., Karlson, A., Bederson, B.B.: A review of overview+detail, zooming, and focus+context interfaces. ACM Comput. Surv. (CSUR) **41**(1), 2 (2009)

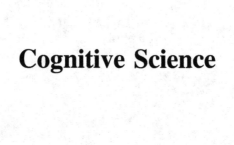

Cognitive Science

The Cognitive Sciences of Cyber-Security: A Framework for Advancing Socio-Cyber Systems

Michael D. McNeese[(✉)] and David L. Hall

The Pennsylvania State University, University Park, PA, USA
mmcneese@ist.psu.edu

Abstract. Traditionally, cyber security has been positioned and developed primarily from a computational-technology perspective. Unfortunately, this has been rather short-sighted as it provided solutions that fail to consider many human-related, cognitive, and social factors that underlie solutions of significance. While there have been substantial contributions from technology development that help the overall problem, a more comprehensive and effective approach is now needed that: (a) explores cognitive sciences and collaborative systems as a substantial basis to reify discovery and prediction, (b) produces incisive research results that inform the design of cyber tools and interfaces for active use, and (c) establishes new understanding of cyber situation awareness wherein the distributed cognitive activities of users, dynamic and changing roles of the threat and the environment, collaborative teamwork, and the promise of innovative cognitive technologies are intertwined and realized. This chapter outlines the perspective of social-cyber systems, a transdisciplinary approach designed to enhance information protection, reduce errors and uncertainty, take advantage of teamwork, and facilitate insightful understanding of what awareness and collective induction means for cyber defense and security. The Living Laboratory Framework is used to describe our approach and to implement specific aspects of social-cyber system research that inform dimensions of awareness and induction. Cognitive explorations underlying cyber situation awareness are presented that involve entwining theoretical foundations, models and simulation, and problem formulation - with - ethnographies of practice, knowledge elicitation, design storyboarding and technology prototyping. Integration of these important elements provides the basis of expanding individual cognitive processing into collaborative teamwork and collective induction that afford the goals of obtaining readiness and resilience in social-cyber systems. Finally, the chapter looks towards what future requirements will be necessary to sustain efficacy in protecting valuable resources and services.

1 Background

Cyber security can mean many things to many people but it is clearly one of the most daunting problems that impacts society today. Not only is it a problem associated with the military or intelligence assets of the United States and other countries, the security of our existence as human beings may be at stake if catastrophic consequences of poor

© Springer International Publishing AG 2017
P. Liu et al. (Eds.): Cyber Sitation Awareness, LNCS 10030, pp. 173–202, 2017.
DOI: 10.1007/978-3-319-61152-5_7

cyber security ensue. Cyber security threatens our lives and our lifestyles with ubiquity unparalleled. It may open up our bank accounts for massive loss, threaten the loss and theft of identities, the security of the transportation systems we use, decimate our energy infrastructure, and can make our defenses that thwart nuclear attack nil. Indeed, cyber security breakdowns are one of the most-wicked problems (Churchman 1967) that besiege humanity in the present days.

In today's world cyber security events and situations unfortunately occur on a regular basis, with some having more serious consequences than others. Since the beginning of 2015 major cyber security events have happened. The most recently leaked data on "Ashley Madison" accounts provides a significant example of how cyber security hacking and data access can reach deep into the societal backbone. Ashley Madison represents an online dating site, which essentially facilitates extramarital affairs for adults who are currently married. In July of 2015 the site was hacked by a group called "The Impact Team" wherein the database of 31 million customers was exposed. This made personal information highly vulnerable and has opened-up other problems. One problem is that the database contained 10,000 customers who were government / military workers. It is surmised that this has compromised national security concerns along the lines of extortion-blackmail, placed sensitive projects at risk, and help adversaries further target cyber security attacks on intelligence data [see <http://thehill.com/policy/cybersecurity/251517-cyber-foes-likely-digging-through-ashley-madison-data>]. Because this event just happened, the spreading activation effects are not yet fully known. But this example demonstrates that hacking is not just a one-time hack that exists at the surface but really creates a complex, emerging situation that has multiple, deep layers. The perception of what cyber security is can be very rigidly defined around the computers, architecture, and data but the perspective that is necessary is more expansive, and needs to consider "awareness" around the broader notions of people, behavior, crime, and society in order to develop compelling solutions. Awareness in cyber security is not simply developing new technologies or computational algorithms but must consider the cognitive sciences that underlie intelligence, behavior, and action.

At the heart of cyber security philosophy, policy, and operations is the adversarial imperative, which imparts a threat to take ownership of computer infrastructure, system, and/or files that maintain data, information, and knowledge that is often critical for preservation. Because computational intelligence is distributed in many ways (smart phones, reservation systems, navigation, cameras, military systems and so on) it makes the cyber threat even more serious and potentially devastating. Cyber security operations are targeted upon technology but they are initiated by human intelligence – designed to control or take over human enterprise, social and political entities, and to destroy what we value as humans. In turn cyber security is concocted by humans against humans and is designed to obtain the 'upper hand' of either control, execution, power, or dominance. Because it is foisted against us – strong programs of immunity from its effects must be initiated and sustained with much creativity and innovation. What makes this so difficult is the lightning quick 'change of state' in which cyber security effects can initialize and dissipate. Couple this much a maximum amount of duping, deception, and disruption and one is facing one of the most-wicked problems possible.

This chapter is derived from our joint effort at Pennsylvania State University (along with a team of other universities) to understand what cyber security means from the perspective of situation awareness. For several years we have been engaged in a Multidisciplinary University Research Initiative (MURI) designed in increase our knowledge about situation awareness within cyber security. This is a grant provided by the Army Research Organization (ARO) and represents a broad bandwidth approach to thwarting threat operations that are predicating on awareness (or lack thereof).

As a point of full disclosure the position that presented in this chapter is one that focuses around the worldview of cognitive science and necessarily is human-centered in view and application. Cyber security is considered from the intersections of information, technology, people, and context to derive knowledge about dynamic awareness and how it emerges over time. While we value the worth and usefulness of technology, we have seen within circles of the human factors that technology is often developed without consideration of human, social, or contextual factors that strongly imprint on its use. This chapter is not anti-technology but instead, uses an interdisciplinary nexus to develop technology that achieves situation awareness where the human is informed and can act in their environment in a way that produces tactical or strategic advantage in the course of achieving an objective. The hope behind this chapter is to introduce some alternative ways of interpreting awareness within cyber security, wherein new innovative thinking and creative design can make a difference in our lives.

2 Introduction

It is no surprise that we conceptualize cyber security as an interdisciplinary system of systems where transformative work is both local and distributed but undertaken by human agents engaged with other agents (human or computational) within an often changing environmental context. From this view, cyber security is human centered and requires human-in-the-loop processing, contextually driven by change, and must be approached and addressed through problem-based learning. As part of our MURI progress (over the last 6 years) – we have held on to the basic idea that if an analyst or team of analysts can obtain and maintain situation awareness during the course of problem solving, they will be successful in protecting systems and enhancing cyber defense readiness. The timely integration of information, technologies, people, and context are all important for considering cyber security as an interdisciplinary system of systems, team of teams conceptualization Cyber security is a very challenging problem space that contains multiple layers of complexity that can emerge and evolve quickly in many different ways. Activities within cyber security problem space can be seen as dis-granular and nonlinear as well as it contains virtual non-physical space (e.g., where hackers attack a software-based system designed to protect computer security), as well as physical cyber security elements, often, which are bridged together through human cognition and action. When considered jointly these elements create a demanding context for establishing situation awareness, and produce what has been referred to as wicked problems (Churchman 1967).

Conceptualizing Cyber Security as Distributed Cognition

For the purposes of this chapter it is necessary to begin with what we consider cyber security to be (i.e., a basic definition that characterizes it as a specific area of focus that is real and exists within a situated context). Therein, we will begin with the following definition (McNeese et al. 2011):

> By cyber security we mean a socio-technical system of a vast array of distributed computers, servers, and analysts designed to protect users from: (a) compromised systems and vulnerabilities perpetrated by adversarial threats and (b) defined and acted upon by humans for humans using computer-based tools.

While this definition is straightforward and specific and describes what cyber security 'is' - it is now four years old and may be too static of a definition. To update this definition, we now believe that cyber distributed cognition occurs in what we might term cyber-worlds – a virtual interactive world that can be veiled, hidden, and often deceptive; that consists of multiple, dynamic layers that can change dimensionally, representationally, numerically, and in many other ways within milliseconds (i.e., lightning quick). Cyber worlds contain socio-cyber systems that consist of a series of human-environment transactions wherein a team of teams utilize many tools and infrastructure inclusive of intelligent computational agents acting as teammates, web-based sensor data fusion, the internet of things, cyber visual analytics, and social network prediction. Socio-cyber systems are exactly the contexts that cyber analysts work within to address, manage, and attack where the adversary seeks to gain entrance to destroy data, exploit information, and/or take control.

Traditional notions or models of cognition get stretched and changed in cyber-worlds as there are unique information-context interdependencies that emerge and change rapidly in time and space within the social and physical environment. Space in this context is different from typical physical context wherein physics play out laws of nature. Space in cyber worlds is bound within the constraints of "what is possible" given the software boundaries, the disguise that data may take on, and the lightning speed of rapidly changing states within this unique kind of conceptual space. This is different than tracking a physical threat of the battlefield wherein movements of targets are subject to $D = R*T$ physics and other constraints. Change of this magnitude means cognition and awareness addressing the current state of cyber operations is more difficult to comprehend, and perhaps learn. Information half-life (recency) becomes incredibly hard to decipher especially in non-routine situations. This is the world we expect a human to understand and comprehend to thwart cyber threats as they manifest in different kinds of modalities and environments (e.g., smart phones, banking systems). As indicated with the above definition cyber worlds must include human interpretation and that interpretation is assisted by technologies that bring forth new tools, interfaces, and simulations that enhance our ability to be active responders, to 'see' differently, and to predict patterns before they come to fruition. The demands placed on cognition are not just analytical but include the ability to induct, to learn deep elements of patterns that form in cyber worlds, to create and intuit, and to discern when deception is in process.

Worldviews of Cognitive Understanding. The world of cyber security takes place within a complex environment (as they denoted above as a cyber-world) that may be conceptualized from a number of different worldviews (mathematical, computational and information science, business intelligence, eco-systems, criminological-terrorist studies, social informatics, information fusion, big data analytics, cognitive-psychological science, to name a few). Historically, situation awareness (Endsley 1995) has primarily been addressed from a cognitivist worldview where an analyst utilizes "cognition as being in his/her head" and then applies it as apropos. This view is predicated on older human information processing approaches to cognition (Newell and Simon 1972) where cognitive understanding is equitable or analogous to a computer elements reading data into a central processing unit (e.g. image translation, memory storage) then appropriating responses via output mechanisms). Cognivistic models have been around approaching 60 years (Newell et al. 1958) and perhaps much longer if one considers philosophic predecessors (e.g. Descartes 1664). The cognitivist view has been challenged as too microscopic (micro-cognition is often too static and relies on a homunculus in the head (but who directs this master controller?); micro-cognition under-estimates the impact of the environment or context that affords action, and often micro-cognition fails to consider the social/teamwork aspects of cognition in terms of emergent dynamics.

In turn, another perspective has emerged which may be termed an ecological-contextualistic worldview. Historically, this view has evolved from the early work of James Gibson (1979) based on his research in direct perception which in turn focused on human-environment transactions, and the role of affordances and effectivities have in specifying information. Action and perception of are jointly determined by an actor within a context (Greeno 1994). A contextualistic approach (Hoffman and Nead 1983) looks at cognition as also being distributed outside the head in the environment. A human often constructs or picks up information in the context of work (direct perception) and learns through repeated use of affordances and effectivities (invariance). Mace (1977) captured the essence of an ecological-contextualistic worldview when he stated "ask not what is inside your head but what your head is inside of". Problems can be seen as exercising opportunities as specified by information in the environment if one has the correct effectivities to act on the affordance when it exists. This places problem solving clearly within an ecological "situated cognition" perspective (Brown et al. 1989; Young and McNeese 1995). Hutchins (1995) is representative of a similar perspective termed "distributed cognition" which is indicative of how cognition forms in context, and provides the foundation that cyber security activities can be wholistically framed as distributed cyber cognition.

Distributed cognition is heavily coupled to perceiving change in the contextual environment that specifies information. Therein, most of these approaches emphasize the role of perception, perceptual differentiation, and the ability of people to understand what that change represents in cyber-worlds in terms of transactions necessary for the agent to accomplish intentions. Perceptual apparatus is bound to the body (e.g., eyes, ears, limbs) – termed embodied cognition (Wilson 2002) – and is the basis for dynamically moving through and experiencing the context as it unfolds. Cooke et al. (2013) has adapted similar ideas as applicable to interactive team cognition providing an ecological basis for team activities especially as pertinent to cyber security applications. Likewise, McNeese (1986) first used the terms macrocognition and macroawareness to describe cognitive activities that are broadly defined and interactive with the natural environment. More recently Klein et al. (2003) and others have extended macrocognition theory as a basis to understand and design solutions to naturalistic decision making problems that are present in many fields of practice. The worldview that this chapter takes is closely aligned with these approaches for individual, team, and 'team of teams' activities, rather than older more traditional perspectives of cognition.

When perception in and of itself cannot pickup information specification directly from the environment, then a person's own cognition and in particular meta-cognition (thinking about thinking) come more into play to make sense of and respond to situations. The environments that are meaningful for success also include social transactions that are distributed within a team or across teams, therein ecological contextualistic worldviews necessarily gravitate towards social connectedness and virtual transactions where information specification in teams is prevalent (or could be prevalent).

The meaning of awareness. As researchers who have historically focused on socio-ecological development of cognitive technologies it is incumbent to ponder what situation awareness or awareness represents in the cyber security/cyber defense field of practice. Some believe that answers will be found when there is an increase in the capacity in data accessibility. Others suggest awareness comes through "intelligence" built into computer algorithms or by reducing uncertainty via probabilistic or machine learning computation. Concomitantly, other worldviews suggest that improvements in awareness come through visualization, visual analytic displays, or through the massive amounts of information that are hidden in "big data" waiting to be data mined. Other perspectives – if even considered – place awareness solely in the mind through consideration of attention and memory activation processes (traditional cognition). More recently, researchers have suggested awareness emerges out of the team mind (Salas et al. 2012). While our work has touched on each of these perspectives at some point across the last six years of our Army Research Office ARO MURI grant; each one considered in isolation is significantly lacking as it fails to portray the big picture, see McNeese et al. (2006), (or what some refer to as the Common Operational Picture of Cyber Situation Awareness in Security).

There are multiple kinds of awareness present in socio-cyber systems, emergent across time and space, represented in various ways to human and agent; distributed across cognition. This is our collective view of what awareness means within cyber worlds. Hence, we refer to this niche as Cyber Distributed Cognition. Based on our own work the following elements are considered primary research missions within this niche:

I. Opportunistic Problem Solving in Cyber Operations
II. MetaCognitive Reflections about the Threat
III. Learning and Spontaneous Access of Knowledge in Context

These missions are both interactive and iterative with each other holistically. Because we believe that cyber situation awareness is an immersive, evolving state that draws from cognition into the context as opposed to merely static knowledge state in the head, our missions point to different ways of thinking about awareness as it plays out within cyber distributed cognition. The missions also formulate some of the backbone of discovery that underlie our actual research objectives during the course of the MURI grant.

Cyber security operations can be punctuated with changing events, volumetric data exchange, and rife with uncertain circumstances. While many procedures are straightforward and known new data can flow into the environment, which causes assessment and awareness to be a high priority. This kind of environment presents the human analyst with ample opportunity (but with associated risks) to engage in opportunistic problem solving (Hayes-Roth and Hayes-Roth 1979). Cyber-worlds can also be nuanced in different ways wherein there may high levels of interdependence, overlapping layers, distributed information, and other forms of isomorphism. Yet it is frequently the case that individual analysts may have their attention diverted into a black hole of exploration and discovery when they are engaged in sensemaking and putting together patterns to determine affordances and effectivities. This presents a kind of bias that is opposition to collaboration. This may be especially true when individual analysts are not in the same physical locale, that is, when they are distributed. Opportunities for collective induction (Laughlin 1999) may exist but knowledge may remain hidden and not shared for maximum utilization (see Stasser and Titus 1985). In cases such as this unique knowledge may remain hidden and inaccessible by other analysts who actually could use it connect the dots to form the big picture. When collective induction is limited, then opportunistic problem solving may suffer and in turn solutions may be minimalistic or not produced at all. If collaboration involves integrative roles wherein distributed information is linked in cyber operations (as it often can be) then a more deleterious effect can occur especially if the distributed information has temporal contingencies and consequences associated with it.

The individual or team of analysts do not just come to a problem or situation without any experience. Typically, they will be place on the job with some level of training and in various circumstances analysts fall on the continuum between novice and expert. As part of their experience, learning is very important as it exposes an analyst to varying situations that may hold some degree of similarity or common elements where previous knowledge can be automatically (spontaneously) accessed and used opportunistically in the midst of a problem. This type of information may be specified directly through perceptual pickup wherein the analyst or team of analysts recognize cues that heed access to cases, stories, or segments of previous experience. Understanding by stories or cases or segments may rely upon metacognitive activities in that analysts may see something that reminds them about how they solved a similar situation in the past. Thinking about how they think is termed metacognitive activity and can occur at anytime but especially is salient when perceptual pickup stirs partial recognition.

Without awareness in cyber distributed cognition, an analyst can have a dim perception and consequently lack a basis for how to adapt or respond to a situation that involves cyber activities. We refer to this kind of state as mindlessness, in contrast to mindfulness. When situations are ill-defined, non-routine, and uncertain it can produce a state akin to "blooming, buzzing confusion" (James 1981) wherein there is a fuzzy fog and focus is sparse. It may be experienced from several sources such as; (1) not paying attention to primary and secondary cues within the environment wherein recognition-primed decision making (Klein 1999) is lacking, (2) information over-loading is experienced wherein focus is scattered, (3) stress or affective levels shuts down the neurological apparatus, or (4) time pressure requires a very fast response. When two or more of these sources combine simultaneously an analyst may devolve into what we refer to as cogminutia fragmentosa (McNeese and Vidulich 2002) whereupon attention is channelized into small strands, and is perceived in piecemeal fashion, and mindfulness is never obtained. If this happens during a live event then mistakes, errors, or even failure can be eminent. Therein, a cyber-world should facil-itate human centered interaction to prevent mindlessness and facilitate mindfulness in order that awareness might evolve to high levels.

Framing the Problem Space – Use of the Living Laboratory (LLF). As mentioned one's worldview can intimately determine what is a problem and what is not a problem dependent on a researcher's perspective. Because we view cyber SA as distributed, cognitive work that is mutually influenced and effected by the context of action it is incumbent to utilize our own Living Laboratory Framework –LLF- (McNeese 1996) to discover and explore problems within cyber distributed cognition. Figure 1 shows the Living Lab Framework. We utilize the interdisciplinary framework to conduct research through multiple levels of analysis and design. The framework emphasizes the mutual relationships and cyclic nature of theoretical and practical constraints of work. The Living lab emphasizes the idea of exploring real world contexts by understanding worker or team-centered problems that emerge during complex operations. This is an

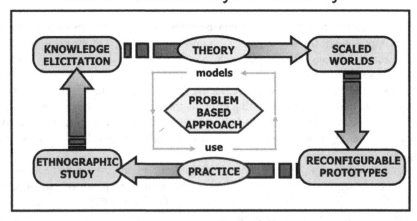

Fig. 1. The living laboratory framework

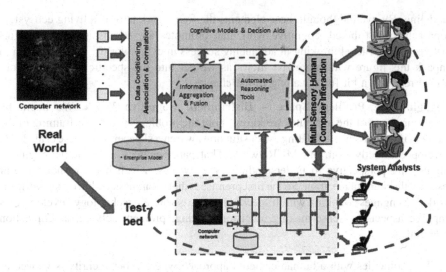

Fig. 2. Instantiation of LLF for Cyber SA MURI Grant

approach that is reflective of the ecological-contextualistic worldview. It has been classified previously as a cognitive systems engineering methodological framework (McNeese and Vidulich 2002). Figure 2 shows a more specified instantiation of the LLF as we utilized it for the MURI grant.

As one can see the central heart of the framework is that of discovering - defining – exploring problems to learn new ways of solving problems. Clearly this framework then enables a problem-based learning (Bransford et al. 1999) approach to human centered cyber SA. Problems come into focus through a variety of means. This is captured in the framework by the interactions of the four elements: (1) ethnography, (2) knowledge elicitation, (3) scaled world simulations, and (4) reconfigurable proto-types. Problems can be informed from the top-down -through theoretical positions- and from the bottom-up - through practice. Practice in the real world as we know is coupled to extant problems that occur as users experience them in differing ways. This excites the bottom-up processes in the LLF that focus on what gets done in cyber security (in particular, cyber situation awareness) and how people utilize technology to accomplish work. As related earlier much of this work is distributed and complex. Concomitantly, problems are also coupled with theory or theoretical positions taken by researchers.

Theory provides a view of what could happen in cyber security by postulating hypotheses about how human-cognitive agents transform their world. Because our worldview necessarily incorporates human-in-the-loop processing of cyber security, practice is typically known (heeded) by the experience that an agent (analyst, operator, or user) encounters while involved with distributed work. At the core of the LLH then is the coupling of theory-problems-practice and the ways they are informed by feed-back from the four elements that can provide additional enhancements of data/information/knowledge. As learning ensues in a given element it feeds-forward to setup processes in other elements as well, and also improves comprehension. Research coupling among these elements also may yield secondary increases regarding use and modeling. By cycling though these elements the framework affords a living ecosystem approach to distributed, cognitive work that promotes an interdisciplinary, transformative, systems-level thinking in advancing success in cyber-worlds. We will return to unpack this figure with more specificity as we get into the specific activities of our MURI research a bit further along in the chapter.

Engaging the Problem Space – Distributed, Cognitive Work. We begin by reviewing some of the attributes we know about the problem space. Our framing of the problem is best taken as 'situating cyber situation awareness' paper (McNeese et al. 2011) developed directly from our MURI work. That paper enabled a distinctive cognitive engineering perspective to understanding cyber-worlds, which has continued in our research throughout the grant. So the first premise is that awareness within cyber worlds is work that engages cognition within specified contexts wherein technology developments improve aspects of sense-making, decision making, problem solving, and/or action potential.

This coincides with a human centered approach where cyber security is viewed as first and foremost as distributed, cognitive work wherein tools and technologies support cognitive work to improve performance (eliminating problems, enhancing capabilities, removing constraints, adapting response). Taking that as our baseline, lets delve in more depth as to what this means. The attributes we find embedded with the cyber security world embroil around difficulties humans have as agents engaged with a complex context. Figure 3 summarizes these problem attributes on a general level and the consequences that emerge for humans.

Typical Problems Encountered

- *Emerging Context in Time and Space*
- *Information Overload*
- *Information Interdependencies*
- *Shallow Common Ground*
- *Reasoning with Uncertainty*
- *Cultural – Ontological Conflicts*
- *Impoverished Visualization*
- ***Situation Awareness – if present - disappears under stress***

Potential Resulting Consequences:
* Articulation and Information Sharing Deficits
* Weak Decision Making Quality
* Performance Confusion and Breakdowns

Fig. 3. Problems encountered in distributed work settings

Exploring Cyber Distributed Cognition Using the Living Lab Framework
Considering the above problems and issues that are pertinent within cyber security operations, there are three specific areas (premises) we wish to look at:

(1) Cyber-situation awareness as distributed cognitive work as performed in a given context, field of practice,
(2) Cognitive work will focus on human-systems integration centered on information fusion for both hard and soft sensor data,
(3) Cyber operations potential can improve with apropos teamwork (both within and across team performance).

Given that our theoretical approach within the Living Lab Framework is distributed cognition and given we have defined what some of the problems are in practice, we will now look at other components of the framework that have been explored the last several years: (1) knowledge elicitation, (2) ethnographic exploration, (3) scaled world developments, and (4) prototype technologies. The LLF is not pre-specified in a linear, assumed order but rather is adaptable to the circumstances the researcher must work within. This chapter reviews outcomes associated with distributed cyber security, socio-cyber systems, and awareness by summarizing accomplishments within two distinctive but related trajectories: qualitative research and quantitative research. Both of these trajectories as part of the LLF are mutually informative and provide feedback cycles to further 'knowledge as design' as more results become available. While there are multiple research accomplishments within each track this chapter focuses on recent work. We begin with qualitative research.

3   Qualitative Research: Knowledge Elicitation/Ethnographic Data

One of the challenges for research in cyber-security is the access problem of experts. Unfortunately, much of the work in cyber security operations is classified and therein unattainable. To overcome this early in the MURI we were able to; (1) participate in a workshop at Arizona State University with some cyber analysts who provided invaluable information to general levels of thinking about cyber analyst work and what situation awareness amounted to –from their experiences, (2) interview/observe different kinds of cyber analysts from different venues (university, business) and in a war game exercise, (3) collect results from a survey given to 112 cyber security experts, and (4) conducted interviews from students from our College who were participants in a recent student regional cyber security exercise. In addition, we had the benefit of faculty members who had prior professional experience and cyber/network analysts.

Through our various contacts we have derived early ideas about cyber work and further elaborated the spectrum of problems that are extant and relevant. We have previously published aspects of # 1, 2, and 3 above (Tyworth et al. 2013) so will not reiterate everything mentioned there. Many of the problems mentioned earlier in the introduction are present in cyber activities, and we have discovered from triangulating across these sources of data that cyber security: (a) involves a hidden – often ill-defined threats, (b) takes place in a notational environment with much context switching present, (c) location and spatial cognition is emphasized (thinking about space in the computer is different than physical space), (d) representation of locations (where cyber attacks occur) especially with temporal constraints is often a problem (this motivated our development of a visual analytics workbench), (e) tracking of problems-situations range from location-time-space representations translatable into semantic descriptions (data-information-sensor translations), (f) there is often collaborative and intuitive reasoning preset wherein human and machine tools related to situation awareness may be most useful), (g) more data is not necessarily useful as it can produce overload and obfuscates comprehension, (h) tools are not very good – they do not deliver what was promised (often this has to do with scale up problem), (i) having to reason and process more information can result in fatigue and burnout (which contributes to mindlessness), and (j) there is often isolation – no common ground present and therein collaborative problem solving is not really supported in any effective way.

We discovered that implications associated with awareness - given these problems – are important. Situation awareness can come and go dependent on what information is known or unknown at a given point in time and this acts as hidden knowledge across team members in the team setting. As complexities grow the focus of intentions can become blurred, disjointed, and channelized (more evidence of mindlessness in operation). Understanding attacks can be confusing when SA comes and goes and when these attacks are multiple and distributed over time. While there are more insights discovered that represent some of the main findings, this qualitative section focuses more on the recent qualitative study with students. (See Tyworth et al. (2013) for more information regarding other qualitative work that imbues individual and team-based distributed cyber cognition.)

Regional Student Competition. One of the primary objectives for recent work in cyber distributed cognition was focused one the use of a Cyber Threat regional exercise which our SRA students participated in as student teams. This objective represents more of a need for qualitative data directly taken in the form of knowledge elicitation interviews, which can then be used to propagate initial concept map-based models.

Preparations and Development. We were given an opportunity to have access to a College of Information Sciences and Technology Security Club project wherein members competed in the Mid Atlantic Collegiate Cyber Defense Competition. This allowed us as researchers to develop a qualitative study to determine how they would problem solve and make decisions when presented with an engaging Cyber Security Threat Situation. As part of the competition they were asked to participate in a challenge problem.

Challenge Problem. The following paragraph describes what they did on the challenge problem in the regional competition:

The work they performed was typical cyber-defense activities. They were given remote access to two Linux and two Windows-based servers to defend from live "red-team" attackers. They were also provided dynamic injects of tasks they were asked to perform – typical systems administration tasks, account creation, database updates, etc. They had full administrative access to the systems they were defending, so they could do anything they wanted. Typical tasks included enumerating and securing accounts with administrative access (changing from default passwords), identifying and updating software with patches, modifying configuration of software to turn off unneeded services, etc. During the exercise, the students needed to identify what was wrong (configuration, patches accounts, services), figure out if attackers were utilizing those vulnerabilities to compromise systems, and turn off attacker access if they were able to locate that the attacker had gained access.

Methods. The participants for the qualitative study were recruited from the team of students that were participating in the National Collegiate Cyber Defense Competition (CCDC). After the project was described to students. Informed consent forms were signed, and the participants were questioned about their team experiences, training and preparation activities, and understanding of the competition and their teammates. The interviews were recorded and notes were also taken to supplement the digital recordings.

When all of the interviews were completed, the digital recordings were sent to a transcription service that transcribed the data word-for-word. In instances where the recording was inaudible the handwritten interviewer notes were used for clarification. All of this data was analyzed by two of the researchers collaboratively. Key phrases were pulled from the transcript and put into a spreadsheet. Once the key phrases were identified, the same researchers worked together to identify themes and categories in order to create the coding scheme (see Table 1). This coding scheme was again collaboratively used to classify each of the key phrases previously identified. In cases in which a classification did not exist, the coding scheme was modified and the process continued as normal.

Results. The outcome of the coding scheme application resulted in specific frequency of occurrence of codes across all interviews. This highlights the nature of distributed cognition, situation awareness, and individual and team cognition as it relates to students identifying, exploring, and solving the challenge problem(s).

In addition to understanding the content of the entire set of interviews vis-à-vis the coding scheme, a plan was derived to produce a descriptive model of the student's distributed cognition to ascertain how situation awareness emerged within knowledge, context, and process. The use of concept mapping (Zaff et al. 1993) was chosen as a flexible, lightweight kind of cognitive model and was collaboratively formulated by the same researchers who coded the interviews - by utilizing the raw text of the interviews and the frequency occurrence produced by the results of the coding scheme. An overall plan was generated to produce an integrative, overlay model of cognition (see Fig. 4).

To initiate this plan, the first phase accomplished included creating a declarative concept map to represent some of the major findings in the coding scheme (as applicable to the actual interview text phrases) to come up with a first-level model of knowledge underlying distributed cognition in cyber operations teamwork. The declarative concept map in turn represents element # 1 in the overall overlay: *intention*. The other elements (*solution path*, *teamwork in evidence*, *cognitive processes demonstrated*) would also need to be developed to completely in the next phase of future work to completely propagate the entire overlay cognitive model. The first phase model (see Fig. 4) is heavily informed by the activity of planning and re-planning, and determining what role uncertainty plays in accomplishing the overall challenge problem. As we perused this initial concept map there was much to be learned in how

Table 1. Coding scheme used to analyze interviews

4	**Problem Solving**	Activities necessary for identifying, addressing, and resolving issues
4.1.	*Strategies plan of action*	
4.1.1.	Shared across the team	
4.1.2.	Individual strategies	
4.2.	*Processes*	Articulated written or unwritten plans necessary to address problems
4.2.1.	Actual	What were some of the processes of problem solving
4.2.2.	Adaptive	Flexibility of processes when new information was presented or something was found to not work
4.3.	*Problem Monitoring*	Activities and techniques for tracking and documenting problems
4.3.1.	Initial identifications of problem	
4.3.2.	Updating problem	
4.4.	*Process Monitoring*	Tracking and documenting of the processes for problem solving
4.4.1.	Strategies	is there monitoring of those actions used to problem solve
4.4.2.	Outcomes	are the results desired or appropriate to the task
4.5.	*Reassessment*	
4.6.	Errors	What happened when there were errors?
4.7.	Tools	
4.7.1.	Information Technologies	
4.8	Priorities	
4.8.1	Updates to	
5	**Planning**	Activities for the purpose of having the necessary skills, personnel, and knowledge to be successful
5.1	*Team based planning*	Activities coordinated among the team for planning purposes

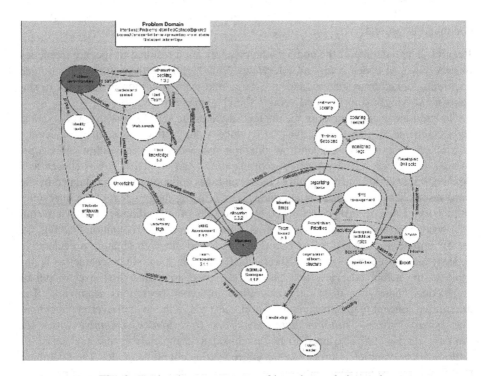

Fig. 4. Declarative concept map of intentions-solution paths

individuals and teams formulate what the challenge problem consists of, and in turn how to begin tackling it. All of this is valuable for understanding comprehension of cyber threat activity, and how this might be improved with new cognitive technologies that would enable information fusion and potential gains through collaborative teamwork.

Implications. It is evident that students working together in teams often struggle to understand how they will solve the problem given to them and how they can work together to reap the benefit of their collective talents. In newly formed teams this is difficult process as it minces strategic knowledge resident in teamwork processes with specific knowledge needed to solve the problem at hand.

Furthermore, the management of their intentions becomes a reified issue in that they have to spend time figuring how to work as individuals but yet as an interactive team, including defining "function allocation" (i.e. Who will do what when with what tools?). Although this was a first-level concept map specifically focused more on planning – it is the first of several concept maps that could be generated as part of the layered representation.

4   Quantitative Research: Simulations, Design Prototypes and Experiments

Much of the work within this trajectory is interrelated as we often design scaled worlds (and the scenarios within) as human in the loop simulations to address specific research problems-issues-constraints initially revealed by novices and/or experts engaged in specific problem spaces (e.g., novice Security and Risk Analysis (SRA) students engaged in the Mid-Central Regional Exercise as reported in the previous qualitative work section). So at the most fundamental level scaled worlds have been designed to take broad problem spaces that exist in practice and scale them down into experimentally tractable simulations that are can be controlled and manipulated according to objectives. The goal is to have an experimental simulation that represents many of the elements of the cyber operations context (such that it appears as a real work environment) but is adaptable for testing and evaluation purposes. To that end, most of our simulations-scenarios are adapted for either testing the theory-based understanding (distributed cyber cognition and awareness) or for evaluating the intervention of an innovative prototype within the scaled world (socio-cyber systems) to see if it influences individual or team performance. Once a prototype is tested and design to the point it positively influences performance in the scaled world, then it is at the state of readiness for application within the real world context it was designed for. If the LLF has evolved technologies to this point they are then inserted into the real world context for actual application testing and the cycle of understanding begins again. At this point we have not actually placed prototypes into actual practice as they still need further testing under different conditions.

The simulations are absolutely designed from our worldview in the sense that they represent human-environment transactions and are strongly ecologically contextualistic. The transactions needed occur when some form of 'change of state' emerges from the context which requires a human to perform in a certain way to cause positive change in addressing problems-plans-subproblems-outcomes. Indeed, all of the simulations we have designed represent changes in the cognitive-contexual continua that a person or team must contend with. Affordances for action are created based on emerging events that create changes in various states which can then be resolved by application of different types and amounts of resources (effectivities). Certain team roles restrict who may do what at what time but together this syntax creates complexity representative of real world cyber situations that are often time-based. Awareness comes from comprehending the emergent situation based on assessment of events within situations, and how well resources are producing positive effects in resolving events. The development of socio-cyber systems often springs off of developing new technologies that specify information about an affordance to make it more visible or known, extending the conditions under which an effectivity is appropriate, advancing awareness based on expectations of state changes, and sharing of hidden knowledge to create a bigger imprint of the common operational picture at any point in time. Tasks can require analytical inquiry at the individual level but also may demand information sharing and collective induction. By simulating real world events and simulations much can be known that was not previously considered. This brings forth 'knowledge as design' and generates new ideas and concepts that are relevant to cyber security concerns.

The simulations have built in dependent measures that accumulate the degree to which performance approaches the optical level based on how well individuals or teams resolve the total number of situations-events that occur in the simulation, and to what degree or level they were resolved to. These simulations require comprehension of the problem, awareness of changes that emerge, communications with team members about all aspects of what is going on, and a lot of individual work representative of a particular role they are responsible for. Because the simulations often present dynamic occurring cyber events, the best-laid plans have to be refigured and revised. This emulates the necessity for replanning which is often one of the bugaboos experienced in complexity and problem solving. When replanning is successful human-environment transactions make headway and problems dissipate. In many cases, the distributed social interdependencies are the most important considerations to pay attention to (i.e., where cyber awareness develops and comes into play as to whether performance will increase or decrease) as they create uncertainty, analytical reasoning, are heavily dependent on temporal awareness. The simulation design affords implementation of actual experiments wherein experimental independent variables are manipulated to see the effect upon dependent variables. The simulations in general also manage control variables that are necessary so as not introduce new extraneous variance. Often as mentioned above scaled world simulations tests a given hypothesis derived from the theory under examination, but it can also test different states of a new technology to see how it might interact with other experimental variables as part of an overall study. Therein, the scaled worlds, experiments, and technology prototypes are intimately coupled together for evaluating ideas and concepts within a domain that represents the real world problem specifications.

Specific Cyber Simulations Developed. During the first four years of the MURI grant one of the focus areas was to specify, create, and build simulations that would emulate salient elements of (1) cyber distributed cognition (2) cyber situation awareness (3) innovations in socio-cyber systems. The goal for these simulations was to provide some degree of flexible experimental control that would impact scenario design generation and to provide quantitative testbeds that could be activated for specific human in the loop experiments. In turn we achieved our goals by developing 3 specific scaled world simulators (1) CyberCITIES (2) TeamNETS (3) IdsNETS (4) NETS Dart. The CyberCITIES simulation was our first simulator in the cyber area and the task focused on recognizing and utilizing information surrounding access control within cyber security (Reifers 2010). Because these simulators have been reported and described elsewhere we will not dwell on them here, Tyworth et al. (2013). By all accounts they were successful as providing adequate experiences with different aspects of cyber security operations albeit with certain constraints and assumptions. One of the essential issues for all the simulations is determining how much training to provide for students. Actually the topic of training and learning is an area the simulations might be extended, as training over time produces insights, expertise, and awareness that was not present previously. This argues for actually conducting longitudinal studies that emphasize the learning of metacognitive activities, spontaneous access of knowledge when it is needed, and how to operate and integrate knowledge effectively as a team. While most experiments focus on single shot studies (one and done) it is our belief that the LLF is best implemented when longitudinal simulations are invoked.

All of the simulations focused on both individual and team cognition requirements within an emerging scenario design in which different events had to be assessed and processed with some rigor. These simulations absolutely required interdependencies across the information-role-context coupling, and all of the simulations represented analytical thinking requirements and the need to communicate with teammates in order to obtain acceptable scores. The simulations also provided a 2-way testbed where the outputs from qualitative research could be a basis for developing a scenario that was grounded in reality. Although each of these simulations had limits as to what could be done – they provided a basis for generating situation awareness and situated action within a specified cyber distributed cognition context. Likewise, the simulations were designed so that new prototypes could be configured within the simulation. This enabled human in the loop testing of new innovations, which could be compared with control cases, as well as salient experimental variables that represent some of the problem states and issues we identified earlier (e.g., time pressure).

The simulations are all predicated on client-server technologies wherein command and control are achieved vis-à-vis experimenter's stations. The picture in Fig. 5 shows the laboratory setups of some of the simulations. Individual stations are shown on the top and bottom figures (enabling experiments to be conducted in which participants act as individuals, members of a closely linked and interacting team, or members of a pseudo distributed team environment.) The middle picture of Fig. 5 shows our Extreme Events Laboratory which supports 3-D visualization experiments, utilization of 3-D sound (i.e., experiments with sonified data interaction) and combined visualization/sonification interactions.

Simulations were designed to absolutely be distributed in the sense that they could provide distributed space (team members are connected via interfaces and chat rooms but remotely located from each other), distributed information (information has to be fused together at individual and team levels to address task demands), and distributed context (in some simulations context switching must occur which challenges awareness).

Human in the Loop Experimental Studies

As part of the nexus between theory-problems-technology feedback loop within the LLF we have utilized this set of simulations for experiments that help to inform and understand cyber distributed cognition in general and how awareness evolves within socio-cyber systems in particular. The goal of human in the loop experiments is to test individual and team cognition under variously constrained conditions to evaluated theoretical perspectives, hypotheses that aim to discover new possibilities in opportunistic problem solving, and to develop and test innovative solutions to problems that are difficult. The set of experiments we have designed and implemented are a mere subset of what is possible to look at given the simulation capabilities, but are the ones we have data on to date. These studies taken as a whole demonstrate that cognition-context-communications-computation-teamwork all play roles in successful problem solving to varying degrees. The design, implementation, and evaluations we produced using the Team NETS, Ids-NETS, and DART NETS simulations have been previously described in Tyworth et al. (2013) but are captured here to provide additional edification as to how our new simulations can be used. The following exert describes experiments that were undertaken to further the understanding of cognitive science within cyber operations:

"We have conducted experiments using the scaled- world simulations. One set of experiments examines transactive memory and CDA. To conduct these experiments, we have updated NeoCITIES scaled-world simulation (c.f., Jones, McNeese, Connors, Jefferson, & Hall, 2004; McNeese et al. 2006) to better support the dynamic and rich nature of the cyber security environment. The new simulation, the NeoCITIES Experimental Task Simulation (NETS), has been extended to support richer scenarios and complex decision making. The current implementation of NETS (referred to as idsNETS) has been implemented using intrusion detection data to mimic the role of an intrusion detection analyst. We have plans to extend the NETS functionality to be able to simulate scenarios from the other operational domains we identify in the future.

For our own research, we are addressing the issue of the formation and maintenance of transactive memory systems in synchronous distributed collaborations. To study this, a new version of the NETS simulation was designed (teamNETS) to simulate collaborative problem solving tasks within a cyber-environment. This version of the simulation was extended with numerous enhancements to better support our research questions and transactive memory research at large. Within the study, each team member is assigned a particular specialty, and in order to achieve high performance, it is necessary that they communicate and share relevant information to solve different types of events. From this study we hope to gain an understanding of how these transactive memory systems are formed in distributed collaborations, and how new systems can be designed to better support this process.

Transactive Memory was first conceptualized by Wegner (Wegner 1986) as an "interpersonal awareness of others' knowledge" and can be conceptualized as a specialized form of Cyber Situation Awareness, where rather than focusing on, or being aware of, aspects within the cyber environment, your awareness is grounded in the cyber knowledge, activities and behaviors of your collaborators. An effective Transactive Memory System can give a human quick and coordinated access to another person's specialized expertise (Lewis 2004). Numerous

Fig. 5. Laboratory environments for cyber operations

studies have shown a positive link between a team's Transactive Memory System and its performance in collaborative tasks (c.f., Ellis 2006; Moreland and Myaskovsky 2000; Pearsall and Ellis 2006).

Whereas Transactive Memory is an important thread within team research it is mainly approached from a management or organization psychology lens, often only considering the humans. Since its inception, technology and information have evolved dramatically, though Transactive Memory has remained fairly constant. Research has focused primarily on exploring its effect in new domains, and extending the concept as a research tool, but no one has examined how new technologies have changed how we, as humans use this transactive memory. In order to bring Transactive Memory into the 21st century, it is imperative that we understand how transactive memory has changed with synchronous distributed collaboration systems, social networks, and crowd-sourced knowledge repositories, to name a few.

A second set of experiments is being conducted to look at the impact of task load on the ability of participants to establish and maintain cyber-SA and prioritize tasks. Maintaining cyber SA is, in part, dependent on the ability to prioritize attention. Cyber defense analysts must attend to alerts associated to potential threats and respond to them within time constraints, requiring a prioritization of events in accordance to their threat level. However, high levels of cognitive workload may limit the ability of analysts to focus their attention on priority tasks. For example, unexpected surges in threat level in some events may not get noticed in time. An interface that provides information on anticipated threat level could facilitate analysts' ability to attend to unexpected surges.

In this set of experiments, we explore the effect of a workload-preview on performance in a dual-task cyber- security event monitoring context using our NETS-DART scaled-world simulation. The simulation provides a dual- task environment. The primary and secondary tasks represent internal and external networks in an organization. All participants are presented with two types of scenarios – regular scenarios and surge scenarios. The difference between the two is that surge scenarios consist of secondary-task events that grow in threat-level and exceed that of concurrent primary-task events. Experimental results are expected to provide insight on the effect that workload previews have on attention- allocation, task management and cyber-SA in multi-task cyber-security contexts. (pp. 8–9)"

After completing the previous simulations (TeamNETS, IdsNETS, and DART NETS), we embarked on the development and test of simulation designed to be strongly linked to actual cyber security operations. This resulted in the newest and most current development of a scaled world simulation termed Cybernetic Team Simulation (CYNETS). The following section describes ongoing work that led to CYNETS becoming a reality.

CYNETS Simulator Proof of Concept. At this point in the chapter we turn now to the most recent proof of concept simulation that was designed, CYNETS.

Preparations and Development. Inherent in our simulation – CYNETS - was the desire to create scenarios that built off of realistic hard data to provide a solid scaled world feel wherein the collective demands on distributed teams would be bound to both hard and soft data integration. Also, we desired a simulator with a scenario that required discovery-information seeking, team communication/coordination, cognitive processing, and therein a task that was ill/defined and uncertain to a degree that would enable the necessity of developing cyber SA.

CYNETS Task. The work they performed was typical cyber-defense activities. They were given remote access to two Linux and two Windows-based servers to defend from live "red-team" attackers. They were also provided dynamic injects of tasks they were asked to perform – typical systems administration tasks, account creation, database updates, etc. They had full administrative access to the systems they were defending, so they could do anything they wanted. Typical tasks included enumerating and securing accounts with administrative access (changing from default passwords), identifying and updating software with patches, modifying configuration of software to turn off unneeded services, etc. During the exercise, the students needed to identify what was wrong (configuration, patches accounts, services), figure out if attackers were utilizing those vulnerabilities to compromise systems, and turn off attacker access if they were able to locate that the attacker had gained access.

Simulation Data. To develop hard data fusion elements, the experimental simulation data was created in the lab environment from a similar perspective. The simulated data was fabricated from a network of computers in the laboratory that simulates an active network of computers from a fictitious organization called "ABC" (see Fig. 6). The ABC network includes three servers and 25 workstations. The data that was provided to simulation exercise analysts included a 24-hour period of logon/logoff log data from a Windows 2012 server for the entire network.

In this 24-hour period, accounts were logged on and off of computer systems to create actual log entries in the Windows Security Log of the server. While the actual events of successful logon and logoff events are entered into the Security Log of the authentication server, these are not the only events that are generally displayed there. A windows domain treats computers in a similar way to the way it treats users. They must also log on and off. However, a systems authentication is more automated. Also,

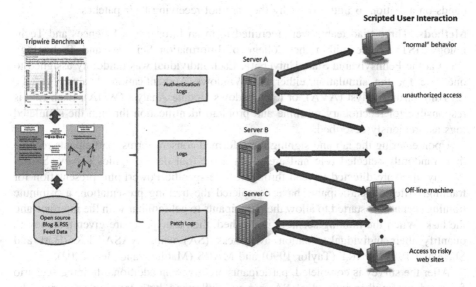

Fig. 6. ABC simulated network

as a user authenticates and accesses networked services, other authentication records are also in the log to include every time a networked user accesses a different network device. This noise of normal activity often clouds the real issues of authentication failure and account misuse. The data set that was presented to simulation participants had some level of normal noise, but generally was limited to successful logon, successful logoff and unsuccessful logon events. Embedded in the presented authentication data was a series of failed logon attempts, followed by an eventually successful event. This simulated a password-guessing activity that resulted in a compromised account.

Additionally, the same 24-hour period was used and a number of viruses were copied on to the computers. The antivirus program was allowed to detect these files and take appropriate action – either delete or quarantine the files with the malicious code. Together with the updates of new antivirus definitions, these two types of records were presented in the antivirus data. To simulate unsuccessful antivirus actions, anti-virus alerts were fabricated repetitively on one system. This mimics the behavior of some antivirus applications – where a suite of malware is installed on a system that re-installs other parts of the suite if they are removed. The undetected malware is indicated because of the repeating successful removal of several sets of other parts of the suite. Together with an outdated set of virus definitions, an analyst is led to the conclusion that the system must be infected with malware that is not detected by the old set of definitions.

The final set of data is patch management. In this case, we created a set of records of normally applied updates. However, we also intentionally left one system offline for a period to show the lack of updates being applied to that system. Additionally, we filled the hard drive of another system to prevent it from having patches applied. This system showed "failed updates", primarily because the drive was full. A network analyst seeing records from these systems would be able to interpret that the systems needed hands-on attention to figure out why they are not receiving their patches.

Methods. Three triad teams were recruited from an Information Sciences and Technology (IST) course within the College of Information Sciences and Technology (IST) at the Pennsylvania State University. Each individual was randomly assigned to one role for the simulation either (1) Windows Authentication Analyst (WAA), (2) Anti-Virus Analyst (AVA), or (3) Windows Update Analyst (WUA). Each role is responsible for reactionary machine and problem identification through the simulated logs as previously described.

Upon entering the lab and signing the informed consent forms, participants receive their randomly selected role and are given a pre-trial demographics survey. Subsequently, they are directed to read through a role-specific PowerPoint presentation for training. After all participants have completed the training presentation, a 5-minute training scenario is started to allow the participants to get familiar with the interface and the task. When the training scenario is finished, the participants are given a survey to quantify their individual situation awareness (SA) using NASA-TLX (Hart and Staveland 1988), SART (Taylor 1990) and MARS (Matthew and Beal 2002).

After the survey is completed, participants are given an additional training scenario followed by another individual SA survey. Following both training scenarios, the participants are given a quick debrief about the scenario and the proper response. Next, the first performance scenario is started and once complete is followed by the same individual SA measures but with the added Shared SA Inventory (SSAI) (Schielzo et al. 2009). Subsequently, participants are asked to complete the second performance scenario and the same individual SA and SSAI surveys. Upon completion of the final survey, participants are debriefed about the fictitious nature of the scenarios and thanked for their service.

Results. The simulation was tested initially with 3 teams to assess feasibility and capture the performance measures mentioned above. Everything worked well in the simulation, and students were able to perform in the role of individual and team cyber analyst duties in determining routine and threat activities as part of their task. While the initial proof of concept was conceptualized, implemented, and tested- and met the expectations of the experimenters, more robust testing and experimentation is desirable. This is discussed further in the future work section below.

Implications. The CYNETS scaled world simulation represents the development of a challenging cyber operations environment that emulates real world threat assessment that involves distributed cognition across individual and teamwork functions. As such it provides a capability for extending understanding of hard (and potentially soft data fusion) within an emerging milieu. The implications are that the study of the problems mentioned at the beginning of this report can be brought into the lab setting and studied for further illumination of situation awareness within cyber defense. Further work on cognitive technologies that are human-centered in design can be embedded within the information architecture underlying the simulator designed to undergo precise human-in-the-loop testing to determine how they improve human/team performance.

Innovative Prototype Technologies

Visual Analytics Test-bench. During the research on the Multidisciplinary University Research Initiative (MURI) on cyber situation awareness, we conducted research on tools and visualization aids for cyber analysts. There are numerous visualizations that have been developed to aid the visualization and analysis of network systems (see for example Stall et al. (2014) and Shrvavi et al. (2011)). In particular, N. Giacobe (Giacobe (2015)) developed a prototype cyber analyst workbench illustrated in Fig. 7. The tool extends the typical concept of providing network-type displays (e.g., overlays of computer network topographies on geographical map displays, network "traffic" displays, attack maps, link diagrams, etc.), to include linking text-based data (e.g., cyber-network sensor data and reports on cyber-attack activities), with social network information (indicating potential threat perpetrators), timeline information, and ongoing analyst hypotheses and notes. The aim was to explore how a cyber-analyst might conduct situation assessment, analogous to the concepts of situation analysis performed by analysts for traditional non-cyber military operations. Indeed, Giacobe explored the applicability of the Joint Directors of Laboratories (JDL) data fusion process model for cyber security applications (Giacobe (2010)).

Complex Event Processing

In addition to visualization aids, research under the MURI grant explored automated tools to detect cyber events and activities. The concept of Complex Event Processing

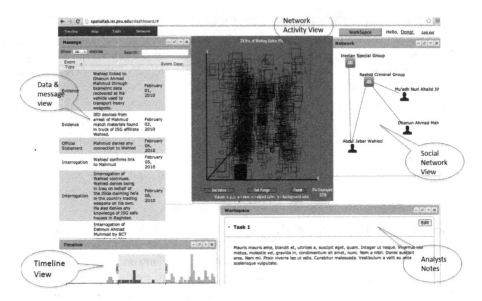

Fig. 7. Prototype analyst workbench (Giacobe (2013))

(CEP) has emerged from the business community and crisis management. The concept involves developing an explicit and implicit representation of conditions, observables, and contextual information that provide evidence for an emerging activity or event. Rimland and Ballora (2014) explored the application of CEP to detection of cyber-attacks. Their architectural approach is illustrated in Fig. 8. In addition to considering the CEP approach, they also explored the transformation of cyber data into sounds (sonification) in order to improve the interface with analysts (viz., transforming network conditions into sounds that analysts could more readily detect anomalies).

Discussion/Future Work

The work undertaken represents further effort to open discovery, understanding, and prediction as to how situation awareness emerges in distributed cyber operations (both individually and in teamwork). While this is a lofty goal, the research described above (coupled with our five previous years of MURI research) has begun to make necessary in-roads in these areas. In particular, we have designed, implemented and provided an initial proof of concept for the CYNETS scaled world simulation involving distributed information fusion surrounding an emergent adversarial threat situation. While the first experimental design and test of the simulation only involved the incorporation of hard data fusion, the scaled world is designed to include soft data fusion in future studies to further extrapolate nuances of cyber situation awareness as cyber operations are employed in both routine and non-routine opportunistic problem solving sets.

Our use and testing of the scaled world using scenarios involving human-in-the-loop testing with Security and Risk Assessment (SRA) students within the College of Information Sciences and Technology validates that it is possible to create a realistic emulation of cyber security using typical data expressions and use from day-to-day

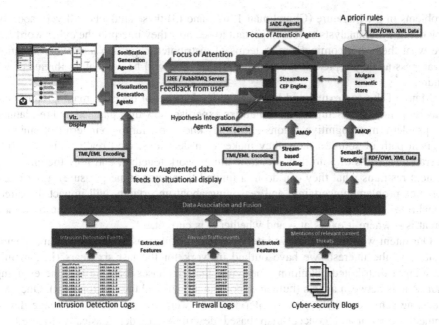

Fig. 8. CEP processing architecture for cyber SA

cyber analyst activities. The simulation affords analysis of individual cognitive processing as well as team cognitive processes to comprehend and discover specific problems and issues that arrive in predicting correct answers or solvation of complex problems. Having the availability of this type of simulation gives an additional tool to breakdown the reasons for individuals and teams not coming up with the absolute correct answers. This purports a "failure-driven learning" approach wherein over time correct answers may be discovered through use and interaction.

Concomitantly, it gives an ability to assess and analyze why wrong answers or procedures occurred potentially giving rise to detect and isolate bugs in cognitive models, and/or barriers to learning how cyber situation awareness comes into existence. Learning why SA does not envelop in the individual and in turn the group provides the basis upon which human-centered cognitive technologies can be developed (as opposed to just blindly throwing technology to the wall to see what sticks).

In addition to developing and testing the CYNETS simulation we were provided an additional unique opportunity to have access to IST students participating in a regional cyber security exercise. This access allowed us to interview students especially as to how they plan to attack a cyber threat situation (again both individually and in teams) and allowed a different kind of exploration as to how students identified, defined, investigated, and solved problems (or not) but from an alternative mode of understanding in contrast to an experimental design and simulation-based study. It is important because; (1) it was deemed state of the art for student teams (circa 2015), (2) it was provided by governmental officials who are fully aware of the embedded issues and constraints and therein represented what would be indicative of wicked problems in the literature (Churchman 1967), and (3) these students will very soon be practicing cyber analysts so it is important to see how they interpret the cyber word and see what their shortcomings are in terms of distributed cognition and cyber situation awareness as they represent the new generation who will be combating threats of the future.

Many of the contextual and human-centric elements of decision making came into play (e.g., how they setup teams and utilize expertise, how they planned and re-planned the problem (metacognitive actions), how they knew how far to go in terms of pursuing a given path of solution, how they make team decisions, etc.) really influence their overall awareness of who they are, how things work together, and how the emerging context restrains what they can do in a limited timeframe (time pressure). Like many complex problems uncertainty and reasoning about uncertainty will impact the directionality of interdependent problem elements and how they become aware of what a threat is – where it exists at – and whether it is current.

Our intent with the qualitative interviews of students was to apply a coding scheme relative to the interests we have outlaid in work for the last six years (i.e., mainly pursuing a distributed cognition worldview that emphases learning and the evolving transactions between agents (human or computational) and the environment). Once our encoding scheme was applied to interviews we were able to use it to engage development of an initial concept-map based descriptive model (basically focused on planning and how people tackle the problems resident in the exercise). Concept maps afford descriptive based cognitive models which can be flexibly used in different ways but mainly as lightweight knowledge representation typologies emanating from knowledge elicitation activity (Zaff et al. 1993). We will discuss more about this below in the future work section.

Our overall goal with the modeling part of the Living Lab Approach, however, is to generate what we refer to as a layered, declarative concept map. This models declarative (and to some extend strategic) knowledge resident in a novice or expert cyber analyst for a given challenge problem within a specified context. As such it employs both cognitivistic and contextualistic layers of understanding and thinking as a person or team evolves through solvation of the problem presented. Because the map is heterarchical and is entrenched within the concept-relation-concept syntax it is maximally flexible and not over constrained. The coding scheme and concept maps of interviews of novice-level students can be useful to contrast and compare against expert concept maps for further elucidation, and inspire specific requirements for training.

In summary, much has been discovered. However, still more needs to be discovered about distributed cognition, information fusion, and teamwork as it contributes to establishing situation awareness in cyber defense. The approach taken here has always been to keep cycling to various components of the Living Lab as opportunity presents itself with eventually the intent to intervene in real world practice with; (a) effective cognitive technologies that truly impact positive use or (b) Innovative training for individuals and teams involved in complex cyber security problems. We turn now to discuss potential future work that directly follows directly from our research activities from this last year.

Future work. If one steps back from what has been accomplished, it clearly sets up some new research channels and extensions that could come into effect. We will briefly discuss what needs to be done in the next phase to further establish this line of research.

First, for the experimental research we feel that the next step is a full-scale experimental study involving CYNETS. Our hope would be to run an experimental design wherein hard fusion is crossed with soft fusion access. In this case soft fusion represents specific intelligence gathered on the threat that emerges during the course of the scenario. This would complement the hard fusion component and provide an additional dynamic in the teamwork component. This would provide a fuller scale test and actual experimental evaluation for publishing (assuming significant effects were obtained). The orchestration of the soft fusion element could be information provided only to one team member at a given point in time (simple soft data fusion) or unique information could be given to all three team members at different points in time (complex soft data fusion). There is experimental evidence that suggests team members only share that which is unique, which if true really limits the collective induction possibilities in the cyber context. Our intent would be to try to utilize ROTC students (as a kind of more DoD-aware student base) and compare with IST/SRA students (who are probably more aware of the technology and security-risk aspects of cyber systems).

Second, the coding schema data can be further propagated as a more integral concept map that involves layered representation to couple together different perspectives on knowledge that underlies situation awareness and distributed cognitive process. The first step would be to produce additional declarative, procedural, and strategic knowledge-based concept maps according to the planned overlay concept mapping typology (see Fig. 4). In the tradition of the AKADAM techniques (see Zaff et al. 1993) it is the intent to use the lightweight concept map model as the basis for; (1) establishing user needs and (2) defining new interface or cognitive technologies to obtain what Perkins (1986) refers to as 'knowledge as design'. The trajectory would be to use the entirely propagated layered concept map across every element as a basis for prototyping new designs that improve situation awareness in individual and distributed cognitive activities.

Third, the results from the experiment can be merged with the qualitative study to mutually inform each facet of our research (e.g., the research independent variables can be directly derived from qualitative data, and likewise the results of experiments can inform better cognitive models of individual cyber analysts and teams of analysts as they engage situation awareness in this kind of context.

Finally, another future goal would be to expound on descriptive lightweight models and create new middleweight models in the form of abstraction hierarchies and the cognitive decision ladder (Rasmussen et al. 1994). These models emphasize both structure and function more than concept maps but are given to make extant the actual contextual variants as well as providing representation of insights when learning proceeds. This is important because both kinds of models set up the cognitive systems engineering of adaptive resiliency systems of awareness in cyber operations which is needed where evolutionary uncertain information fusion foments across a highly distributed environment. Eventually, the goal would be to learn from the discoveries inherent in student exercises as well as the experimental designs in a way that really strengthens and reinforces the cognitive models and ensuing technologies that are waiting to be developed for the next generation.

References

Bransford, J.D., Brown, A.L., Cocking, R.R.: How People Learn: Brain, Mind, Experience, and School. National Academy Press, Washington, DC (1999)

Brown, J.S., Collins, A., Duguid, P.: Situated cognition and the culture of learning. Educ. Res. **18** (1), 32–42 (1989)

Churchman, C.W.: Wicked problems. Manage. Sci. **14**(4), B141–B142 (1967)

Cooke, N.J., Gorman, J.C., Myers, C.W., Duran, J.L.: Interactive team cognition. Cogn. Sci. **37** (2), 255–285 (2013)

Descartes, R. (1664). L'Homme (treatise of man). Facsimile of the original French, together with an English translation by Hall, T.S.: Harvard University Press, Cambridge (1972). An abridged translation, by Stoothoff, R. is also available in Cottingham, J., Stoothoff, R., Murdoch, D. (Trans. & eds.) The philosophical writings of Descartes, vol. 1. Cambridge University Press, Cambridge (1985)

Ellis, A.P.J.: System breakdown: the role of shared mental models and transactive memory in the relationship between acute stress and tem performance. Acad. Manag. J. **49**, 576–589 (2006)

Endsley, M.R.: Toward a theory of situation awareness in dynamic systems. Hum. Factors J. Hum. Factors Ergon. Soc. **37**(1), 32 (1995)

Giacobe, N.A.: Application of the JDL data fusion process model for cyber security, in Multisensor. In: Braun, J. (ed.) Proceedings of the SPIE Multisource Information Fusion: Architectures, Algorithms and Applications, vol. 7710 (2010)

Giacobe, N.A.: A picture is worth a thousand alerts. In: Proceedings of the 57th Annual Meeting of the Human Factors and Ergonomics Society, San Francisco, CA, pp. 172–176 (2013)

Giacobe, N., Hall, D.-L.: Research opportunities and challenges for cyber systems risk management, 30 June 2015, 27 p., technical report for Penn State Applied Research Laboratory (2015)

Gibson, J.J.: The Ecological Approach to Visual Perception. Houghton Mifflin Company, Boston (1979)

Greeno, J.G.: Gibson's affordances. Psychol. Rev. **101**(2), 336–342 (1994)

Hart, S., Staveland, L.: Development of NASA-TLX (Task Load Index): Results of empirical and theoretical research. In: Hancock, P., Meshkati, N. (eds.) Human Mental Workload, vol. 52, pp. 139–183. North-Holland (1988)

Hayes-Roth, B., Hayes-Roth, F.: A Cognitive model of planning. Cogn. Sci. **3**, 275–310 (1979)

Hoffman, R.R., Nead, J.M.: General contextualism, ecological science and cognitive research. J. Mind Behav. **4**(4), 507–559 (1983)

Hutchins, E.: Cognition in the Wild. MIT Press, Cambridge (1995)

James, W.: The Principles of Psychology. Harvard University Press, Cambridge (1981). Originally published in 1890

Klein, G.: Sources of Power: How People Make Decisions. MIT Press, Cambridge, MA (1999)

Klein, G., Ross, K.G., Moon, B.M., Klein, D.E., Hoffman, R.R., Hollnagel, E.: Macrocognition. IEEE Intell. Syst. **18**(3), 81–85 (2003)

Laughlin, P.: Collective induction: Twelve postulates. Organ. Behav. Hum. Decis. Process. **80**(1), 50–69 (1999)

Lewis, K.: Knowledge and performance in knowledge-worker teams: a longitudinal study of transactive memory systems. Manage. Sci. **50**(11), 1519–1533 (2004)

Mace, W.M.: James J. Gibson's strategy for perceiving: Ask not what's inside your head, but what your head's inside of. In: Shaw, R.E., Bransford, J. (eds.) Perceiving, Acting, and Knowing. Erlbaum, Hillsdale (1977)

Matthew, M.D., Beal, S.A.: Assessing situation awareness in field training exercises. US Army Research Institute for the Behavioral and Social Sciences (2002)

McNeese, M.D.: Humane intelligence: a human factors perspective for developing intelligent cockpits. IEEE Aerosp. Electron. Syst. **1**(9), 6–12 (1986)

McNeese, M.D.: An ecological perspective applied to multi-operator systems. In: Brown, O., Hendrick, H.L. (eds.) Human Factors in Organizational Design and Management - VI, pp. 365–370. Elsevier, The Netherlands (1996)

McNeese, M.D., Cooke, N.J., Champion, M.: Situating cyber-situational awareness. In: Proceedings of the 10th International Conference on Naturalistic Decision Making (NDM 2011), 31 May–3 June, Orlando, FL (2011)

McNeese, M.D., Mancuso, V.F., McNeese, N.J., Glantz, E.: What went wrong? What can go right? A prospectus on human factors practice. In: Proceedings of the 6th International Conference on Applied Human Factors and Ergonomics (AHFE 2015) and the Affiliated Conferences, AHFE, Las Vegas, NV, July 2015

McNeese, M.D., Pfaff, M., Connors, E.S., Obieta, J., Terrell, I., Friedenberg, M.: Multiple vantage points of the common operational picture: Supporting complex teamwork. In: Proceedings of the 50th Annual Meeting of the Human Factors and Ergonomics Society, San Francisco, CA, pp. 26–30 (2006)

McNeese, M.D., Vidulich, M. (eds.): Cognitive systems engineering in military aviation environments: Avoiding cogminutia fragmentosa. Wright-Patterson Air Force Base, OH: Human Systems Information Analysis Center (HSIAC) (2002)

Moreland, R.L., Myaskovsky, L.: Exploring the performance benefits of group training: Transactive memory or improved communication? Organ. Behav. Hum. Decis. Process. **82**(1), 117–133 (2000)

Newell, A., Shaw, J.C., Simon, H.A.: Elements of a theory of human problem solving. Psychol. Rev. **23**, 342–343 (1958)

Newell, A., Simon, H.: Human Problem Solving. Prentice-Hall, Englewood Cliffs (1972)

Pearsall, M.J., Ellis, A.P.J.: The effects of critical team member assertiveness on team performance and satisfaction. J. Manag. **32**, 575–594 (2006)

Perkins, D.N.: Knowledge as Design. Erlbaum, Hillsdale (1986)

Rasmussen, J., Pejtersen, A.M., Goodstein, L.P.: Cognitive Systems Engineering. Wiley, New York (1994)

Reifers, A.: Network access control list situation awareness. (Unpublished doctoral dissertation). The Pennsylvania State University. University Park, PA (2010)

Rimland, J., Ballora, M.: Using complex event processing (CEP) and vocal synthesis techniques to improve comprehension of sonified human-centric data. In: SPIE Proceedings, vol. 9122. Next-Generation Analyst II, 22 May 2014

Salas, E., Fiore, S.M., Letsky, M.: Theories of Team Cognition: Cross-Disciplinary Perspectives. Routledge, New York (2012)

Scielzo, S., Strater, L.D., Tinsley, M.L., Ungvarsky, D.M., Endsley, M.R.: Developing a subjective shared situation awareness inventory for teams. In: Proceedings of the Human Factors and Ergonomics Society Annual Meeting, vol. 53, p. 289 (2009)

Shiravi, H., Shiravi, A., Ghorbani, A.: A survey of visualization systems for network security. IEEE Trans. Vis. Comput. Graph. **18**(99), 1 (2011)

Stall, D., Yu, T., Crouser, R. J., Damodaran, S., Nam, K., O'Gwynn, D., McKenna, S., Harrison, L.: Visualization evaluation for cyber security: trends and future direction. In: Proceedings of the Eleventh Workshop of Visualization for Cyber Security, pp. 49–56 (2014)

Stasser, G., Titus, W.: Pooling of unshared information in group decision making: Biased information sampling during discussion. J. Pers. Soc. Psychol. **48**, 48–1467 (1985)

Taylor, R.M.: Situational awareness rating technique (SART): The development of a tool for aircrew systems design. Situational awareness in aerospace operations, AGARD-CP- 478. Neuilly Sur Seine, France: NATO-AGARD, 3/1-3/17 (1990)

Tyworth, M., Giacobe, N., Mancuso, V., McNeese, M., Hall, D.: A human-in-the-loop approach to understanding situation awareness in cyber defense analysis. EAI Endorsed Trans. Secur. Saf. **13**(2), 1–10 (2013)

Young, M., McNeese, M.: A situated cognition approach to problem solving. In: Hancock, P., Flach, J., Caid, J., Vicente, K. (eds.) Local Applications of the Ecological Approach to Human Machine Systems, pp. 359–391. Erlbaum, Hillsdale (1995)

Wegner, D.M.: Transactive memory: a contemporary analysis of the group mind. In: Mullen, B., Goethals, G.R. (eds.) Theories of Group Behavior, pp. 185–205. Springer, New York (1986)

Wilson, M.: Six views of embodied cognition. Psychon. Bull. Rev. **9**, 625–636 (2002)

Zaff, B.S., McNeese, M.D., Snyder, D.E.: Capturing multiple perspectives: a user-centered approach to knowledge acquisition. Knowl. Acquisition **5**(1), 79–116 (1993)

Impact of Team Collaboration
on Cybersecurity Situational Awareness

Prashanth Rajivan[✉] and Nancy Cooke

Human Systems Engineering, Arizona State University, Mesa, AZ, USA
{pnrajiva,Nancy.Cooke}@asu.edu

Abstract. Information complexity and expanse of cybersecurity space surpasses the cognitive ability of individual analysts to be truly situationally aware. Team level situation awareness in cyber security can be described as the coordinated perception and comprehension of significant events in the network by all team members that serve as the basis for effective response actions. Effective teamwork is imperative to transform individual analysts' disparate cognition and situation awareness into team level, collective cognition and situation awareness. We employed a hybrid methodology that makes opportunistic use of a mix of field observations, simulation, modeling, and laboratory experimentation to study and improve team situation awareness in the cyber security domain. Findings from experiments summarized in this chapter demonstrate the important role of teamwork at every level of cyber security defense and the detrimental effect of team process loss on overall cyber defense performance.

Keywords: Teamwork · Collaboration · Communication · Human factors · Cyber security · Simulation · Modeling · Cognitive Task Analysis · EAST

1 Introduction

Situation awareness (SA) is to be cognizant of relevant changes in the environment either happening at the moment or forthcoming [15]. The concept of situation awareness (SA) was originally used to refer to an individual pilot's awareness of changes relevant to the flight. Translating this into cybersecurity defense context, situation awareness would refer to an individual cyber defense analyst's (human operator defending an organization from cyber attacks) awareness of changes to network/system activity that might constitute an attack/breach.

Situation awareness is a dynamic cognitive process whereby an individual or a group of individuals need to continuously modify and update their SA with new information from the environment [16]. However, even a medium or semi-large sized organization would typically have to manage massively interconnected network of systems (both mobile and non-mobile) and software services containing several known (yet unpatched) and unknown vulnerabilities. Computer networks

© Springer International Publishing AG 2017
P. Liu et al. (Eds.): Cyber Sitation Awareness, LNCS 10030, pp. 203–226, 2017.
DOI: 10.1007/978-3-319-61152-5_8

are predominantly monitored for security attacks through signature-based sensors that produce large amounts of alerts that could be rife with false alarms. In addition to unreliable attack event data, large amounts of data in the form of system logs and network traffic data are also collected for analysis and attack detection purposes. Hence, information environment in cyber security can be characterized as a big data problem for human analysts who have to process the large amounts of information to detect attacks. Such a level of complexity, information overload and expanse of cybersecurity space surpasses the cognitive ability of a single analyst or system to continuously process and update information to be truly situationally aware.

Cyber security detection task, therefore, requires a large group of human analysts and a multitude of technology to divide and work round-the-clock to effectively defend large computer networks from continuous cyber attacks/breaches. In the information overloaded cyber security environment, technological solutions are undoubtedly crucial for achieving good situation awareness and for attack detection but currently it is not feasible to develop security solutions (e.g., host/network intrusion sensors, network mapping software, security analytics and visualization) to solely have complete security awareness and respond to threats reliably. The human analyst and technology must operate interdependently to triage and analyze the large amounts of threat information to detect attacks. Human analysts are especially essential for developing hypotheses about emerging threats and for using contextual knowledge to prioritize threats based on severity and to respond to attacks appropriately. It is important to recognize that the "awareness" in situation awareness resides neither with the analyst alone, nor with the technology alone, but with the joint human-technology system [25].

Attack surface is constantly evolving especially with new vulnerabilities detected every day on a growing amount of hardware and technology. It is not feasible even for an expert individual analyst assisted with highly intelligent technology to have all the knowledge and expertise or pay attention to such widely disparate threat vectors. Hence, a highly collaborative team of analysts with diverse knowledge, skills and experience is necessary to keep organizations abreast of evolving threats. Furthermore, attacks are increasingly multi-step (a combination of techniques used to deliver, exploit, command and control) and therefore events observed by different analysts could be pieces of a larger attack that spans different parts of network or could be pieces of redundant attacks observed by different analysts at different parts of the network. Attacks can also be stealthy, strategic and can include non-technical attack vectors such as social engineering. Pertinent information to detect such attacks are often distributed across time and space (different network end points and systems) and would require inputs from many other teams to successfully detect and respond. Hence, situation awareness necessary to detect advanced forms of threats is difficult to achieve and requires members of different teams and analysts working across work shifts to collaborate and share information with each other. This requires understanding how different components of this system (individual operator, team of operators and technology) work together interdependently to achieve situation awareness and also the human-system gaps impinging these interactions. Hence, complete security situation awareness is improbable or difficult to achieve through interactions only between an individual analyst and his/her technology. Individual analysts within a team and organization, supported by technologies conducive to human collaboration, would need to effectively communicate, and share information and knowledge with each other to detect highly sophisticated cyber attacks of this time and the future.

Furthermore, security analysts and technology do not operate in vacuum but within the context of a complex sociotechnical system that is organizational security. In addition to large networks of computers and a manifold of threat detection software, this sociotechnical environment include several human operators and stakeholders (e.g., security defense analyst and responder) working in different roles, capabilities and at different times of the day. For example, analysts would typically have to work with system administrators, data stewards, physical security teams, security training teams, software vendors, end users, employees, privacy teams and even legal teams to maintain the security posture of the organization.

Finally, information sharing and collaboration between organizations about emerging threat vectors are also crucial to inhibit the spread of novel attacks (such as zero-day vulnerabilities and attacks) to different organizations. Information disclosure between organizations could involve disclosure of newly detected vulnerabilities, disclosure of attacks/breaches or disclosure of initiatives taken to proactively deter identified attacks. A large body of work has led to web based tools that enable information disclosure between organizations. Furthermore, governments have developed information sharing and analysis centers to encourage cyber security information exchange. However, confidentiality, legal implications, cost of disclosure and brand reputation largely inhibits information sharing between organizations. Nevertheless, information sharing and collaborative initiatives between organizations and between government agencies are necessary for large scale security situation awareness which is in turn critical to the overall security posture of an entire nation.

The Iranian Airbus tragedy of 1988 in which a commercial flight full of passengers was mistakenly shot down by USS Vincennes [6] is a classic example of the effects of poor teamwork. Although, till date, there are no widely publicized reports about attack detection failure due to lack of teamwork between analysts within an organization, there are some preliminary evidence from observations of cyber defense exercises that point in that direction [19,21,37]. Such adverse events in the cyber environment that stem from lack of human collaboration could be avoided by working proactively to improve teamwork between analysts. Efforts to improve teamwork and collaboration within organization and between analysts have been minimal. However, there has been some work to improve information sharing between organizations partly because it is a much more publicized policy issue. As we have enumerated, effective human collaboration and information sharing at every level of the cyber defense process is vital for developing a more secure Internet ecosystem. Therefore, it is important to measure and improve team level security situation awareness at every level of cyber security. In this chapter, we explore the role of human collaboration and information within the cybersecurity system and the impact of collaboration on achieving security situation awareness.

2   Team Cognition

Team cognition can be defined as cognitive processes such as learning, decision making and situation awareness occurring at the team level [34]. Not surprisingly, team cognition has a significant effect on human performance especially in complex socio-technical environments [7,10,34] such as cyber security. The three major theoretical perspectives used for explaining team cognition are: shared cognition or shared mental models, transactive memory, and interactive team cognition.

2.1   Shared Mental Models

The shared cognition or shared mental models view has been around for more than two decades and is the most widely adopted approach used to explain team cognition [1,7,22,34]. It adopts the concept of mental models (individual) and extends it to explain cognition in teams. Mental models can be defined as "mechanisms whereby humans are able to generate descriptions of system purpose and form explanations of system functioning and observed system states, and predictions of future system states" [33, p. 7]. Cannon-Bowers, Salas, and Converse [2] first developed the concept of team mental models based on their study of expert teams: "When we observe expert, high performance teams in action, it is clear they can often coordinate their behavior without the need to communicate" [1, p. 196]. Shared cognition [1,7] theory suggests that team performance is dependent on the degree to which the knowledge and understanding of the task and the situation is similar across the members of the team. In simple terms, it requires the members of the team to be on the "same page". The shared cognition model is often critiqued for its simplistic view of team cognition given that it is unlikely that all individuals have identical knowledge structures [10]. Similarly, it is not feasible for all analysts in a team (even in a small team) to share the same knowledge and awareness of the threats in the network due to the massiveness of computer networks and information complexity inherent in cyber security defense. There could however be overlapping knowledge and information between analysts that could play a role in overall team performance, but would still require a significant amount of interaction between analysts to transform individual cognition into team level cognition.

Cross-training, wherein members of a team are trained on each others team roles, is often used to foster shared team cognition [34]. Training cyber defense analyst teams for shared cognition through cross training is not pragmatic because cyber threat landscape is evolving and it is not possible for an analyst to know, learn and have experience on all the emerging vulnerabilities, threats, adversarial tools and techniques. Furthermore, it will be difficult to cross-train cyber defense analysts because analyst's roles in general are almost homogeneous with subtle differences in terms of skills and experiences (largely tacit). Also, cross-training analysts conducting different roles such as triage analysess, correlational analyses an and forensics analyses is also difficult considering the highly technical nature of each role. Therefore, cross training for cyber defense teams is not practical.

2.2   Transactive Memory

In everyday life, we often use memory systems outside of our own minds (i.e., calendars, notes and directories) to remember things such as meeting times and phone numbers. To formalize this type of memory which is distributed across individuals and systems, Wegner [42] introduced transactive memory. Transactive memory considers each individual in a group a memory system holding distinct information and knowledge along with the awareness of what others in the group know. Transactive memory is similar to external memory, but instead of remembering to look at book for a certain information, we just remember that our team mate is an expert on a topic and that asking her or him will give us the same information in a faster and more comprehensible manner. Therefore, instead of trying to train every analyst to know everything, analyst team members can leverage each others' expertise to achieve their goals. However, this type of team behavior is also contingent on good team interactions mostly in the form of team communication.

2.3   Interactive Team Cognition

Cooke and colleagues [8,10] proposed a theory of Interactive Team Cognition (ITC) which states that team cognition can be observed in team interactions. This is contrasted to the earlier theory of shared team cognition [1] which states that team cognition is the sum of the knowledge of individual team members. ITC does not however dispute the importance of individual knowledge for effective performance, but argues instead that team cognition is not solely tied to the knowledge of the individual members of the team. ITC goes further to posit that team cognition is not a final product but an ongoing activity that constantly updates and clarifies individual and team cognition. This is in contrast to the shared mental models perspective that views team cognition as emerging from relatively static knowledge structures of individuals and therefore measures of cognition and performance are aggregated from the individual level. Hence according to ITC, team cognition has to be studied and measured at the team level through observation of team level processes such as communication. Communication is the key medium through which a team of humans form relationships, collaborate and share information. Communication could be conducted through various forms such as face-to-face communication, non-verbal communication and even through virtual mediums such as telephone networks and internet networks. Whatever the form be, communication is a key element in the team process. Communication in cyber security defense teams is also multimodal. Finally, according to ITC, team cognition is unique to each context and therefore needs to be studied for each context and importantly, in the context. ITC fits well as a theoretical driver to measure and improve team cognition in the cyber defense environment because threat landscape in cyber space is constantly evolving and therefore team level interactions between analysts should be an ongoing activity. Such consistent interactions would enable the analysts to have good security awareness of their network and to take the appropriate response. This would eventually lead to good cyber defense performance. It should also be noted that interactions between analysts need to be less biased to gain good security situation awareness [27].

3   Team Based Situation Awareness

There are several definitions of situation awareness (SA), however the definition which is widely used is "the perception of the elements in the environment within a volume of time and space, the comprehension of their meaning, and the projection of their status in the near future" [15, p. 97].

Situation awareness conceptualized at the team level is called team situation awareness (Team SA). Team SA is viewed as an important factor to be considered in designing human-machine systems and interfaces [36]. Endsley defines team SA as "the degree to which every team member possesses the SA required for his or her responsibilities" [17]. According to this perspective, the team's performance depends on the level of situation awareness in each of the team members and one member's poor SA can affect the team's performance. However, this model of team SA does not go far enough [18]. It may be relevant to homogeneous groups, but not to heterogeneous teams and this perspective may not suffice as team increases in size [9]. If a team is truly an interdependent group, then each team member will have different, though perhaps overlapping, perspectives on the situation. In a complex and dynamic world, it is likely that two or more perspectives on the team will need to be fused in order to have SA that extends beyond an analyst's screen of alerts. The fusion takes place through some form of team interaction often communication. For example, one analyst may be aware of a denial of service attack on a network server and once this information is integrated with another analyst's awareness of two other similar attacks on a different network a bigger picture emerges. Without the interaction and integration, the team as a whole cannot perceive all the threats, comprehend them, and project appropriate responses.

In short, team SA is much more than the sum of individual SA [35]. This follows from the perspective of Interactive Team Cognition [8] that espouses that cognitive processing at the team level occurs through team interactions situated in a rich context. This view of team cognition can be contrasted with others that focus on the aggregate of individual knowledge (e.g., [24]). Thus by placing the focus on team interaction, team situation awareness can be described as the coordinated perception of change in the environment by team members that serve as the basis for effective action [18]. According to this view, team SA means, members of a team becoming aware of different aspects of the situation and knitting the pieces of the puzzle together through communication or other interactions to achieve team situation awareness and to take appropriate actions [35]. This view [11] suggests that team members through team interactions transform individual knowledge to collective knowledge and in the process achieve team situation awareness. Hence it is important to study team level interactions to detect team level process loss and biases among cyber defense analysts to truly improve team level situation awareness.

Team cognition and its processes have been profusely investigated in other domains such as medical teams, air traffic control and intelligence analysis. Therefore, there is a large collection of literature on cognitive biases that affect team cognition in such complex domains. In contrast, research in the cyber security domain have predominantly focused on the technical side of the problem, even though it has been widely characterized as a socio-technical problem [14,23]. Studies to explore the human side of the cyber problem are minimal and mostly have focused on the individual analyst because the task on first sight seems to be an individual cognitive task. Champion et al. [3] found that team processes such as communication and collaboration play important roles in the outcome performance, which is detecting potential cyber attacks. There is very little work done so far to explore the various aspects of team cognition of cyber defense. Due to the complex, heterogeneous and dynamic nature of cyber defense, it would be more suitable to study team level interactions of analysts and identify factors that improve team level interactions and team performance.

4   Living Lab Approach

The methodology that we employed to study team level processes in cyber security was a hybrid methodology that makes opportunistic use of a mix of field observations, simulation, modeling, and laboratory experimentation. The methodology centers on the use of synthetic task environments [12] or simulations that represented a compromise between field studies and artificial laboratory experiments. The methodology that we used to conduct research on teamwork in cyber defense is presented in Fig. 1. Multiple methods were used in an integrated fashion so that results from one method provided input to another method. At the heart of this approach was the use of Synthetic Task Environments (STEs) for laboratory experimentation.

4.1   Cognitive Task Analysis

The methodology starts in the field with Cognitive Task Analysis (CTA). Gaining a good understanding about how the operators in the real world perform the cyber defense task was essential for conducting research in a setting that is faithful to the real world. CTA was used to understand the tasks and the cognitive processes and requirements underlying those tasks at individual and

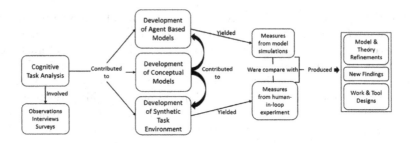

Fig. 1. Overall methodology used to study team processes in cyber defense

team levels. As shown in Fig. 1, the findings from the CTA provided input for all other methodological steps including modeling, STE development, development of measures, and simulation-based human-in-the-loop experiments. The CTA is also a good source of research questions and hypotheses to be tested in later experiments.

Access to cyber defense analysts at their workplace was often restricted due to confidentiality policies and also due to workplace time restrictions. Hence, field studies to understand the different roles, responsibilities and team process in cyber defense was achieved through field observations of cyber defense exercises conducted at both academic (with students) and organizational (defense organization) levels. In exercises organized by defense organizations, roles and responsibilities of team members were found to be structured and rigid whereas the roles of team members in academia based cyber defense exercises were loosely defined (responsibilities are exchanged as the exercise evolves). However, in both venues, we observed that there was a team leader assisted by team members either monitoring networks for intrusions or taking response actions to already discovered intrusions. In academia based cyber defense exercises, leadership role was often shared whereas in other non-academia based defense exercise, leadership was centralized. Most of the defense activities in both venues were live activities such as monitoring for attacks, analysis of activity logs and response to attacks. Offline activities such as code and malware analysis was only a small part of these exercises. The team sizes at cyber defense exercise were observed to be usually a larger 10 person team. However, a survey we conducted with 130 people working in cyber defense (predominantly working at academic settings) indicated that cyber defense team size varied between a 3 person team and 5 person teams with members of the team working on different roles.

In cyber defense exercises, the amount of team interactions widely varied between teams and admittedly some teams in academia based exercises demonstrated higher level of interactions due to the competitive nature of these exercises. However, the amount of communication and collaboration between real world cyber defense analyst teams was still not clear and therefore we sought expert (cyber defense managers) opinion through interviews. Experts' anecdotes indicated that even though analysts worked in groups, there was a lack of communication and collaboration within cyber defense analyst groups (working in group doesn't automatically mean there is teamwork). They hypothesized that existing reward policies and lack of team training could be the contributing factors. There was preliminary evidence from observational study conducted by Jariwala and colleagues [21] that teamwork could lead to better performance in cyber defense analysis. It is difficult to collect valid measures of team performance and team process measures from cyber defense exercises due to lack of experimental control and due to lack of priority given by current cyber defense exercises towards improvements to human factors and team processes. Hence, evidence from controlled experiments are required to validate the effectiveness of teamwork in the cyber defense context.

Perception of teamwork in cyber security defense was found to be positive among both cyber defense analysts and security managers. Security managers reported to value teamwork that leads to automation of tasks and collaborations that lead to detection of attack signatures not seen before [40]. Positive emotions reported towards teamwork indicated that teamwork is highly valued in cyber defense. However, as opposed to other emergency response teams such as EMS (Emergency Medical Support), collaboration in security must be initiated by the individual analyst i.e., an analyst initiates collaboration on detecting an attack that needs more than one person's knowledge or expertise to solve [4]. In many other domains, the task is well structured with each member of the team playing a particular role and requiring the individual members to work as a team on the task from the beginning. Therefore, even though teamwork is perceived positively by the cyber security community, it is currently not a natural part of the task (part of the reason why collaboration and teamwork is minimal in cyber defense). A significant amount of extra effort is required to foster collaboration in security through team training and collaboration tools.

4.2 EAST (Event Analysis of Systemic Teamwork)

As part of the CTA, we conducted an EAST (Event Analysis of Systemic Teamwork) analysis [41] of cyber security systems. This framework characterizes an organization in terms of tasks, information, and a social system. The output of the analysis is in the form of graphics that represent these various aspects of the system that can be examined and compared qualitatively and quantitatively. EAST provides a high-level view of the large sociotechnical system. The assumption is that with adequate models of cyber security systems we can understand how different system configurations (variations in team coordination, management structure, task allocation, information needs, and social networking practices) impact cyber situation awareness and ultimately, cyber security. Three organizations participated in this part of the CTA. Organization A was a cyber security organization within the military. Organization B was a cyber security unit within a large information technology company and Organization C was a cyber security unit within a small information technology company.

The models were informed by one or two sources of data. In all three cases a Subject Matter Expert (SME) from each organization consented to be interviewed about their units. Interviews took approximately one hour each.

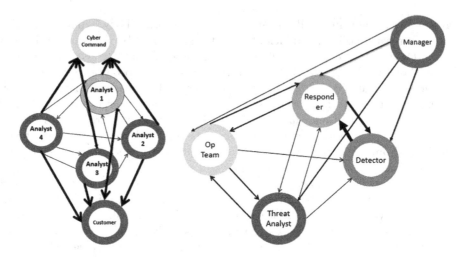

Fig. 2. ORG A - social network diagram

Fig. 3. ORG B - social network diagram

Results of the interviews were used to tailor surveys targeting analysts at each of the three organizations. Survey questions were aligned with the task, information, or social aspects of each organization. There were no survey responses returned from Organization A, and 7 and 1 responses respectively from Organizations B and C. The interviews, supplemented by these surveys as available, were instrumental in deriving the EAST models that are shown here.

Interview Results: Organization A. The organization A (ORG A) interview revealed that the 50 cyber security analysts work mostly independently with little to no teamwork or collaboration among them (See Fig. 2). However, the analysts do exchange information with each other using chat and shift-change meetings. Additionally, the analysts operate under a hierarchical chain of command and have the roles of manager, team leader, and analyst. In general, analysts stay with the same customer and hence do not rotate assignments. The process of analyzing and reporting incidents is fixed, with analysts gathering information, documenting findings, and reporting to cyber command (for review, achieve) and their customers (other DOD sites). Lastly, analysts leave the ORG A team largely due to burn out (average turnover rate is 1–1.5 years). The ORG A team's main goal is to discover and report on all possible intrusions that are against prevailing policies. In order to accomplish this goal the analyst's main tasks are: hand-off meetings, customer assignments, review of events, gather batches of alerts, review alerts, dispatch those alerts, and then gather a new batch of alerts. These tasks are done sequentially with one task not being more important than the other. Analysts gather needed information using online references, dictionary, work flow systems, and other resources (Fig. 4).

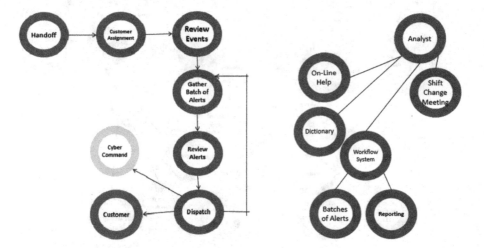

Fig. 4. ORG A - sequential task network

Fig. 5. ORG B - information network diagram

Interview Results: Organization B. The ORG B team of fourteen analysts consists of detectors (6), responders (6), a threat analyst and a manager working closely together with the operations team (See Fig. 3). Communication among the detectors and responders is most common, but overall the team seems to communicate across all levels. The subject matter expert also stated that the analysts routinely collaborate on a team level. Furthermore, some of the analysts' roles are interchangeable, whereas others are not. For instance, a responder can perform a detector's job, but not the other way around.

The overall goal of the team is to ensure zero data loss. Interrelated measures are taken to wade off cyber attacks. These measures are: detection, monitoring, response, proactivity, design for security and availability, and server handling (see Figs. 5 and 6). In particular, the detectors are responsible for classifying the alerts into "buckets" of good, bad, or neutral ones, whereas the responders further investigate the alerts (bad ones first, then neutral ones). The threat analyst models what is going on in the network and the operation team answers questions responders may have (difficult alerts). They also train detectors and responders. The survey revealed some interesting findings (see Fig. 7 for summary). For instance, though the importance of teamwork was expressed among the analysts it was not part of their daily routine. Also, analysts did not work under time constraints this was a 24-hour operation, so if something did not get done in the previous shift, then the next shift would take care of it. In addition, the analysts reported that they did not have difficulty processing and integrating information while assessing critical incidents.

Interview Results: Organization C. This response team consists of four security specialists (see Fig. 8). Their roles and responsibilities are: Information

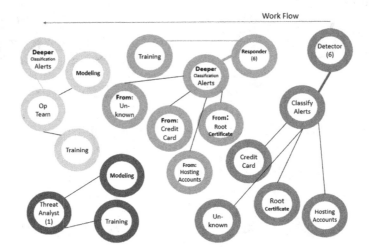

Fig. 6. ORG B - sequential task network diagram

Security Specialist (monitoring logs, audits, etc.), Information Security Engineer (vulnerability scans, analyzing information, responding to security escalations), Information Security Architect (design), and Chief Security Officer (policy setting, process and procedures, customers). The analysts collaborate on a daily basis and some analysts can perform dual jobs, but in general they do not rotate out of their positions. However, they do move up with experience. Furthermore, the analysts' tasks are interrelated, completed in parallel, and repeated almost constantly. Log files, Wikis, and other tools are used by the security specialists (see Fig. 9).

A Summary of Organization B Computer Incident Response Team (CIRT) Survey Results

Social Questions
- Detectors and Responders communicate most throughout the day
- Face-to-face or chat is preferred
- Preferred communication tool is chat
- Consulting on alerts is the most common communication
- **Importance of teamwork expressed but most do not work in teams**

Task Questions
- Alerts are most common task
- Process is well documented
- There is **no time constrains** on handling the alerts – 24 hour operation, next analyst takes over what previous one didn't finish
- Individual Detectors and Responders seem to handle specific alerts (specialization within their roles)

Information Questions
- Log files most common form of passing along information; **Notepad** used to keep track of IP addresses when analyzing a threat
- Responders and Detectors pass the most information to one another

Critical Incident Questions
- Evidence is key for decision making and is therefore not difficult
- Rule could be written (opportunity to automate)
- **All analysts reported that they did not have difficulty processing and intergrading information while assessing critical incident**

Specific Roles Questions
- Responders and Detectors work closely together
- Escalating an Alert:
  - Detectors consult with Responder
  - Responders can implement change
  - Threat Analyst consults with Responders and Engineer

Fig. 7. ORG B - summary

Overall Summary. Some stark differences between the Organization A: computer incident team and the two private security teams exist. As somewhat

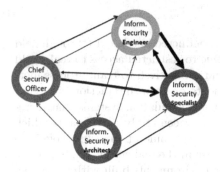

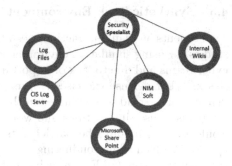

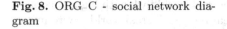

Fig. 8. ORG C - social network diagram

Fig. 9. ORG C - information network diagram

expected, the organizational structure is much more rigid within the military computer incidence team compared to the other two teams. For example, analysts at Organization A generally do not rotate assignments or switch roles. Yet, both private security teams do so (to a certain extent knowledge permitting). Likewise, most Organization A tasks are completed sequentially and are dependent on each other, whereas many tasks in the other two teams are done constantly and in parallel. This rigidity-organizational and task related-may be one of the reasons why Organization A security analysts burn out more quickly. However, there are also some similarities between all three security teams. For one, most tasks are not time constrained since security monitoring is done 24/7. Hence, alerts not classified in one shift will be classified in the next. Moreover, all three security teams reported that all tasks are equally important. Lastly, looking at teamwork and collaboration one finds a wide range of answers. The Organization A analysts do not collaborate or work in teams, the Organization B analysts collaborate, but there is little teamwork, and the Organization C analysts seem to collaborate and work as a team (see Fig. 10).

A Summary of Organization C - Computer Incident Response Team (CIRT) Survey Results

Social Questions
- Chief Information Security Officer talks to everyone, in particular with the Information Security Specialist.
- Communicates about high priority, unknown, and difficult alerts; hunches/speculations, deliberations, and final reports.
- Finds team work extremely important.
- Face-to-face communication = most of the time.
- Phone preferred over Chat, Wikis, etc.

Fig. 10. ORG C summary of survey results (Only the Chief Security Officer answered some of the survey questions.)

4.3 Synthetic Task Environment

Experiments on team interactions need to be conducted in context (through field studies) or using simulation environments. Due to restricted access to real world cyber teams and due to lack of importance currently given to team process metrics in cyber defense exercises [19], experiments on team interactions in cyber defense can instead be conducted in the lab using simulation systems that recreate realistic user interactions and work flows between study participants which would in turn require the participants to exercise some of the same cognitive process involved while conducting cyber defense in the real world [12]. Synthetic task environments (STE) are such simulation environments built with the objective of recreating the cognitive aspects of the real world task with highest fidelity possible, giving less focus towards the appearance of the real world environment [12]. STEs tend to have mixed fidelity with the task and cognitive requirements being higher fidelity than equipment and interfaces.

Results and findings from cognitive task analyses we conducted served as input for the development of STE called CyberCog [29]. The STE provided an experimental context that preserved the cyber defense task environment. The entire cyber defense task flow was not replicated in the STE, because the objective was also to provide an environment for experimentation that was better controlled than the field. It can be thought of as an abstraction of cyber defense environment. In addition to being guided by the CTA, the selection of features to extract from the field and to be brought into the lab was based on research questions and technological constraints. As the STE itself was being developed, task scenarios that served as the experimental task and measures of performance, process, and cognition in this context were also developed. CTA data provided input for these developmental activities and together with the STE they became the lab based experimental context from which we collected human-in-the-loop data. Participants in our experiments used this synthetic task environment (CyberCog) to perform different cyber defense tasks. However, usage of the STE to collect measures comes with the added burden of training the study participants for the specific task which has to be simplified, carefully designed and tested.

4.4 Agent Based Modeling

Findings from both Cognitive Task Analysis (CTA) and human-in-loop experiments provided inputs for developing computational models and simulations. They were used in tandem with experimentation to extend empirical results to situations that are difficult to test empirically (e.g., 100 operators, team interactions occurring over longer time periods) and for theory building to explain empirical findings. A multi-agent simulation system [28] was used to model the dynamic, team-level interactions between the analysts because multi-agent simulations are generally used to study macro level social phenomena emerging from micro level interactions between agents (can be simple rule based agents or more sophisticated cognitive-model based agents). The focus on macro-level interactions is consistent with the theory of interactive team cognition.

CTA and lab experiments provided theoretically grounded parameters for multi-agent simulations. Simulations using different combinations of parameter values were conducted which is infeasible to study through lab based team experiments. The models developed were validated by comparing the human-in-loop experimental results against the results from the multi-agent model simulation which leads to findings that ultimately can be applied back in the actual domain. In addition, the findings from modeling and experiments can feed back to refine the models and to ask new experimental questions.

These living lab methodologies described were applied to measure the effect of lack of collaboration (collaboration loss) during triage analysis and effect of team process loss during correlation analysis on cyber defense performance. As described earlier, it is important to study and measure team level interactions to detect team level process loss and biases that would affect situation awareness in cyber defense. Team interactions during triage analysis and correlation analyses were specifically studied because they are the fundamental and commonly conducted tasks in cyber defense [13]. Triage analysis is the first level task in the cyber defense task hierarchy and most of the upper level defense analysis and decision are based off the information fed by triage analysts. Subsequent to triage analyses involves correlational analyses of the threats and suspicious events discovered through triage analyses. An improvement in team performance at the triage and correlational analyses level would have a positive effect on overall cyber defense performance. Next we summarize the experiment and models used in these experiments.

5   Team Collaboration Loss

5.1   Human-in-the-Loop Experiment

Triage analysis is usually the first step in the cyber defense analysis process. During triage analysis, analysts monitor the large number of network events flagged by sensors to determine if events are indeed suspicious or if they are simply false alarms [13]. Findings from triage analyses feed further analyses for responding to attacks. Therefore, it is imperative to improve analyst performance on triage analysis. Triage analysis entails constant monitoring of large numbers of events that could correspond to a disparate array of known and unknown attacks requiring the analyst to have a wide range of security expertise and to constantly acquire new expertise. A group of analysts are often tasked to perform triage analyses, but they don't necessarily have to collaborate and work as team. The task is generally seen as an individualized task with each analyst working on parts of the flagged network event data set. However, we hypothesized that there can benefits to teamwork even at the triage level.

To demonstrate the importance of teamwork in triage analysis, we investigated the effect of teamwork/cooperation versus Individual-work/competition on triage analysis performance [31]. The synthetic task environment (STE),

CyberCog [29], was originally built for this experiment. The CyberCog system was built to recreate the different aspects of triage analysis task as it was performed in the real world, but in a controlled mode. CyberCog was a three-person synthetic task environment that simulated the triage process in cyber defense analysis. The CyberCog system presented a simulated set of network and system security alerts which participants had to categorize as either benign or suspicious. The classification is based on other simulated information sources such as network and system activity logs, a user database, a security news website, and a vulnerability database. Alerts used in this system were simplified versions of their real world counterparts to make them understandable for our experimental participants who were not familiar with the domain or the task. Simplified does not imply that the alerts were easy to analyze but simply meant that they are presented in a form that was free from technical jargon. Simplified data were used to make the task easy for participants to quickly learn through training.

In this experiment, team members were trained with both diverse and overlapping triage analysis knowledge such that each team member had some unique triage analysis expertise necessary for optimum overall cyber defense performance in the experiment. Team members were either incentivized to work individually or to collaborate to detect as many attacks as possible through triage analysis. All team members had access to information that describes each others' expertise.

We found that participants' performance on difficult to analyze alerts (or "hard alerts") in the team/cooperation condition was significantly better than participants' performance in the individual/competition condition. No difference in performance was detected on easy to analyze alerts. The participants had to put more cognitive effort into analyzing "hard" alerts when compared to other alerts. To accurately analyze the hard alert types, the specialized training provided prior to the start of the experiment was necessary. It was difficult and time consuming (not impossible) for a non-expert to learn (through resources provided) and analyze the hard alerts during the analyses process. In contrast, the remaining easy alert types were intuitive even to non-experts and therefore the participants in the individual/competition condition were able to demonstrate similar performance compared to participants in the team/cooperation condition when analyzing "easy" alerts. So we hypothesized that teamwork could be leading to essential peer-to-peer learning that was allowing participants in the team/cooperation condition to perform better.

Cyber defense performance can be improved through improved team work between cyber defense analysts. Teamwork between analysts could be improved by rewarding analysts to collaborate, through team training and by providing tailor made collaboration tools. However, teamwork might not be desirable in all instances but it would be during novel events such as during zero-day attacks and large scale attacks that are complex and overwhelming when countered individually. Novel attacks (such as zero-day attacks, Advanced Persistent Threats) are not an everyday event and are difficult to predict but demands coordinated teamwork. Hence, consistent efforts to measure and improve team processes in cyber defense analyst teams is necessary to enable the team to work together effectively when required. Cyber security analysts should be made aware that collaboration is not only important for overall organization's security posture, but can also lead to mutual benefits in terms of self-rewards, knowledge expansion and to reduce one's workload.

5.2   Agent Based Model

Developing lab based, human-in-the-loop experiments of team process in cyber security is a long and arduous task primarily due to the technical nature of the task. Therefore, an agent based model was built to replicate and extend the experiment presented in the previous section to explore the effects of different collaboration strategies and team sizes on triage analysis performance [32]. Parameters for the model was based on findings from CTA, the human-in-the-loop experiment and past literature in cognitive science. The model was validated by comparing the results from simulation against results from the experiment. Results from model simulations indicated that, in novel triage analyses situations, collaboration can expedite the required learning process through low cost exchange of knowledge. Moreover, results from the model simulations indicated that collaboration between a heterogeneous group of people (people with different knowledge structures) can lead to better triage analysis performance in comparison to collaboration between a homogeneous group of people (people with similar knowledge structures) because diversity in knowledge could be conducive to analysis of a multitude of attacks. Team size was also found to play an important role in triage analysis performance. A large group of heterogeneous team members could lead to excessive knowledge exchange which can be counter productive in terms of gaining expertise.

Hence, it can be inferred that, fostering and rewarding small groups of heterogeneous (in terms of background knowledge and experience) analysts to collaborate and triage alerts can lead to improved triage analysis performance. Collaboration in the team can be sustained through frequent team training.

6   Team Process Loss

6.1   Human-in-the-Loop Experiment

Triage analysis is usually followed by the attack correlation task [13] wherein the attacks/events flagged to be suspicious are correlated to detect patterns and relationships between events that could be either temporally or spatially distributed, and could be part of attacks carried out at a larger scale. Attack correlation is a crucial contributor to the overall cyber situation awareness because it contributes to the comprehension aspect of situation awareness.

Attack correlation is a cognitively difficult task to conduct due to the vastness of computer networks and information complexity of cyber security. Attack correlation is essential in detection of advanced forms of threats (APT - Advanced Persistent Threats) such as multi-step attack, zero-day attacks and stealth attacks.

Currently, there is a scarcity of methods and technologies to proactively detect multi-step attacks and APTs even though the breadcrumbs of the attack emerging in a network are available, observed, and most often reported by the analysts. Currently, it is also in-feasible to program an expert system to correlate and integrate such seemingly disparate information and detect an emerging large scale attack. However, it is feasible for the human analysts to collaborate, share information and incorporate the contextual information essential to correlate and integrate the seemingly disparate events that are part of a large scale emerging attack. On the other hand, humans have biases and cognitive limitations that prevent them from doing such complex correlations and integration.

Training, motivating and rewarding analysts to work as a team solely may not ensure effective team work and information flow especially in correlation tasks. Pooling individual analyst's expertise would be crucial to attack detection especially in novel attack situations (e.g., zero day attacks) and in detecting multi-step kind of attacks. However, past literature in organizational psychology and cognitive science shows us that teams by default are ineffective in pooling novel information. Teams are known to repeatedly discuss and pool information which is also commonly known to a majority of the team members. They are known to be ineffective in using the unique knowledge available with each team member in making decisions. This process loss is popularly known as information pooling bias or hidden profile paradigm [38]. This effect has been observed in a wide array of teams such as medical teams [5], military teams [26], and intelligence analysis teams [39] and jury teams [20].

Therefore, we investigated the presence of team process loss in the form of information pooling bias in cyber defense analyst teams conducting attack correlation tasks [30]. We also demonstrated that collaborative visualizations, designed considering human cognitive processes, can be effective in minimizing this bias and improving cyber defense analyst team performance [30]. Furthermore, agent-based modeling was used to theorize about internal cognitive search processes in human analysts that result in such biases during their team discussions [30].

Results strongly indicated that all the teams who participated in the experiment exhibited the bias while performing the correlation task. They were found to spend a majority of time discussing attacks that were also observed by other members of the team, whereas they spent only a low percentage of time discussing attack that were known uniquely by each team member, but were correlated and were part of a large scale multi-step attack. Such a biased team discussion in attack correlations could lead to ineffective detection because sometimes integrating the seemingly disparate unique and isolated events could be crucial to detecting large scale multi-step attacks such as advanced persistent threats (APT) [30].

Detection performance was observed to improve in teams who used cognitive friendly collaborative visualization tools during their discussions [30]. Teams without visualizations on an average detected 30% fewer attacks in comparison to teams with the visualization. The difference in detection performance was from the detection and correlation of increased number of unique attack types by teams with visualization. These findings indicated that the information pooling bias can be minimized in cyber defense analyst teams conducting attack correlation tasks by using tailor-made collaboration tools developed taking into consideration the cyber defense analysts cognitive requirements [30].

6.2   Agent Based Model

An agent based model (ABM) was developed to theorize about the cognitive search processes used in the head of an analyst who is trying to search for information to contribute to an ongoing discussion [30]. Cognitive search processes were particularly chosen for theory exploration because they were suspected to be the key component behind the bias because if the team members conducted a depth first type of search, it would lead to a tunneled and narrow focused discussion spending most of the time discussing the same topic and being myopic about other potential large scale attacks. Hence it was hypothesized that humans, by default, use heuristics based on local search/uphill search process [30] to search for information in their memories in order to contribute to the ongoing discussion, leading to the information pooling bias. Furthermore, when the ongoing topic of discussion does not appear in the current search neighborhood, it can cause humans to not recognize the presence of related information available in other part of memory spaces. Therefore, assistance is needed in the form of visual interventions to stimulate recognition memory to help find that relevant information to bring to the discussion.

Three search models were developed and explored: Random Search, Local Search and Memory-Aided Local Search. The random search model was the null model for which agents' do random walks in search of information to contribute to the discussion and was developed for comparison purposes to evaluate whether the models of interest (local and memory-aided) were not producing a stochastic behavior. Results indicated that both local search models and the memory-aided local search model deviated significantly from the null model (random search) and therefore it can be inferred that local and memory-aided local search models were not behaving in a random fashion [30].

In the local search model, agents conducted local neighborhood search and moved in an uphill manner in search of information to contribute to the discussion. In the memory-aided local search model, agents were aided in finding regions in its memory space where it would be possible to find relevant discussion information and once they knew the region to examine, they did local/uphill search in that region in search of information to contribute to the discussion. It was observed that agents in the local search model spent more time discussing shared information more than agents in the memory-aided local search model. Similarly it was observed that agents in the local search model spent less time discussing unique information compared to agents in the memory-aided local search model.

The models themselves do not convey much information and hence have to be compared and validated against the complementary human-in-the-loop experiment. The agents in the "local search" model were observed to demonstrate biased team discussion as observed in the human-in-the-loop experiment. Furthermore, the agents in the "memory-aided local search" model were observed to demonstrate less-biased team discussion as observed in teams with visualization in the human-in-the-loop experiment.

These results are particularly insightful because we can now suspect that human analysts could be using simple heuristics based cognitive search process during team discussions thereby causing them to have such a bias. On the other hand, they could be lacking a global view due to low recognition memory which is essential to see the connections between seemingly disparate but connected information. Therefore, in such contexts, we need tailor made, cognitive friendly collaboration tools and visualizations that will enhance human cognitive search processes which is essential for attack correlation analysis.

7   Summary

Cyber defense is complex, dynamic, overloaded with information and to make things worse, it is rife with uncertainties. Effective human collaboration and information sharing at every level of the cyber defense process is essential to maintain an organization's security posture. Simply bringing a group of analysts together does not automatically ensure teamwork. Analysts have to be incentivized, trained and aided with appropriate tools to foster effective collaboration between them. Moreover, cyber defense analysts teams and other closely associated teams must be experimentally studied to detect team-level process losses. Improvements to teamwork and team interactions can augment security situation awareness which is essential for overall cyber security defense performance.

Time restrictions and confidentiality policies inhibits naturalistic field studies on cyber defense teams. Therefore, it would be beneficial to use field study opportunities for studying work flow of cyber defense analysts and cognitive processes underpinning their work flow. Findings from such field studies can then inform synthetic task simulation development (synthetic task environments) for running controlled human-in-loop experiments in the lab. Measures and findings from such experiments can further be explored, extended and validated through multi-agent modeling and simulations. We presented experiments conducted using these methodologies for studying teamwork on two different cyber defense tasks: triage analysis and correlation analysis.

Cyber defense analysts in the real world have to triage a large number of security events. Regular, known security events can be analyzed by individual analysts and would not require a team effort. Events that are novel, difficult to analyze, non-intuitive (e.g., events associated with zero-day attacks) and emerging in nature (forewarning events that prelude larger multi-step or APT kinds of attacks) are often "hard" to analyze accurately due to lack of prior knowledge and evidence. To analyze such difficult and uncertain events, diverse expertise and knowledge would be necessary which can be quickly and efficiently achieved through teamwork among a heterogeneous group of analysts. Applying the extra effort to communicate and collaborate with other team members for analyzing uncertain and novel events could be perceived as an inconvenience or even as an added cost. However, as we see from the results, instead of trying to reason and analyze all of the alerts, the analysts can achieve higher performance by handing-off uncertain alerts/events with other appropriate analysts to leverage each others' unique expertise. Collaborating to analyze all alerts may also be detrimental to performance as shown in our results. Hence, carefully designed team training methods would help analysts to determine when to initiate collaboration, who to collaborate with and also when to pursue analyses individually. Finally, results from the experiment also indicated that teamwork and information sharing could significantly reduce analysts' workload.

Attack correlation which follows triage analyses involves fusion of disparate attack information (e.g., attack source, vulnerabilities and systems exploited, attack path and so on). In addition to the inherent cognitive load associated with the task, the multitude of parameters necessary to identify relevant attack patterns would be distributed both temporally and spatially. Such a task surpasses the ability of an individual analyst to efficiently make attack correlations to detect an attack. Therefore, the correlation task is simplified by employing teams of analysts to collaborate during attack correlation phase. However, past literature in organizational psychology and cognitive science shows us that teams by default are ineffective in pooling novel information which is pivotal to correlation analyses. Teams are known to repeatedly discuss and pool information which is also commonly known to a majority of the team members [38]. Empirical results from our experiments indicate that cyber defense teams conducting correlation tasks would also be affected by such biases causing sub-optimal decision making [30]. Hence, even though collaboration among human analysts is essential for effective attack correlation, the teams also have to be facilitated with tools to mitigate or reduce such cognitive biases (e.g., confirmation bias and information pooling bias). It can be further theorized that such collaboration tools can enhance the information search process in-the-head leading to less biased decision making as shown through our model results. Less biased information exchange would significantly augment team level security situation awareness.

The research summarized in this chapter used a combination of human-in-the-loop experiment and agent-based modeling to investigate team cognition in cyber defense demonstrating how such a multi-faceted, multidisciplinary approach is effective and insightful for team research in cyber security defense domain. This chapter demonstrates the benefits of teamwork in cyber defense through exploration of team interactions and team level cognitive biases in two different cyber defense tasks. But there are host of other factors too such as trust, confidentiality and organizational security policies that would be affecting teamwork which requires further explorations.

References

1. Cannon-Bowers, J.A., Salas, E.: Reflections on shared cognition. J. Organ. Behav. **22**(2), 195–202 (2001)
2. Cannon-Bowers, J.A., Salas, E., Converse, S.: Cognitive psychology and team training: training shared mental models and complex systems. Hum. Factors Soc. Bull. **33**(12), 1–4 (1990)
3. Champion, M., Rajivan, P., Cooke, N.J., Jariwala, S., et al.: Team-based cyber defense analysis. In: 2012 IEEE International Multi-Disciplinary Conference on Cognitive Methods in Situation Awareness and Decision Support (CogSIMA), pp. 218–221. IEEE (2012)
4. Chen, T.R., Shore, D.B., Zaccaro, S.J., Dalal, R.S., Tetrick, L.E., Gorab, A.K.: An organizational psychology perspective to examining computer security incident response teams. IEEE Secur. Priv. **5**, 61–67 (2014)
5. Christensen, C., Abbott, A.S.: 10 team medical decision making. In: Decision Making in Health Care: Theory, Psychology, and Applications, p. 267 (2003)
6. Collyer, S.C., Malecki, G.S.: Tactical decision making under stress: history and overview. In: Making Decisions Under Stress: Implications for Individual and Team Training. American Psychological Association, Washington, DC (1998)
7. Converse, S.: Shared mental models in expert team decision making. In: Individual and Group Decision Making: Current Issues, p. 221 (1993)
8. Cooke, N.J., Gorman, J.C., Myers, C.W., Duran, J.L.: Interactive team cognition. Cognit. Sci. **37**(2), 255–285 (2013)
9. Cooke, N.J., Gorman, J.C., Rowe, L.J.: An ecological perspective on team cognition. Technical report, DTIC Document (2004)
10. Cooke, N.J., Gorman, J.C., Winner, J.L., Durso, F.: Team cognition. In: Handbook of Applied Cognition, vol. 2, pp. 239–268 (2007)
11. Cooke, N.J., Salas, E., Kiekel, P.A., Bell, B.: Advances in measuring team cognition. In: Team Cognition: Understanding the Factors That Drive Process and Performance, pp. 83–106 (2004)
12. Cooke, N.J., Shope, S.M.: Designing a synthetic task environment. In: Scaled Worlds: Development, Validation, and Application, pp. 263–278 (2004)
13. D'Amico, A., Whitley, K., Tesone, D., O'Brien, B., Roth, E.: Achieving cyber defense situational awareness: a cognitive task analysis of information assurance analysts. In: Proceedings of the Human Factors and Ergonomics Society Annual Meeting, vol. 49, pp. 229–233. SAGE Publications (2005)
14. Dutta, A., McCrohan, K.: Managements role in information security in a cyber economy. Calif. Manag. Rev. **45**(1), 67–87 (2002)
15. Endsley, M.R.: Toward a theory of situation awareness in dynamic systems. Hum. Factors J. Hum. Factors Ergon. Soc. **37**(1), 32–64 (1995)
16. Endsley, M.R.: Level of automation effects on performance, situation awareness and workload in a dynamic control task. Ergonomics **42**(3), 462–492 (1999)
17. Endsley, M.: Final Report: Situation Awareness in an Advanced Strategic Mission (nor doc 89–32). Northrop Corporation, Hawthorne (1989)
18. Gorman, J.C., Cooke, N.J., Winner, J.L.: Measuring team situation awareness in decentralized command and control environments. Ergonomics **49**(12–13), 1312–1325 (2006)
19. Granåsen, M., Andersson, D.: Measuring team effectiveness in cyber-defense exercises: a cross-disciplinary case study. Cognit. Technol. Work **18**(1), 121–143 (2016). http://dx.doi.org/10.1007/s10111-015-0350-2

20. Hastie, R., Penrod, S., Pennington, N.: Inside the Jury. The Lawbook Exchange Ltd., Clark (1983)
21. Jariwala, S., Champion, M., Rajivan, P., Cooke, N.J.: Influence of team communication and coordination on the performance of teams at the ICTF competition. In: Proceedings of the Human Factors and Ergonomics Society Annual Meeting, vol. 56, pp. 458–462. SAGE Publications (2012)
22. Klimoski, R., Mohammed, S.: Team mental model: construct or metaphor? J. Manag. **20**(2), 403–437 (1994)
23. Kraemer, S., Carayon, P., Clem, J.: Human and organizational factors in computer and information security: pathways to vulnerabilities. Comput. Secur. **28**(7), 509–520 (2009)
24. Langan-Fox, J., Code, S., Langfield-Smith, K.: Team mental models: techniques, methods, and analytic approaches. Hum. Factors J. Hum. Factors Ergon. Soc. **42**(2), 242–271 (2000)
25. McNeese, M., Cooke, N.J., Champion, M.A.: Situating cyber situation awareness. In: Proceedings of the 10th International Conference on Naturalistic Decision Making (2011)
26. Natter, M., Bos, N., Ockerman, J., Happel, J., Abitante, G., Tzeng, N.: A c2 hidden profile experiment (2009)
27. Puvathingal, B.J., Hantula, D.A.: Revisiting the psychology of intelligence analysis: from rational actors to adaptive thinkers. Am. Psychol. **67**(3), 199 (2012)
28. Railsback, S.F., Grimm, V.: Agent-Based and Individual-Based Modeling: A Practical Introduction. Princeton University Press, Princeton (2011)
29. Rajivan, P.: CyberCog a synthetic task environment for measuring cyber situation awareness. Ph.D. thesis, Arizona State University (2011)
30. Rajivan, P.: Information pooling bias in collaborative cyber forensics. Ph.D. thesis, Arizona State University (2014)
31. Rajivan, P., Champion, M., Cooke, N.J., Jariwala, S., Dube, G., Buchanan, V.: Effects of Teamwork versus group work on signal detection in cyber defense teams. In: Schmorrow, D.D., Fidopiastis, C.M. (eds.) AC 2013. LNCS, vol. 8027, pp. 172–180. Springer, Heidelberg (2013). doi:10.1007/978-3-642-39454-6_18
32. Rajivan, P., Janssen, M.A., Cooke, N.J.: Agent-based model of a cyber security defense analyst team. In: Proceedings of the Human Factors and Ergonomics Society Annual Meeting, vol. 57, pp. 314–318. SAGE Publications (2013)
33. Rouse, W.B., Morris, N.M.: On looking into the black box: prospects and limits in the search for mental models. Psychol. Bull. **100**(3), 349 (1986)
34. Salas, E., Cooke, N.J., Rosen, M.A.: On teams, teamwork, and team performance: discoveries and developments. Hum. Factors J. Hum. Factors Ergon. Soc. **50**(3), 540–547 (2008)
35. Salas, E., Prince, C., Baker, D.P., Shrestha, L.: Situation awareness in team performance: implications for measurement and training. Hum. Factors J. Hum. Factors Ergon. Soc. **37**(1), 123–136 (1995)
36. Shu, Y., Furuta, K.: An inference method of team situation awareness based on mutual awareness. Cognit. Technol. Work **7**(4), 272–287 (2005)
37. Silva, A., McClain, J., Reed, T., Anderson, B., Nauer, K., Abbott, R., Forsythe, C.: Factors impacting performance in competitive cyber exercises. In: Proceedings of the Interservice/Interagency Training, Simulation and Education Conference, Orlando, FL (2014)
38. Stasser, G., Titus, W.: Pooling of unshared information in group decision making: biased information sampling during discussion. J. Pers. Soc. Psychol. **48**(6), 1467 (1985)

39. Straus, S.G., Parker, A.M., Bruce, J.B.: The group matters: a review of processes and outcomes in intelligence analysis. Group Dyn. Theory Res. Pract. **15**(2), 128 (2011)

40. Sundaramurthy, S.C., Bardas, A.G., Case, J., Ou, X., Wesch, M., McHugh, J., Rajagopalan, S.R.: A human capital model for mitigating security analyst burnout. In: Eleventh Symposium on Usable Privacy and Security (SOUPS 2015), pp. 347–359 (2015)

41. Walker, G.H., Stanton, N.A., Baber, C., Wells, L., Gibson, H., Salmon, P., Jenkins, D.: From ethnography to the east method: a tractable approach for representing distributed cognition in air traffic control. Ergonomics **53**(2), 184–197 (2010)

42. Wegner, D.M.: Transactive memory: a contemporary analysis of the group mind. In: Mullen, B., Goethals, G.R. (eds.) Theories of Group Behavior, pp. 185–208. Springer, New York (1987)

Author Index

Printed in the United States
By Bookmasters

Printed in the United States
By Bookmasters